International Studies
in Honor of
Tomás Rivera

Edited by
Julián Olivares

Arte Público Press
Houston

International studies in honor of Tomás Rivera

...ts from the Texas Commission ...or the Arts, a Federal Agency.

Arte Público Press
University of Houston
University Park
Houston, Texas 77004

All rights reserved
Copyright © 1986 Arte Público Press
ISBN 0-934770-60-3
LC 84-072306

Printed in the United States of America

Tomás Rivera
1935-1984

Photo courtesy of the University of California, Riverside.

Revista Chicano-Riqueña
A Review of Hispanic Literature and Art of the USA
Vol. XIII Fall-Winter 1985 Nos. 3-4

Publisher: Nicolás Kanellos

Editors: Julián Olivares and José Saldívar

Book Review Editor: Patricia Mosier

Advisory Board: Miguel Algarín   Michael Olivas
                 Jaime Carrero   Rosaura Sánchez
                 Sylvia Cavazos Peña   Ntozake Shange
                 Rolando Hinojosa   Evangelina Vigil-Piñón

Contributing Editors: Norma Alarcón, Ron Arias, Rodolfo Cortina, Víctor Hernández Cruz, Jorge Huerta, Tato Laviera, Luis Leal, Nicholasa Mohr, Carlos Morton, Juan Rodríguez, Gary Soto.

Program Director: Cristelia Pérez; Business Manager: Sabrina Hassumani; Advertising: Tomás Vallejos; Fund Raising: Silvia Novo Pena; Art Director: Narciso Peña; Staff: Maricela Oliva, Estela Castillo, Mybao Nguyen.

Revista Chicano-Riqueña, at the University of Houston, appears quarterly and publishes poetry, fiction, art, plays, essays, articles and reviews. Submissions should be addressed to *Revista Chicano-Riqueña*, University of Houston, University Park, Houston, TX 77004. Submit articles in duplicate with SASE.

Yearly Subscription Rate: individuals, $15; institutions, $20; single copies and back issues, $5.00.

Revista Chicano-Riqueña is published by Arte Público Press, which is supported in part by the National Endowment for the Arts, the Texas Commission for the Arts, Tenneco Oil and Exploration, Inc., and the Burkitt Foundation. *Revista Chicano-Riqueña* is a member of The Coordinating Council of Literary Magazines and COSMEP.

Revista Chicano-Riqueña is indexed in *Index of American Periodical Verse, MLA International Bibliography, Chicano Periodical Index, Popular Culture Abstracts, Hispanic American Periodical Index* and *Sumario Actual de Revistas*.

Contents

In Honor of Tomás Rivera, *Julián Olivares* — 7
Legacy, *Evangelina Vigil-Piñón* — 15

Tomás Rivera: Recollections and Essays

Tomás Rivera: Remembrances of an Educator and Poet, *Rolando Hinojosa-Smith* — 19

Thoughts on Tomás Rivera, *Américo Paredes* — 24

. . . *y no se lo tragó la tierra:* With Tomás Rivera in Spain and Personal Memories, *James H. Abbott* — 26

Tomás Rivera: The Ritual of Remembering, *Luis Leal* — 30

Tomás Rivera: Witness and Storyteller, *Eliud Martínez* — 39

Language and Dialog in . . . *y no se lo tragó la tierra*, *Nicolás Kanellos* — 53

The Search for Being, Identity and Form in the Work of Tomás Rivera, *Julián Olivares* — 66

Invisible Women in the Narrative of Tomás Rivera, *Patricia de la Fuente* — 81

The Patriarchal Ideology in "La noche que se apagaron las luces," *Sylvia S. Lizárraga* — 90

The Discourse of Silence in the Narrative of Tomás Rivera, *Lauro Flores* — 96

Chicano and Hispanic Literature of the United States

Growing Up Chicano: Tomás Rivera and Sandra Cisneros, *Erlinda González-Berry* and *Tey Diana Rebolledo* — 109

Fragmentation in the Chicano Novel: Literary Technique and Cultural Identity, *John C. Akers* — 121

Bilingual Poetry: A Chicano Phenomenon, *Susan E. Bassnett* — 137

The Presence of Native Americans in Chicano Literature, *Heiner Bus* — 148

Chicano Literature: A European Perspective, *Dieter Herms* — 163

Hispanic Literature in the United States: Self-Image and Conflict, *Eliana S. Rivero* — 173

A Closing Note, *Nicolás Kanellos*   193
Appendices: Two Letters   194
Contributors   196

In Honor of Tomás Rivera

Tomás Rivera was born in Crystal City, Texas, the son of migrant workers. He became a migrant worker himself. Through his own grit and *search*, he finished college, earned a doctorate in Spanish literature and established himself in academia, becoming in a very short time Chancellor of the University of California, Riverside. But he never forgot the experiences of the migrant laborer's life; they determined his life. Like sand in the cuffs of his overalls, he carried them in his memory and wrote a novel documenting this migrant life that stands today as a masterpiece of Chicano literature: . . . *y no se lo tragó la tierra*.

As a person, educator and writer, Tomás Rivera did much for humanity, his people and Chicano Literature. It was his encouragement and participation that helped establish *Revista Chicano-Riqueña*. Tomás Rivera died, still a young man, in 1984 and returned to the earth of Crystal City, a gem of a man.

For personal reflections on Tomás, I refer you to the remembrances of Rolando Hinojosa and James Abbott. For those who did not know Tomás personally, Américo Paredes speaks for all of us. The essays collected here in honor of Tomás Rivera speak eloquently of his worth and stand as a tribute to the legacy he left us.

Rolando Hinojosa's "Tomás Rivera: Remembrances" takes us on a peripatetic dialogue with Tomás. As we walk with them through the streets of Texas, Mexico, New York, California, New Orleans, we are privileged to share the intimacy of two *amigos estrechos*. We feel their warmth and their concerns about education for Chicanos, share their recollections of good times and hard times. We discover that Tomás was not only Rolando's closest friend, but to no surprise, "knew how to be a friend."

Américo Paredes' "Thoughts on Tomás Rivera" express the sentiments of those of us who did not know Tomás Rivera personally, but feel that we do know him well through his fiction and poetry, where "he left much of what was the best of him." Uppermost in Tomás' thoughts was the welfare of his people; in society, education and literature, he sought for a "sense of community among all *mejicanos*."

Many of us have known or suspected an autobiographical basis to the stories Tomás relates in his novel. James H. Abbott, in his essay ". . . *y no se lo tragó la tierra*: With Tomás Rivera in Spain and Some Personal Memories," uncovers the anecdotes which Tomás related to him and which Tomás later transformed into some of the stories of his novel. Abbott comments on Tomás' exceptional memory and the distance he achieved between the anecdotes and their narration. Above all, Abbott confirms for us Tomás' acute sensitivity, love of humanity and sense of humor.

Remembering forms the basis of two essays by Luis Leal and Eliud Martínez. Leal's "Tomás Rivera: The Ritual of Remembering" confirms that an important characteristic of Chicano literature is the capture of the past. He emphasizes that this retrieval is not motivated by mere nostalgia, but—especially for Rivera—is a ritual of remembering that precedes the ritual of cleansing and prophecy. Rivera noted that the reconstruction of Chicano life and culture depends on the concepts of *la casa, el barrio, la lucha*. Leal comments on these concepts, these cultural matrices, in the works of Chicano poets that Rivera esteemed and also applies them, in the technique of remembering, to Rivera's novel and, most notably, to Rivera's own poetry.

Martínez's "Tomás Rivera: Witness and Storyteller" speaks of the traditional *narradores del pueblo*, the town storytellers who witness life and are endowed with an extraordinary capacity to remember and to chronicle orally or through the written word. Martínez notes this tradition in Rivera's novel, especially in the boy protagonist who becomes aware of a mysterious, inexplicable calling, which he acknowledges at the novel's conclusion. Rivera's storytelling art is characterized by objectivity of observation and subjectivity of selection. The stories, Martínez perceives, speak for themselves, but certain scenes, monologues and snips of conversation allow the author to indirectly comment and express his compassion.

Rivera once spoke of the *tension* that characterizes literature and life. Borrowing the Orteguian idea that a human life is like a dramatic work of art, a struggle to *create* that person that one perceives himself to be or can be, Martínez applies three factors, equally Orteguian, which produced a dramatic tension in Rivera's life. Vocation, circumstance and fortune became articulated in the creative life of Tomás Rivera and dictated a different direction from the life of witness and storyteller.

The essay by Nicolás Kanellos was presented as a paper at a symposium on Tomás Rivera in 1973. Twelve years have not blurred the significance of this document which is made public on this occasion. Kanellos applies his expertise on *teatro* to Rivera's *tierra*. The "Language and Dialog" of the novel is made of the same true-to-life language that characterizes Chicano theatre; furthermore, through their vivid language, the Chicano characters relate and interpret their lives in a most *dramatic* manner. The multiple voices and registers of emotion, and especially the anonymous dialogues, much like a Greek chorus commenting on characters and incidents, make this novel "one of the most powerful pieces of Chicano art." Kanellos draws particular attention to the novel's vignettes that, like the *teatro* skits with their stock characters, are "dramatic capsules that present typical scenes and archetypal characters of Chicano life with humor, pathos and social satire." The three levels of descriptive narrative, dialog and monolog correspond, respectively, to the three levels of society, family and individual psyche; and, as a composite, they dramatize the total culture of the Chicano migrant workers.

My own discussion looks to three essays by Rivera and takes from them the concepts of labyrinth, the *other*, memory, discovery and volition, and applies them to his novel and his epic poem "The Searchers" as instrumental in "The Search for Being, Identity and Form." With Rivera's novel, I compare the opening and closing stories, "El año perdido" and "Debajo de la casa." In the first, the child protagonist, searching for the past, enters the labyrinth of discovery. At the end, he recuperates the past and recognizes the history and collective conscious of his people. This realization confirms his being and secures his identity with the *other*, which is his collective humanity. Form is not only the protagonist's *formation*, but, by noting the stories' symbolic action, we perceive them as allegories of creation. The novel's conclusion is open-ended, leaving the protagonist as an author *en potencia*, whose novel will depend on his volition and owe its unique form to the folkloric tradition from which it emerged.

The motif of the search becomes an odyssey and dominant theme in Rivera's epic "The Searchers." Here I apply the concepts discussed above in an examination of the poet's unique eternalization of time, by which the dead and the living coexist simultaneously in a "fiesta of the living." Through this simultaneity of existence, history is experienced in the present and a "passion of prophecy" is transmitted and kept alive. But it is the search and discovery of form that makes possible the rescue of the dead, the recuperation of a search to realize a prophecy, and the salvation of the living.

Traditional depiction of Hispanic women, especially by Chicano authors, as *good* or *bad, innocent* or *seductress* has resulted in their diminished realistic portrayal, either raising them to totemic proportions or reducing them to marginal figures. Patricia de la Fuente and Sylvia Lizárraga offer penetrating insights into Rivera's feminine characterization. In her "Invisibile Women in the Narrative of Tomás Rivera," Patricia de la Fuente perceives that his stereotypical portrayal of women reflects the values of the period in which *tierra* was written and, as such, the diminished feminine characterization should not impinge on the honesty of the author's perception of reality. This critic prefers to see the absence of characterization not as a flaw but as "evidence of a creative force operating within certain limits imposed by the author to achieve his artistic purpose." De la Fuente notes four categories of "invisible" women, each of which includes examples of the basic good/bad dichotomy. The Chicana/Anglo dichotomy appears to be the most significant and offers insights into the narrator's values. The actions of Anglo women, for example, suggest independence from masculine domination, often with tragic results. As a deliberate narrative technique, female stereotypes are used as an index of male psychological reality, as "stage props to create a series of emotional conflicts" for Rivera's male narrators.

The "seductress" is the subject of Sylvia Lizárraga's essay on "The Patriarchal Ideology in 'La noche que se apagaron las luces.' " As a mirror of social conventions, it is uncommon to find in literature women who break with social mores and do not pay for their transgressions, often with their lives. Such a woman is Juanita, the antagonist of this story who is held responsible for her boyfriend Ramón's suicide. In society's accusation of Juanita's infidelity to Ramón and to the social conventions expected of women, Lizárraga—in an interesting parallel with the Grisóstomo and Marcela episode of *Don Quijote*—sees implicit Rivera's condemnation of the patriarchal ideology for the damage it causes to both sexes.

Rivera's novel, written in the late 60's and published in 1971, during the height of the Chicano Movement, "documents" the lives of migratory workers of the 40's and 50's. While this documentation of past experience, of itself, is not a factor in perceiving the novel as predating the Movement, Lauro Flores maintains that "The Discourse of Silence" is a significant factor for just such a perception. The documentation of the migrant life is filtered by the author through a "spiritual dimension" which gives emphasis to feelings and the human condition. The result of this emphasis is a "dense subjectivity" and the emergence of a "quasi-existentialist vision of the world well within the currents of modern subjective prose." The characters' feelings are rarely externalized; indeed, due to their passive and silent nature, the characters' silent discourse—in which they "think," "recall," "forget," "see," "feel"—manifests an "interiorization of experiences as the only possible recourse that the characters can visualize to be able to order the confusion unfolding around them." When they do try to share their feelings and experiences, their efforts are characterized as limited and sometimes feeble attempts of communication. The discourse of silence, thus, proclaims alienation and situates the characters in a period before the Chicano Movement. The author's characters, Flores affirms, "inhabit a harsh world in which exploitation and denial are still the fundamental traits of their existence and which leaves them no other exit but to express their anguish through a discourse of silence."

Rivera's *tierra* and Sandra Cisneros' *The House on Mango Street* are growing-up stories, and can be said to belong to the genre of *bildungsroman*. Erlinda González-Berry and Tey Diana Rebolledo, in their essay "Growing Up Chicano: Tomás Rivera and Sandra Cisneros," demonstrate that, in contrast to the formation of the male hero, the genre demands that the young female heroine "integrate her destiny with that of a man who will protect her, defend her and create a life for her."

These works of Rivera and Cisneros are similar in that both are a collection of smaller texts which can be read separately but which, together, are structurally and thematically related through the protagonists, and in which the *house* serves as labyrinth and center of consciousness. The differences consist in the point of view, which in *Mango Street* is consistently that of the young girl, and the rites of passage leading to sexual awareness in *Mango Street*'s protagonist, Esperanza. She suffers negative experiences which awaken her to her female sexual vulnerability. With regard to writing, Cisneros' protagonist is more clearly conscious of its use in the act of self-exploration than is Rivera's, who, only at the novel's conclusion, reveals a narrative self-consciousness. Finally, the essential difference is whereas Rivera's character and protagonist search for a lost paradise denied because of social injustice, racism and economic suffering, Cisneros' young protagonist—identifying herself with the victimized heroines of fairy tales—rebels against societal and cultural codes that would subordinate her to the male. In this determination, she breaks with the traditional female *bindungsroman*.

The retrieval of the Chicano past, discussed in many of the above essays is admirably realized through the narrative technique of fragmentation. John C. Akers' essay on "Fragmentation in the Chicano Novel: Literary Technique and Cultural Identity" makes an important distinction between the Chicano and Hispanic American novels. He demonstrates that narrative and structural fragmentation do not signal the chaos and disintegration that various critics maintain for the latter; rather, in the Chicano novel, it is a technique to discover meaning and integration. In the novels of Raymond Barrios, Rolando Hinojosa, Miguel Méndez, Tomás Rivera, Alejandro Morales and Ron Arias, Akers affirms that fragmentation is a "vehicle of recollection and vicarious return." In contrast to traditional narrative methods, fragmentation enables a writer to widen his scope, discover a vast array of experiences in various temporal settings, fix images and affirm identities, and allow segments of reality to be secured on their own grounds as well as being comprehended in their totality. Fragmentation, then, is a "consciously chosen path" that allows the novelist to retrieve and appropriate "what is rightfully his" and to "bring readers to a deeper experience of the unique cultural identity of the Chicano."

In a discussion of U.S. Hispanic literature, we must ascertain which are the Hispanic groups, who are their writers and how do their works express their experiences and ethnic consciousness. Eliana Rivero's essay, "Hispanic Literature in the United States: Self-Image and Conflict," attempts to answer these questions.

Chicanos, Nuyoricans or Neoricans (mainland Puerto Ricans) and a distinct generation of Cuban Americans are the groups that have contributed the most to an awareness of the Spanish-mestizo heritage in the United States. What they have in common, Rivero points out, is that their literature is "the mirror for a hybrid social being," who, while seeking cultural reaffirmation and self-identity, is caught in "the conflict of not being 'fully Hispanic' or 'fully American.' " A principal aesthetic manifestation of this search and conflict is the bilingual medium, which conveys a sense of ambiguity and, sometimes, rootlessness. Chicanos and

Nuyorricans, in the process of self-search, recreate myths—Aztlán, Borinquen—in order to establish cultural space. With regard to Cuban Americans, their literature is often a nostalgic cultural production of their country of origin, but is presently showing signs of a "transition from emigrés or exiles to members of an ethnic minority in the U.S."

Hispanic literature of the United States has reached readers and scholars beyond our borders. Symposia on Hispanic literature are held throughout the world and our literature is now included in many American Studies programs. Indeed, such has been its impact that concepts of "American" literature have been revamped. It is especially noteworthy that it has been the Europeans, and not the mainstream Americans and their institutions, that have recognized U.S. Hispanic writers for their artistic excellence and relevance to the American heritage. In this vein we include three essays from our European colleagues, Susan E. Bassnett of England, and Heiner Bus and Dieter Herms of West Germany.

Susan E. Bassnett's "Bilingual Poetry: A Chicano Phenomenon" begins by pointing out that Chicano poetry is heir to two different traditions that are in conflict. In the Anglo-Saxon world, poetry exists only in its written form and is produced by a minority for a minority, which tends to be middle class and academic, often ideologically leaning to the right. In the Latin American tradition, poetry is both written and sung, word and *canto*, intimately involved in the struggle for freedom and national unity, and whose functionaries are sometimes ambassadors and politicians. As heir to these two traditions, Chicano poetry is involved in a dynamic dialectic whose major manifestation and synthesis is realized in bilingual poetry.

Bassnett distinguishes between two types of bilingualism, vertical and horizontal. In the latter, two languages have equal status for the speaker, whereas in the former the languages co-exist in a hierarchical relationship. For many Chicano poets, then, achieving linguistic parity is of central importance. From a position of vertical bilingualism, they move towards the horizontal, and "out of their particular struggle comes the most original and startlingly creative texts in Chicano literature: Chicano poetry." Bassnett demonstrates that, through this bilingual dialectic, such poets as José Montoya, Ricardo Sánchez, Ernie Padilla and Alurista "have been able to work with form and content, rather than simply concentrating on the overt 'message' contained within the text."

Heiner Bus' essay on "The Presence of Native Americans in Chicano Literature" notes that, while it is commonplace to establish a bond between the Native American and the Mexican American, the Native American theme is relatively rare in Chicano literature. Yet, when it is undertaken by Chicano writers, it is done with intensity and respect for another ethnic minority. Although the profound exploration of the individual components of each group has yet to come, Bus does note signs of such an effort in the writings of Nash Candelaria, Sergio Elizondo, Rudolfo Anaya, Alurista and Pat Mora. The writers' treatment of the Native American theme is "related to the individual choice of subject and point of view"; however, there are certain elements or attitudes held in common.

Nash Candelaria and Rudolfo Anaya emphasize the common roots of Chicanos and Native Americans. In the search for identity, these authors rely on the interplay of Chicano and Indian mythologies and their storytelling traditions. Alurista sees both groups as victims of a "new colonialism" and advocates a mutual defense and protection of Native American values. Bus notes that Pat Mora and Sergio Elizondo look at Native American heritage from a more detached and less "historical" perspective. While Mora's perspective is mainly one of admiration, Elizondo uses "the Native American experience as a means to find new values to build a new world liberated from the oppression of the past." In contrast with much mainstream American literature, Chicano literature's treatment of the Native American theme avoids usurpation, tends away from romanticizing it and perceives Native American culture as part of a common history and a remarkable achievement.

Dieter Herms' "Chicano Literature: A European Perspective" advances the application of Lenin's "two culture theory" to the study of minority literature. This theory, based on the division between the ruling and bourgeois classes, and the working class, Herms finds especially applicable to a country indeed made up of two distinct cultures: the ruling white Anglo culture and the U.S. minorities.

Perceived humanistically, Herms sees this "two culture theory" as fitting between and partaking of Joseph Sommers' historical-dialectical theory and Juan Bruce-Novoa's theory of the space of Chicano literature. This theory "adds to the ideological context of literature the positive emotional"; the ideological and aesthetic qualities of a text (the textual dialectic of form and content) are necessary steps to the *social reconstruction* of the text. This approach, Herms maintains, "addresses itself to complexity of form capturing the complex reality of our time." From a two culture perspective, three works emerge as modern Chicano masterpieces: . . . *y no se lo tragó la tierra, Floricanto en Aztlán* and *La carpa de los Rascuachis*.

Although this approach does not arrive at results drastically different from other theories of Chicano literary criticism, Herms emphasizes that what it can do is "focus more sharply on the anti-imperialist, democratic, socialist, humanist, protest and subversive trends of Chicano literature," as well as address itself to the problems of distribution and reception of literature. Herms affirms that, in the end, Chicano literature is a "literature of peace," not bent on any political dogma but concerned with "survival."

Indeed, Tomás Rivera has taught us all how to *survive*, and through us he *survives*. This is his *legacy*.

Julián Olivares
Houston, 22.X.85

Legacy

for Tomás Rivera

a man of prophecy
has moved on
ahead of our times
there were no parting words
no "Adiós, amigos, me despido."
only his vision
the passing of the torch:

and the poet's hand
burns hot
secrets must be revealed
pen cutting deep
into the blank page
¡escarba!
¡escarba!
como el campesino
a pico y pala
el tesoro allí está
escondido
preservado para el uso
de otras generaciones
todavía no nacidas

Evangelina Vigil-Piñón

Tomás Rivera

Recollections and Essays

Tomás Rivera: Remembrances of an Educator and a Poet

Rolando Hinojosa-Smith

Of all the lines in Tomás Rivera's most sustained poem, "The Searchers," it appears that the following passage from section VII reveals a good part of that valued friend's life and vision:

> We were not alone
> after many centuries
> How could we be alone
> We searched together
> We were seekers
> We are searchers
> and we will continue
> to search
> because our eyes
> still have
> the passion for prophecy.

And these next lines go along with that self-reliant, passionate spirit which I saw in those 13 years we knew each other:

> when we walked
> all over Minnesota
> looking for work
> No one seemed to care
> we did not expect them to care

A first and casual reading may mislead the careless reader into seeing the preceding as words and evidence of a cold personality; his wasn't a cold personality, but he did stress hard and uncomplaining work and, above all, excellent quality at the task on hand. Indeed, a careful reading of "Searchers" will illustrate those strong, enduring human values which he possessed and which all of us admire, if not exactly follow and set for ourselves.

My writing in this instance, and not as a by the way, is more of a memorial to the man and to our friendship and less of a testimonial to his valuable literary contribution. A personal thing, then. It will be anecdotal but as devoid of sentimentalism as I can make it; sentiment, on the other hand, is another matter.

When we first met in the Fall of 71 on the campus of Southwest Texas State University (his alma mater of which he was subsequently designated a Distinguished Alumnus), we fell into a six to seven-hour walking talking conversation that was to mark our usual pattern of walking and talking. We skipped the scheduled conference at San Marcos and walked and talked for some 20 miles that day.

Once, we walked and talked from the Hipódromo in Mexico City to the Polanco District, no mean walk, until we caught a cab in front of the Jewish Temple just off Avenida Moliere. In New York we took longer walks: once from midtown (the Sheraton on Seventh) to Mulberry Street in Little Italy and then across to Chinatown to celebrate some 6,000 years of Chinese history as our country was celebrating its 200th anniversary. We also took other long walks from New York's midtown up to Yorktown and back to the 59th Street Bridge and from there to the Park, down Fifth Avenue and then across to the Taft or the Hilton. We did the same on Los Angeles' surface streets; in San Francisco; Bloomington, Indiana; and on another occasion, from the University of the Americas to Cholula and back again; on the return walk of this one, we stopped to talk with an 83-year-old man working a one-hectare *milpa*. We walked into the middle of the cornfield, said hello, sat down, and listened to that old man as he told us of a trip he had once made to Puebla as a boy. Puebla was less than 20 miles from where we sat.

Oh, we'd take cabs and buses, too, but we preferred walking. Tacitly, then, we both sensed a feeling of freedom in the cold of a New York winter or trooping up and down in the hills of Berkeley and San Francisco or in the heat of April in a Phoenix-to-Tempe hike we once undertook.

We also sat and talked, of course; and we listened to music—to some of Lydia Mendoza's usually—and we'd comment on the talent of the teen-age Lydia in the '30's who was then as she is now: singing and earning her own livelihood in the 1980's.

Our talks, among other things, consisted of admiration for people who worked hard as our working-class parents had; of the talent and patience of the preceding generation; of duties in school administration on both our parts; and as always, on writing: I'd talk of Anthony Powell and Heinrich Böll and he'd come up with Hippolyte Taine and León Felipe.

Nights and days of personal talk of family, too; and then, one night, at the Royale in New Orleans in February of '83, after our two-man show at Tulane (we'd laid in a six pack of Beck's Dark) he said something on this order:

"Roland, I made a list of the places we've been to in the last 12 years. Are you ready? We've lived about a year together in motels, hotels, university accommodations, etc. . . ."

I burst out laughing, but demanded proof, nevertheless. And there it was: the list. This, naturally enough, led us to more talk and to more people; the reminiscences of the near death we both experienced on an airplane trip in 77; of lectures given and places visited together; and of strange readings we'd been invited to.

I reminded him of a reading we once did in a small northern California town: a wind storm was raging, and it was cold. We were in an old house bought by farm workers, and the firewood crackled and snapped so strongly, we had to raise our voices to read, and also to be heard above the voices of some people arguing in another room about buying themselves another keg of beer or something; there were kids playing and rolling on the floor, and then, to top it, Tomás had forgotten to bring his reading glasses. I sat there, next to the fire, listening to "Pete Fonesca"—one of my favorites and his—and as I sat there, I thought he'd rewritten it completely. No such thing: he was saying it from memory; the forgotten glasses were in the motel somewhere.

On another occasion, we were taken to read at an elementary classroom. Unannounced, as it turned out. This was out in Sacramento. It must've been eight o'clock in the evening, and the people there were wrangling about some budgetary item or other and there we were, in the middle of it. Just like that. We were then introduced and the people applauded. As we left, Tomás nudged me and pointed to the classroom: the people were at each other's throats again. Not literally, you understand, but we could hear them well enough as our host—with no explanation or apology—said that was one of the best times *he'd* ever had. Tomás and I fell laughing into the car and, as usual, I caught the hiccups.

Most of the time, though, it was a reading at a too serious academic locale or in some controlled conference or symposium. At other times, on meetings of a more immediate academic importance: we sat on the Board of Directors of the National Council of Chicanos in Higher Education (NCCHE) to decide, in great part, upon the fate of talented young men and women who were to go on in their graduate and post-graduate studies. This apportioning of limited money made it difficult to decide among so many talents in need, but it was more than worthwhile: we were in the service of something, not of someone. And there was fun and almost childish glee and, yes, the pride we felt when a José Limón received his Ph.D. in Anthropology from the University of Texas at Austin or a Ramón Saldívar won his in English from Yale or a Yolanda Julia Broyles won her doctorate in German from Stanford, and the others who went on to Cal, Harvard, Michigan . . .

We met disappointments in some of our selections, but they met no recriminations from us on that account. We didn't expect thanks nor did we get them, and so once in a while, over a dark Beck's I'd quote him a line from "The Searchers":

> No one seemed to care
> we did not expect them to care.

And then there were the exchanged notes and letters over those 13 years regarding more news on family, work, and as always, on writing. And as regards writing, as time went on: more of mine and, to our loss, less of his.

There were also the home visits and that winter quarter term I taught at UCLA when I spent my weekends at his home in Riverside in 1981. And there was Concha, wife, friend, and companion, and their children whom I saw go from elementary school and, for the two oldest, Ileana and Irasema, on through their undergraduate degrees at UT; and Javier who played peewee football in San Antonio, who gathered rocks in El Paso, and who then took up painting, and settled for composing music of his own. Once, and quite by accident since we didn't mean to pry, we discovered that Javier kept some 20 books under his bed, which he read late into the night.

Good times. Watching a track meet at Riverside or seeing the University nine there take on a good University of San Diego squad; and on to Palm Springs to sit in at a Grapefruit League game between Milwaukee and California; watching and enjoying a strong rendition of *The Lion in Winter*; dinners with students at the Chancellor's house. And a typical Saturday workday when we drove to talk to some old folks in Sun City, a drive back to a woman's organization in Riverside, and finishing the day with an evening talk in San Bernardino to a group of civil servants.

Hard times, too. I learned he'd suffered small betrayals and hurts, and some not so small. But above all, there was love. Love for his family first and understandably so, but also for his profession and for education and for the art of teaching which he loved most of all.

And other shared memories, too. In his memorable . . . *y no se lo tragó la tierra*, the novel shows us a section where the verb *remember* appears and reappears as a litany. His letters to me included past doings and future plans as most letters among friends, but the invariable note would be of something we'd done together: some sharing and remembrance:

Aug. 79: . . . that 74 Symposium in Indiana. Remember?
Apr. 82: . . . remember the bougainvillea you and I planted?, it reaches the eaves now.

And on and on. But remember was used not merely as a call to remembrance; there was something else, and we talked about that, too. I'd said that in our case I took the word as the familiar command form; the present subjunctive in Spanish: *recuerda*. He said he liked that, that this would force him to remember, as he had, when he wrote of that horrible experience we read of in *tierra* when his unsuspecting parents, off on a migrant trip—and so that Tomás would not miss school—paid his room and board at the home of a homicidal couple.

But the anecdotes served more than as a remembrance of time past. There was much to learn in them and to pass on, to apply. Without the preaching, we *reminded* ourselves.

And so, as I sit here and write and rewrite and edit this manuscript, I find I was left with more than a list of memories and anecdotes: I was left a lasting friendship, for Tomás was not only my closest, my best friend, but he also knew *how* to be a friend. This was no casual talent.

He also held friendship, respect, and admiration for two *mexicano* deans: don Luis Leal, now a Senior Research Associate at the University of California at Santa Barbara, and a likewise respect and admiration coupled with friendship for don Américo Paredes, the rightly acclaimed and Distinguished Centennial Professor at UT.

And there was warm respect for colleagues and other friends with whom he worked, among them Arleigh Templeton and Peter T. Flawn, two men who recognized his talent, who put it to work, and who were then more than well-rewarded with excellence in administrative abilities of which Tomás had aplenty.

Much has been been written and made, perhaps too much, of the fact that he was the first Mexican American to serve as Chancellor in the University of California System. It's a fact and undeniable, and it may also be a reflection upon the State of California. But look at these facts: Tomás Rivera won his Ph.D. from the University of Oklahoma in 1969, and he was named Chancellor less than ten years later.

Now *that* was an accomplishment.

On this last move of his to Riverside in 78, he wrote: "Concha's getting tired of all this moving about; it's our seventh move, Roland. . . ."

I think he'd have made another one to his beloved state of Texas, and Concha—that fine person—would have made her usual and willing contribution in this move, too.

There's more, of course, but it isn't a matter of filling page after page here. It's something else; it's friendship, and I choose not to talk it or write it all away. It's akin to love in that it is best when understood and shown; there's no demanding of it if it isn't there.

A great loss? Yes; and for me: irreplaceable. But he's not completely gone in a spiritual way and sense because we, all of us who knew him, will keep him, as he said: ". . . in words and in square objects we call books." But he's also in our hearts and minds, because Tomás Rivera left us more than words in books. Yes. He left us much, much more: he left us himself.

Vale, Tom.

Thoughts on Tomás Rivera

Américo Paredes

I never rode on the back of a migrant workers' truck with Tomás Rivera. I never bent my back over the long rows, tasting my own sweat as it ran down the corners of my mouth, feeling the ache at the small of the back as we stooped side by side down interminable furrows. I never sat beside him in class, in public school or college, keenly self-conscious of my threadbare clothes. Nor, in more mature years, did I ever sit across from him at a small table in some *mejicano* bar, hoisting a few *heladas* while we worked out in detail what was wrong with the world and what we were going to do about it. In fact, I am aware as I write this that I never had a private, face-to-face conversation with him in the years that we did know each other—not at receptions or *cantinas*, not at his home or mine. And that realization pains me with the thought of something irretrievably lost.

Whenever we did meet it was in the midst of a crowd of people, all claiming his attention, so that we exchanged a few formal sentences at the most. It makes me wonder whether I belong with those of his friends whose words are gathered here to commemorate him.

I first met the man about the time I became acquainted with the book, . . . *y no se lo tragó la tierra*. I was then Director of the brand-new Center for Mexican-American Studies at the University of Texas at Austin. José Limón, though still a graduate student at the time, was my very capable right-hand man. He suggested that we try to get Rivera appointed to a joint position in Mexican-American Studies and Spanish and Portuguese. So Rivera came to our campus, and Limón introduced us. Tomás Rivera was a very pleasant person with a ready smile, but there was an air of self-assurance about him as well. The iron determination that had carried him so far, and that would carry him much farther yet—that was not evident in his demeanor; and those who did not know him well may have sometimes been deceived as to the man they were dealing with.

Tomás gave the usual lecture expected from candidates for appointment. But our Spanish Department was not interested at the time in a Mexican-American born in El Cristal, so nothing came from his visit. In the years that followed, I kept up with his academic progress as well as with his writings. I saw him occasionally and (as I have said) usually as part of a crowd. I will always regret the twists of chance that kept me from becoming his friend.

In spite of this, I think I did know Tomás Rivera well. In his fiction and in his poetry, where he left much of what was the best of him. There he will live as long as our people can read the language of their forefathers. But he did more, especially for young Chicanos. He marked a path for them in literature and in practical affairs that gives them a model for their own lives. His life is worthy of emulation and a source of pride for all of us. From the beet fields of Minnesota in 1956, to the chancellorship of a major university campus by 1980 is an almost incredible achievement.

But his accomplishments were not achieved in the spirit of looking out for Number One. He was always conscious of his people, especially the young ones struggling for an education as he had struggled. There always was in him a searching for a sense of community among all *mejicanos* in the United States. Time and again, in his *pláticas* and in writing, he referred to the isolation that existed among *mejicanos* doing creative work. In a talk at the University of Texas at Austin, in March 1983, he spoke about the importance of a sense of community that must be attained by that somewhat amorphous whole known as Chicanos, Mexican-Americans, or *mejicanos*. He felt that such a sense of community was important in the development of a Mexican-American Literature, and conversely he pointed out the "many ways that Mexican-American Literature has established community." Tomás Rivera's work has done much to create such a sense of community among us, adding to the *barrio* experience that has been expressed by other writers a living picture of the roots from which we come.

When he was interviewed for *Chicano Authors: Inquiry by Interview* (Austin, 1980), by Bruce-Novoa, Rivera emphasized the fact that in . . . *y no se lo tragó la tierra* he set out to do more than to describe or narrate. He wanted a document, to leave in unforgettable form "the suffering and the strength and the beauty of these people," to give part of our history in Texas a "spiritual dimension" which he found in the people he had known (148-49). "I felt that I had to document the migrant worker para siempre," he told Bruce-Novoa, "para que no se olvidara ese espíritu tan fuerte de resistir y continuar under the worst of conditions" (150-51). That same indomitable spirit characterized Tomás Rivera, and this important part of him must continue to live. Tomás died when he was at the peak of his creative powers; we will never know how much more he might have done had he lived a longer life. But he left part of himself with us, and that part will not die. He showed us that we can win against great odds, and that we all belong together. And he set it all down, *para siempre*.

... *y no se lo tragó la tierra:* With Tomás Rivera in Spain and Some Personal Memories

James H. Abbott

Tomás Rivera and his prize-winning work, ... *y no se lo tragó la tierra*[1] are directly related, in my memory, to the summer of 1969 when we were directors of a group of students who went to the University of Madrid to take the traditional courses for foreigners. Before beginning summer school, we made a ten-day trip through Andalusia to visit places of historical, artistic, and literary interest, and it was then that we began to know each other outside the university classroom in an atmosphere of daily living, shared hotel rooms, meals, and the confines of a tour bus. In addition to many other things, like Tomás beginning to shyly *tutearme*, the days of close contact gave me an opportunity to recognize in him the qualities which go into the making of a successful creative literary artist, teacher, and administrator. Tomás had an amazingly accurate memory for recalling events, anecdotes, and concrete objects from his earlier years, but memory is not the only ingredient of a successful writer. He must also have an acute sensitivity, a sense of the rhythm of words, and the effect they may have on a reader. His sensitivity gave him the ability to anticipate what had to be done for the program to function efficiently, and because he organized everything well, he avoided problems before they could arise. His sense of humor in dealing with the demands of a summer session abroad made that summer one of the most successful during the life of the program. As part of our responsibilities we attended morning classes with the students and gave supplementary classes in the afternoon. Although our schedule was filled with our multiple duties as advisers, teachers, and administrators, we did manage to find time to talk about a variety of things in a relaxed and free exchange of ideas. Every morning we walked to the campus and had a tonic water before going to class; during the noon meal and at dinner we also talked, and sometimes before our afternoon sessions we had a *botellín* of beer at a sidewalk stand near the Colegio Mayor where we lived on the Paseo de Juan XXIII. During our strolls to the campus, in the dining hall, sitting under the shade trees, or on our trips to downtown Madrid, Tomás told me many things. Like all writers, he had a special interest in the language, and he was somehow amazed and pleased to find out that some words he had thought were used only in the Southwest of the United States were also used in Spain. He commented about the verb *mercar* when he heard it on the street one day, giving examples of how he remembered hearing it as a child, and the noun *mezcolanza* amused him when he saw it on a poster because he had thought it was a figment of my imagination. At times he commented on details of the Hispanic world and Hispanic culture which was a part of his heritage. In Cádiz he smiled when he heard some children counting as they jumped rope, "*Uno, do, tre,*" because he had heard that pronunciation in other countries, and the *garapiñadas* he saw in the same city reminded him of his childhood. During the entire summer no detail escaped him, a fact that attests to his great ability to observe life and its many dimensions and manifestations. The same perception and insight, together with his sensitivity, are evident in his writings.

In addition to commenting on things in Spain, Tomás also told me anecdotes and experiences from his childhood and adolescence. He always told these things with his innate sense of humor, and even in anecdotes charged with sadness and injustice he softened them with a smile so that no personal bitterness showed through. Themes of social protest and injustice which underlie much of what he told me never reached the point of overt expression. It would be impossible to determine exactly what his feelings were at that moment, but in retrospect, it seems that his talent as a narrator gave him a kind of objectivity within the subjective nature of the episodes he told. He was obviously aware of the injustices in the world, but his role as narrator was so important that he did not want to mix it with other aspects of his story telling. There was a kind of ambivalence of subject/object that gave his stories a tone of refusing to present himself as a victim who inspires pity and sympathy, as though he saw himself as both subject and object at the same time.

The alternating author/narrator so evident in . . . *y no se lo tragó la tierra* seems calculated so that the reader cannot clearly distinguish the personal experiences that Tomás actually lived from those that he observed or heard. For example, when he told me of the child who was refused a hair cut (53), he told it in the first person as something he himself experienced. In its published form, however, he writes the same event in the third person, like something he saw happen to another child, and it is not until "Debajo de la casa" (164) that the reader realizes that the author himself was probably the child in the episode. On the other hand, he told in the first person the selection about the glass of water under the bed, as it appears in the novel. Tomás probably alternated or juxtaposed author/narrator/protagonist as part of his own personality. He saw no reason for making a clear distinction, because for him everything was part of a united and inseparable humanity to which he felt himself vitally linked. In any event, it does not seem probable that he would change from first person to third without a valid reason. Not allowing the reader to separate clearly one thing from another corresponds, on another level, to the author's own sense of humor, ironic and picaresque, which occasionally left his listeners puzzled. He once told a reporter that his only defect was, "I'm fat," and he told another one that he ate *menudo* for breakfast.² In Spain, as he shopped for a suede coat for Concha and I looked for clothes, he christened a suit I bought as the "Mary Poppins Suit" because of its tailoring. His evaluation was so accurate that I wore the suit only once or twice, but it still hangs in my closet and I smile when I see it. His humor was never intended to deceive or offend his listener or his reader. He wanted to include everybody in his jokes and thus establish a more human relationship and a channel of communication, which is an important, if not basic, aspect of his literary works and his life. The small anecdotes which deal with a conversation or an event without any apparent importance reflect all of humanity, which Tomás loved and respected. Even the unjust deserved his understanding because they are, at times, victims of the injustice they impose on others, like the old man who killed the child and later took to drink, lost his ranch, and probably went insane (67). Saying that Tomás understood does not mean that he forgave injustice, although at times he pitied those who committed it, because in his humanitarian vision of the world there was no room for long-term personal hatred. This love for humanity was what led him to smile benevolently when he repeated the expression, "No, pos sí," which appears in his writings as it did in his conversations.

The attention that Tomás, the writer, gives to language is evident in all the anecdotes and episodes in his work. He not only observed and captured the speech of the characters he presents, but he also transcribed it accurately, so that it communicates to the reader a feeling of something spontaneous and natural. I remember that when he told me the story about going to Utah, he said, "Iuta está camino a Japón" (21). Although this detail may seem unimportant, it does show that Tomás thought a great deal about what he wrote and was not satisfied until he expressed it in the best way possible. This attention to form is precisely what distinguished his work from a sociological or philosophical treatise, although . . . *y no se lo tragó la tierra* includes these two topics or themes and many others.

The sociological themes are easily discernible in his works in spite of the fact that Tomás did not stress them in a belligerent way. Philosophical themes, however, are all-embracing, and may include the sociological or social criticism. An example of the juxtaposition of themes is "Cuando lleguemos," (148-52) an episode which he did not tell me that summer in Spain, but which is one of the most profound chapters of the collection. The story tells simply of the break-down of a truck and the thoughts of the workers while they wait at night for repair so they can continue their trip to another work area. It is an episode which could have occurred or it may be a summary of several. What distinguishes it from other selections is that the author enters the thought processes of the characters and relates what they are thinking. The narrative form thus removes it from the realm of the purely documentary and anecdotal realism. The title itself leads the reader toward an indefinite future, unlike other selections written in the past tense as accomplished facts already over and finished. In "Cuando lleguemos," although one of the passengers says, "We never arrive," they all think and dream of arriving and what they will do, and this "when we arrive" orients them toward the future and the hope of a better life. They never surrender in the vibrant struggles of life, which makes them, biographically, dynamic human beings. The idea that existence is dynamic is compatible with one aspect of the author's philosophical world view, and taking into account his extensive readings, it is very likely that, consciously or not, Tomás suggests this philosophical idea which he knew well from his readings of Unamuno, Ortega, Sartre, Camus, and many others. What he tells in all of the selections is what Unamuno called *intrahistoria*, but what distinguishes the *intrahistoria* here from other selections is the orientation toward a future in spite of the possibility of "we never arrive." Being always in the act of arriving defines the dynamic man as opposed to the static man in Ortega's philosophy. The characters in "Cuando lleguemos" reflect this aspect of Tomás Rivera, the type Ortega would call a select or dynamic man. "Debajo de la casa" also looks to the future, and it is significant that the narrator says, "I would like to see all these people together. And if I had long enough arms, I could hug them all at the same time." The selection, and the novel, ends when the narrator says of the child, "To relate this entity with that entity and that entity with still another,and finally relating everything with everything else." The child then climbs a tree and tries to establish communication with somebody he imagines in a distant palm. In his works Tomás presents a dynamic people, relates everything with everything else, and establishes a channel for communication.

. . . *y no se lo tragó la tierra* naturally lends itself to various interpretations and different levels of reading. The memories of my personal contact with the author as student, friend and colleague are in perfect harmony with what Tomás was as a person and the stories he told me that summer in Spain. All the qualities that it took to turn memories and experiences into a work of art were evident to me then, before I knew that Tomás was going to publish them. If fate had not interrupted the vital course of his life, there is no doubt that Tomás would continue arriving philosophically, because for him life was "cuando lleguemos," and he would still be remembering, creating, working, telling stories to friends, and embracing all of humanity with a big benevolent smile.

[1]Tomás Rivera, . . . *y no se lo tragó la tierra* (Berkeley: Quinto Sol Publications, S.A., 1971). All quotations are from this edition. Page numbers are indicated in the text.
[2]In *URC* (University of California at Riverside, Aug/Sept., 1979), 2.

Tomás Rivera:
The Ritual of Remembering

Luis Leal

For Tomás Rivera the most important characteristic of Chicano literature is the striving on the part of the writers to capture a fast-disappearing past, that is, the desire to conserve past experiences, real or imagined. In his essay, "Chicano Literature: Fiesta of the Living," he has told us that in Chicano literature there is a preoccupation with the past, which is "a ritual from which to derive and maintain a sense of humanity—a ritual of cleansing and a prophecy," and not the result of "mere nostalgia brought about through a disillusionment with what has happened, nor a disorientation within a value system, nor the exploding of the myth of a moral government."[1]

According to Rivera the ritual of remembering, for Chicano writers, is based on three simple images, *la casa, el barrio, la lucha*, which are the bricks out of which they reconstruct Chicano life and culture, and with which they offer us, in their writings, their own world. With these three elements, Rivera, in his own works, gave us a unique view of that world. "The ritual is simple yet complex. The bond is there, the cleansing is there, both for the Chicano writer and for his reader. These effects of the ritual are produced through simple forms as *la casa* and *el barrio* and by the transgressive and ingressive concept of *la lucha*" (452).

The first form upon which the Chicano writer focuses his attention to rescue the past, *la casa*, symbolizes for Rivera the Chicano family, for whom it is a refuge, a place of intimacy, of privacy: "*La casa* is to me the most beautiful word in the Spanish language. It evokes the constant refuge, the constant father, the constant mother. It contains the father, the mother and the child. It is also beautiful because it demonstrates the strong connection between an image in the mind and an external form" (441).

To illustrate how the Chicano writer has reconstructed Chicano experiences using the image of the house and the concept of the family, Rivera, in the same essay, reproduces poems by Alurista, Ricardo Sánchez, and José Montoya. In the first poem, "la casa de mi padre," Alurista recreates the friendly and open atmosphere that prevails in the Chicano home, where visits by members of *la raza* become a ritual. His father's house was always "open and waiting for La Raza" to offer them its hospitality and entertain them with music:

> corridos y jaranas
> boleros

> baladas tristes

The reader assumes that the poetic voice is remembering the nature of his father's house. In the next poem quoted, "Recuerdo . . . ," by Ricardo Sánchez, the poet makes use of the ritual of remembering to write a composition recreating the figure of his father:

> padre mío
> puro hombre
> un chicano orgulloso . . .

As an activist, he is engaged in *la lucha*, the third of the forms utilized to reconstruct the past:

> east el paso lo respetaba,
> barelas albuquerque lo conoció
> > él entonces era azote,
> > chicano que no se cuarteaba,
> era Pedro Lucero Sánchez
> > su madre era Gurulé por apellido

The third poem quoted, the well-known "La Jefita" by José Montoya, "is representative of the many poems written about the Chicano mother, *abnegada*, whose great warmth and strength have contributed to the solidarity of the family" (443). Montoya also structures his poem as a ritual of remembering; the images of the fields and the *carpas* bring to mind his mother, *la jefita*, with her *palote* making tortillas all night long, without ever resting. Around the mother, the poet skillfully reconstructs the life of the field workers, thus preserving, with poetic images, an aspect of the life of the campesinos.

The fourth poem quoted, "chicano infante," also by Alurista, is dedicated to what Rivera calls "the third person contained within the concept of *la casa*—the child" (444). In this composition, the poetic voice addresses the "chicano infante" and promises to protect him and to see that he is happy:

> tú eres feliz
> > y lo serás (. . .)
> i will see to that
> —you will smile (in the sun)

Smiling in the sun is an act associated with the religious rites of the sun worshippers. With that image, Alurista introduces a motif which gives the "chicano infante" a mythical dimension, since the child will be able to perform a rite inherited from early ancestors, the *sol* worshippers.

El barrio, the second form employed by Chicano authors in the act of ritual remembering, "is an important protagonist in giving, conserving and cleansing the poet" (445). To illustrate this form, Rivera reproduces another poem by Alurista, "nuestro barrio," and "Journey II" of Raúl Salinas's well known epic "A Trip Through the Mind Jail." In these poems, Rivera tells us—and this observation applies to the works of other Chicano authors as well—"the Chicano writer is involved in a ritual that takes him back to primal and basic elements of a specific people" (445). Both poems are structured as a ritual remembering things past. Alurista brings to life his dead grandfather, and thus the poem becomes an elegy where the flowers on the tomb turn into crosses:

>   el recuerdo de mi abuelo
>   —de las flores en su tumba
>   dust
>   polvosas flores
>   blowing free to powdered cruces

Salinas, on the other hand, is motivated to remember by an act that will erase a period of his past, his early school days: "They're tearing down the old school / wherein i studied as a child." The memories that the poet keeps best, and this confirms Rivera's theory about Chicano literature, are those related to rituals:

>   What do i remember best?
>   What childhood mem'ries
>   cling stubbornly to the brain
>   like bubble-gum under a table?

Among those memories are Saturday afternoon Confession, first Holy Communion Day, and singing "God Bless America" ("would you believe?").

The third element, *la lucha*, according to Rivera, is "not only linked to but encompasses *la casa* and *el barrio*. *La lucha* is a struggle of cultures, dignified and undignified, a struggle of man and that which he creates, a struggle to tear away one's own masks and discover oneself" (448). To illustrate this third element, Rivera selected two poems by Alurista and one by Sergio Elizondo. The poems by Alurista, "must be the season of the witch" and "mis ojos hinchados" symbolize a struggle "between culture and technology":

>   la llorona
>   she lost her children
>   and she cries
>   en las barrancas of industry
>   her children
>   devoured by computers
>   and the gears
>   must be the season of the witch

In the second, the theme is *la lucha* for racial equality and the dignity of all men:

> mis ojos hinchados
>   flooded with lágrimas
> de bronze
> melting on the cheek bones
> of my concern
>   rasgos indígenas (. . .)
> dust gathers on the shoulders
>   of dignitaries
> y de dignidad
>   no saben nada

In the poem "My Tale," from his epic *Perros y antiperros*, Elizondo ritualizes, by remembering, the act of unmasking himself and becoming, Rivera affirms, "the sum of his own circumstances" (448):

> Brother, hand me the lira,
> you with the twelve-string.
> I have no hymn of glory . . .
> let's see what we make of this.
> I.
> A soldier I went,
> A man I returned.

Tomás Rivera was very well acquainted with Chicano literature, and therefore he had no problem finding appropriate poems to illustrate his theory. In the essay we have been annotating he tells us that he had been involved with Chicano literature for six years (that is, since 1969), but that he had lived its roots all his life; that he had known and had come to feel a bond with most Chicano writers, and that the poets cited are personal acquaintances; that whenever he read poems by them, he participated fully in their intentions. "For me they evoke my people. One comes to realize that we must love those with whom we live, those with whom we share" (441).

Rivera chose to illustrate his theory with the works of others; his modesty prevented him from citing his own works. The only mention of his own writings to be found in the essay is a quotation from an earlier essay of his, "Recuerdo, descubrimiento y voluntad," in which he tells us that in his novel he gave emphasis to the rhetorical technique of remembering: "En mi obra, . . . *y no se lo tragó la tierra*, hice hincapié en los procesos del recuerdo, del descubrimiento, y de la voluntad. Primeramente esto del recuerdo. Me refiero al método de narrar que usaba la gente. Es decir, recuerdo lo que ellos recordaban y la manera en que narraban."[2]

Since Rivera was quite conscious of the narrative technique of remembering, it is relatively easy to find examples of this procedure in his own works. In fact, it would be difficult not to find them. Beginning with his first known work, the elegiac poem "Me lo enterraron" (1967), the three ritual motifs of the remembering process of the Chicano writer form an intrinsic part of his literary technique. In "Me lo enterraron" the poetic voice reconstructs the relationship between the father and the son by remembering recurrent actions. The family rituals consist of simple daily actions carried out by the father. Every night he brings home *pan dulce* for the children:

> que siempre nos traía pan dulce por las noches

He never went to church but knew how to love:

> que nunca iba a la iglesia, pero sabía amar

He loved his wife very much, a fact that did not stop him from having a *vieja*:

> que amaba mucho a mi madre, pero tenía su "vieja."

Every time the boy would ask for a nickel, the father would kick him, but would atone by crying:

> que me pateaba por un quinto y después lloraba

He always worked, sang, and loved:

> que siempre trabajaba
> y que cantaba, y que amaba.

The poem is structured by assuming that the persons who buried the boy's father did not know his personal characteristics, while he did, and therefore he is able to remember them:

> Ellos no sabían
> que traía un anillote con su M bien grabada
> . . .
> Ellos no sabían
> que me enseñó a llorar y a amar
> . . .
> Ellos no lo sabían
> y por eso me lo enterraron.

At the same time, the boy regrets his father's death, the burial is a ritual action that he wanted to prevent, but could not:

> Yo no, ellos,
> ellos me lo enterarron.

> . . .
> Y no quería.
> Yo no lo enterré.

His unwillingness to have his father buried is symbolic of his desire to have him *en la casa*, to preserve the unity of the family and, especially, to have the daily ritual act repeated. Oscar Somoza detects, in the poetic voice of this poem, "a reference to a past time when he (Rivera) was a boy. It is the act of remembering a relationship of love which is interrupted by a tragedy, the death of one individual."[3]

In the number of *El Grito* which appeared during the fall of 1969, Tomás Rivera published seven poems, among them "Me lo enterraron."[4] The inspiration for the second one, "The Rooster Crows en Iowa y en Texas," can be traced back to the days when, with his family, he was a migrant worker, making the yearly journey from Southern Texas to the Midwest during the early summer and returning in the fall. In his essay, "Recuerdo, descubrimiento y voluntad," Rivera remembers that "there was always someone who knew the old traditional stories—*el gigante moro, el negrito güerín*, etc. Then there were always those who acted out movies, told about different parts of the world and about Aladdin and his magic lamp. An oral literature was, in that way, developed in migrant camps" (71). He did not forget those traditional stories, and in his poem about Iowa and Texas he makes reference to them:

> The rooster crows.
> The alarm rings.
> They eat and go to work.
> "Aladín y su lámpara maravillosa."
> The snow falls.
> The truck runs full of people.
> And we return . . . . home. (58)

In the only collection of poems published by Rivera, *Always and Other Poems* (1973), there is a brief poem, "Past possessions,"[5] which is significant for the simplicity with which the poetic voice remembers and gives expression to childhood days through the use of common everyday images associated with the world of the third member of the family, the boy, in his *barrio* environment. This is a poem that brings back memories of childhood days and forces him to recognize himself in the "other":

> A piece of string
> A broken top
> A crooked kite
> A wooden gun (. . .)
> Quiet . . . noise
> A long thin weed a lance
> A few larger cans a dance

> Boxes
> For cars and houses
> Such trivial things

To the idea of remembering Rivera later added two other concepts, those of discovery and volition. The relationship between these two elements can best be observed in his poem "The overalls," where he again makes use of a common image, this time associated with the working world of the campesinos. With it, he is able to express the void and the emptiness felt as a result of the death of a member of *la familia*, and, at the same time, how the experience of remembering the ritual of the burial leads to personal discovery:

> Frightening
> as the attic hole
> the overalls in the garage, hanging
> and the vapor from the train
> swung to my face
> as the cross that
> shouted the lump
> in the cemetery
> and the sounds of clods
> of earth hitting the coffin
> reminded me of something
> I knew nothing about
> the glancing of tearful eyes
> embracing
> as I sensed
> that I had been born
> the crushing vapor
> and the overalls, hanging
> in the garage
> never to be filled again (*Always*, 11)

It was in his novel, . . . *y no se lo tragó la tierra*,[6] where Rivera best succeeded, through the use of the ritual of remembering, in giving form to the life of the migrant worker. It is here also that he exalts the values of the Chicano family (*la casa*), the community (*el barrio*), and the struggle (*la lucha*). This was best expressed by the author himself in an interview with Javier Vázquez-Castro. The answer to the question, "¿Qué datos autobiográficos podrían alumbrar su obra?" is a revealing one, for it does *alumbrar* the motivation for the writing of the novel, and it helps the critic to interpret his works in general. He also tells us why he gives so much importance to the acts of remembering, discovering, and volition. He said:

El hecho principal es que fui "migrant worker" los primeros

> veinte años de mi vida; entonces lo que yo presencié como niño, como joven, ya como adulto, fue una lucha constante del trabajador chicano en el suroeste y en el medio oeste . . . Precisamente, yo trato de describir en . . . *y no se lo tragó la tierra*, que abarca los años '40 y '50, la explotación del trabajador agrícola . . . para que a través de ese recordar, salga la fuerza volitiva que nos permita vernos como personas psicológica y físicamente completas. De ese modo, descubrimos que siempre habíamos tenido voluntad, y que ello nos daría el empuje final en nuestra búsqueda.[7]

The experiences of his migratory years were best transformed into a literary expression in his novel, a work that has been analyzed by critics from every conceivable aspect.

The technique of remembering is best exemplified in the last chapter, "Debajo de la casa" ("Under the House") where the boy hides and there, in the dark, remembers. The use of interior monologue, which predominates in this chapter, lends itself well to bringing back memories, either by thinking about them, by reproducing remembered conversations—a technique common in the works of Juan Rulfo, a novelist admired by Rivera—

or by the reproduction of public speeches: ". . . soveranos—este día es de suma y magna importancia" (sic) (". . . fellow citizens, this is a most solemn and important occasion," 167). This last device is also utilized to integrate into the narrative historical information: "Fue en mil ochocientos sesenta y dos cuando las tropas de Napoleón sufrieron una derrota ante las fuerzas mexicanas" ("It was in the year eighteen hundred and sixty-two when Napoleon's forces suffered a major defeat at the hands of the Mexican forces," 167). It also serves to document the life of the speaker:

> Luego vino la revolución y perdimos nosotros al último, a Villa le fue bien, pero yo me tuve que venir para acá, aquí nadie sabe en lo que anduve. A veces quiero recordar pero la mera verdad, ya no puedo. (167)
> (Then came the Revolution and in the end we lost. Villa came out of it alright, but I had to come over here. Here no one knows the things I did. Sometimes I try to remember, but in all honesty I can't remember anymore.)

The implication here is that being unable to remember one's past is a tragedy, for then the past history of the Chicano will not be reconstructed and will be lost forever.

Rhetorically, the ritual of remembering, on the part of the boy under *la casa*, serves to recapitulate and give structural unity to the episodes that form the novel, the experiences that have been remembered in the previous chapters. The boy thinks:

> Necesitaba esconderme para poder comprender muchas cosas.

De aquí en adelante todo lo que tengo que hacer es venirme aquí, en lo oscuro, y pensar en ellos. Y tengo en tanto que pensar y me faltan tantos años. Yo creo que hoy quería recordar este año pasado. Y es nomás uno. Tendré que venir aquí para recordar los demás. (168)
(I needed to isolate myself in order to understand many things. From here on all I have to do is come back here in the dark and think about them. And I have so much to think about, and so many years to catch up on. I think that today I wanted to remember this past year. But that's just one year. I'll have to come here to remember all the others.)

And with that promise the novel ends. We do not know if the boy went back to his hiding place to remember the other years. We do know that one of those acts of remembering had to do with an experience undergone by his family in the Midwest, when they had to fight an unexpected enemy, salamanders, symbolic of the forces oppressing the migrant workers; that he also remembered episodes in the life of a very unique person, *el Pete Fonesca*,[8] and that he was going to remember life in *la casa grande*, a work that apparently was never realized.

Tomás Rivera is remembered. *Que en nuestra memoria perdure.*

---

[1] "Chicano Literature: Fiesta of the Living," *Books Abroad*, 49 (1975), 441.
[2] "Recuerdo, descubrimiento y voluntad en el proceso imaginativo literario/Remembering, Discovery and Volition in the Literary Imaginative Process," *Atisbos, Journal of Chicano Research*, 1 (1975), 66; cited in "Fiesta," 440-41.
[3] Oscar Somoza, "Tomás Rivera (1935-1984)," in *Chicano Literature: A Reference Guide*, Julio A. Martínez & Francisco A. Lomelí, eds. (Westport, CT: Greenwood Press, 1985), 333.
[4] *El grito*, 3 (1969), 57
[5] *Always and Other Poems* (Sisterdale, Texas: Sisterdale Press, 1973), 3.
[6] Rivera's novel was published by Quinto Sol Publications (Berkeley, 1971) with an Introduction and English translations by Herminio Ríos C., in collaboration with the author, with assistance by Octavio I. Romano-V. These translations appear in these essays, in some instances with slight modification. In subsequent essays, where translations do not accompany the text, the reader can refer to the translations provided in previous essays; editor's note.
[7] Javier Vásquez-Castro, "Tomás Rivera," in *Acerca de literatura, Diálogos con tres autores chicanos*, (San Antonio: M & A Editions, 1979), 49-50.
[8] "On the Road to Texas: Pete Fonseca," *Aztlan: An Anthology of Mexican American Literature*, Luis Valdez & Stan Steiner, eds. (New York: Alfred A. Knopf, Vintage Books, 1972), 146-54.

Tomás Rivera: Witness and Storyteller

Eliud Martinez

> *Pertenece a la extraña condición humana que toda vida podía haber sido distinta a la que fue.*
>
> *Velázquez,* José Ortega y Gasset

Tomás Rivera's death brought an end to a very demanding career as educator and administrator which often clashed with his vocation as writer. His unexpected death leaves a void. Many tasks and responsibilities which he took on by himself must now be distributed among many. The void underlines a valuable lesson, moreover. A few of us should learn to respect the variety of ways that Chicano intellectuals elect to serve our people. Because there are few versatile persons like himself among educated Chicanos, Rivera tried to be and he succeeded, one must grant, in being many men. On behalf of Chicanos and higher education in the United States he sacrificed his literary art and indeed his life.

After a book of poetry, a few short stories and a novel, which followed his years of productive scholarship, circumstances and accidents of time and place forced Tomás Rivera to make a choice. That choice influenced the direction of his life during the last ten years, and particularly the last five, which he gave to the University of California, Riverside. As an educator he chose to become an administrator, which channeled away time and energy from his writing.

Death makes one pause and reflect about life, and in the case of creative artists, one will usually ponder the value of their creative life and work. In his book about Diego Velázquez, the seventeeth-century Spanish painter, José Ortega y Gasset made an insightful interpretation of the relation of the artist's life to his paintings and his career, both as a member of the king's court and as painter, and he employed an illuminating method of biographical art criticism that applies very appropriately to Tomás Rivera's life, career and literary art.

Three distinctive factors, according to Ortega, tend to shape a human life: *vocación, circunstancia, azar*.[1] To understand an artist, Ortega states, one must understand his life and those three factors—vocation, circumstance, fortune—that interplay in his creative life.

> Above all, a life is an intimate reality which exists for itself, and which, by the same token, can only be apprehended from within *(desde adentro)*. If we change the focus of our vision and see life

from within rather than from without, the spectacle changes. Life ceases to be a series of events which occur with sequential connections. It becomes a drama, that is, a dynamic process whose unfolding is perfectly intelligible.

Seen *desde adentro*, Ortega maintains, a human life is like a dramatic work of art. His premise is that "man endeavors and struggles to create, in the world to which he is born, the imaginary personage which constitutes his true self."

Ortega defines the potential personage in the language of dramatic art. He is the character whom the actor would bring to life, an ideal self whom a living being aspires and struggles to create and realize. This true ideal self which each of us is, he states, is called "vocación."

In life as drama, as a perfectly intelligible dynamic process, the interplay between the artist's vocation and the circumstances of his life creates dramatic tension. If one now thinks about the "dynamic process" of Rivera's life, one cannot avoid thinking of his vocation to write and of the obstacles to writing which his administrative responsibilities placed in his path, especially during the last five years of his life. Ortega's conception of creative life helps make Rivera's dilemmas more clear in our minds: "Our vocation clashes with the circumstances which in part favor and in part impede it. Vocation and circumstances, therefore, are two given dimensions which complement one another in the dynamic system they form, and they can be precisely defined and clearly understood."

In Rivera's case the circumstances of his last few years did not favor his writing vocation. His writing was further impeded by a third factor in this plausibly defined relation of biography and art. Oretega calls it "irracional," "el azar," fortune, by which Ortega means chance, or accident as of birth and place, as in time and history. Consequently, Ortega concludes, the components of each human life can be narrowed down to the three significant factors identified above.

Those who knew Tomás Rivera can easily imagine the excessive demands of administrative responsibilities on the talents and skills, and on the time and energies of an imaginative writer. It is true that some of these demands were of his own making, much to his credit because he felt an immense sense of responsibility and commitment to Chicanos and American education, as the record of his public and private life shows. His life was propelled by a mission and a dream, at the expense of his writing career and his personal life. Those who knew his fast-paced and hectic schedule are aware of the time that he spent at his office and on the road, away from family and away from writing. Given the circumstances that permitted him to represent Chicanos, he must have felt that he had to be everywhere. Concha, his wife, stated that Tomás sacrificed his life for the university, and in my personal opinion he sacrificed his writing also to serve our people.

Other writers and artists can surely appreciate the immensity of these two sacrifices. Yet during his short life, without reaching an age that one normally associates with being one of the elders, Tomás linked his literary art with a storytelling tradition which is natural among certain old Mexican people who witness life, who seem born to remember and destined to tell stories.

Rivera was a witness and a storyteller. He linked Chicano literature with oral history, popular eyewitness accounts and corridos. Like the character of Don Lucas in Yáñez's *Al filo del agua*, like other Chicano writers, like many of the elders we have known in our families, Tomás was a *narrador del pueblo*.[2]

In the depiction of *el viejo* Lucas Macías, Agustin Yáñez has given an excellent portrait of a *narrador del pueblo*, which fittingly describes, except for the matter of age, some of our Chicano writers.

> He is not the oldest—elders abound in the village—but among them he has the best memory and the liveliest wit. He is a repository of municipal and public records of individuals, families, events and deeds. . . . Unable to read, he is obstinate nevertheless about finding someone to read him whatever books, journals and newspapers fall into his hands and which he tirelessly seeks to get his hands on. If he had the money, the first thing he would do is to hire an indefatigable reader. In this way he has forged his philosophy, or better still, distilled it from experience and reading so as not to err in remembering a date or a precedent, in prescribing a remedy, giving legal advice or making predictions. "Philosopher of the wake," they teasingly call him, because he does not miss a one, and at each wake he spills forth a torrent of maxims and opinions. Faithful chronicler, he has no personal history. In life he has been merely a witness and a recorder of things that have happened to other people. He does not even know his own age . . . surely he is over eighty, because he clearly remembers that his father, once a soldier, went off to the war in Texas . . . (125, 109)

El viejo don Lucas is not the oldest of the elders, very likely over eighty, but among the old people he has the best memory. He is a walking custodian of public and municipal records, a faithful chronicler, witness and keeper of the records of what occurs to others. It is extremely significant that don Lucas cannot read or write, but the desire to have someone read to him is inexhaustible. Despite never having left the village he is a walking memory of detailed information, dates, events, the names of personages and historical figures. For him sight and smell are the mainsprings of memory. In the memory of this storytelling witness what is immediate and present has little value except when it resembles or parallels the past or foreshadows the future. The wisdom of the *narrador del pueblo* is natural and is most evident in his ability to express philosophical truths about the meaning of the present in the context of the past and the future.

Don Lucas typifies the exceptional witness and storyteller. Those individuals are born with an extraordinary memory. For them remembering the past is an intuitive calling. Telling stories is their destiny. These storytellers, moreover, who cannot read or write, are very likely unaware that remembering the past is a calling and that it is their destiny to tell what history has omitted, as Carlos Fuentes has said, and preserve spoken things that eventually are forgotten—"lo que el viento se hubiera llevado," as Emerenciano Rodríguez Jobrail has expressed it.

An extraordinary memory is the essential and native-born gift of *narradores del pueblo*, despite or perhaps because of not being able to read or write. As more Chicano writers emerge, they will preserve in writing their own stories, the stories of our mothers and fathers, and of our grandparents who did not have the opportunity to go to school, stories that the wind would otherwise carry away, that would die with the witnesses who cannot read or write.

Tomás too was born to witness, to remember and to tell. An unusual memory is clearly evident in his literary work, which established a model for preserving the oral history of our people, in writing. In this light the itinerant poet, don Bartolo, of . . . *y no se lo tragó la tierra*,[3] expresses Rivera's fondness for the voices of our people and for those among us who have preserved stories orally:

> Bartolo pasaba por el pueblo . . . siempre vendiendo sus poemas . . . Y cuando los leía en voz alta era algo emocionante y serio. Recuerdo que una vez le dijo a la raza que leyeran los poemas en voz alta porque la voz era la semilla del amor en la oscuridad. (163)
> (Bartolo always came through town . . . He always sold his poems . . . And when he read the poems out loud, it was a serious and an emotional experience. I remember once he told the people to read his poems out loud because the voice was the love seed in the dark.)

With *tierra*, a novel of voices, Rivera, in the short space of time that he was among us, left a significant Chicano literary legacy that links the stories of our people with those of Mexico, other parts of the Americas and the world; with *lo mexicano*, Mexican popular culture and folklore, language and thought.[4]

The conception of the Chicano writer as witness and storyteller gains in authority when one considers the affinities of our writers with many Mexican and Latin American writers. Their extraordinary works have served as examples for our own writers, and attest to the fact that as witnesses their vocation has been undeniably to be *narradores del pueblo*: Mariano Azuela, Martín Luis Guzmán, Agustín Yáñez, Juan Rulfo, and Carlos Fuentes of Mexico; Alejo Carpentier and Guillermo Cabrera-

Infante of Cuba; Gabriel García-Márquez of Colombia, among others.[5]

A parable by Jorge Luis Borges, "The Witness,"[6] is useful in clarifying further the conception of the Chicano writer as witness. The message contained in Borges' parable applies to artists in general, of course. But ponder it carefully, apply the message to Rivera as a witness whose short life did not permit him to tell the many stories that he could have told, and we become aware of the extent of our loss.

In Borges' parable a Saxon man, like the child protagonist in the first chapter of *tierra*, is in a state between sleeping and waking, sleeping and dreaming perhaps, resting in a stable which is almost under the shadow of a new stone church. He hears the ringing of the church bells, a new phenomenon that has become one of the customs of the land. But this man, the parable tells us, saw as a child the face of pagan gods of divine horror and exultation, the crude wooden idol hung from Roman coins and heavy clothing; he saw the sacrifice of horses, dogs and prisoners. Before dawn, he will die and with him will die, never to return, the last immediate images of these pagan rites which he saw as a child; and the world will be a little poorer when this man dies. The parable continues:

> Deeds which populate the dimensions of time and space and which end when someone dies may cause us wonderment, but one thing, or an infinite number of things, dies in every final agony, unless there is a universal memory as the theosophists have conjectured. In time there was a day that extinguished the last eyes to see Christ; the battle of Junín and the love of Helen died with the death of a man. What will die with me when I die—Borges asks—what pathetic or fragile form will the world loose?

When Tomás died the world lost his memory of other songs of life, impressions and experiences, from his childhood and youth; and, from more recent years, the memories of things that he witnessed and experienced, silently, like the watchful child-narrator of his novel, storing them up for a later time that was not to come, time not in the fields under a hot sun but in an air conditioned office, in a university setting. Other kinds of hardships, no need to name them, different from those of his early life. These new ones, many of us would not have expected at institutions of higher learning. Education has led Chicanos to a paradoxical discovery of an astonishing new world since the sixties.[7]

The hardships of a middle class professional life demanded of him in the end two great sacrifices: his art and his life. The world lost what the witness saw from the fourth floor of the Administration Building at the University of California, Riverside, during the last five years of his life. We may safely conjecture, however, given the evidence of his literary works, that in the course of discharging his duties and during some of the regularly scheduled meetings that took place in his and other offices, the creative mind of the witness was organizing new stories, planning undoubtedly to let the scenes and the dialogue of men and women of learning and culture speak for themselves.

A writer can easily imagine the mind of the Chancellor drifting to scenes of the past. His writer's mind would have found the contrast to present and immediate scenes dramatic and paradoxical. In some cases, however, he would have seen a continuation of old "things" in a different context. Some people know that he made notes and jotted down observations on the back of official documents and administrative correspondence, to be developed later. Perhaps one day his jottings may see the light of day. Or perhaps another witness will tell the stories of Chicanos in academia which the world lost when Tomás died.

Rightly, we honor the author of . . . *y no se lo tragó la tierra* for many reasons. Among them, he was a pacesetter for younger Chicano writers, and *tierra* promised more. Somewhere among his personal possessions, stored in one of many boxes, there is a novel, about which Tomás did not say much, other than that it was to be called *La casa grande*. Among those close friends he said that it was about many migrant workers who rent a big house. The majority of them were men without women, a few were married men. The single men lived on one floor of the house, but they were always conscious of the presence of women. One can see the writer's vision in the "unfinished" stories at the end of *tierra* pointing to a big novel with a host of characters, perhaps to continue those stories. What happens, he asked once, when men without women share a great house with a few married men who have their wives and daughters with them? It is the subject of a Greek tragedy. I think he said something like that.

We honor other dimensions of the man. We honor the educator who, given the circumstances of his birth and early formative years, found it natural to give our people a special place in his educational goals. He brought credit to all Americans, especially those of Mexican ancestry, when he became the first Chicano—and the youngest in the University of California system—to take charge in 1979 as Chancellor of UC Riverside, a major institution of higher learning in the United States.

At last, one could say, our country has lived up to its democratic ideal of equality, but as it usually happens, some Americans remained skeptical about this nation's ideal. His appointment, nevertheless, represented a supreme achievement for all Chicanos. He demonstrated that it was possible.

Part of his dream as educator was to share with the rest of us and, especially with the younger people who follow in our footsteps, the benefits that American education can open up to our people. As his wife Concha has said, Tomás Rivera wanted a quality education for all people regardless of color or race or gender. This aspiration complemented his mission: to increase opportunities for Chicanos to obtain a quality education. He longed to see an increasing number of university-educated, middle class Chicanos. He dreamed of an unbroken chain of Chicano educators whose mission would be to pass the torch of learning and the love of one's people from generation to generation.

I suggest that *tierra* and his whole life's work attest to this aspiration: Tomás Rivera dreamed of our people's fullest participation in American life and society, playing a significant role in the Americas and in our own country, helping to create harmony and good will among people of diverse cultures and backgrounds, with *pride* in our Mexican cultural inheritance and *education* as the two keys to the future of the Chicanos.

The task of carrying out this mission was as solitary as that of the writer:

> Quisiera ver a toda esa gente junta. Y luego si tuviera unos brazos bien grandes los podría abrazar a todos. quisiera poder platicar con todos otra vez, pero que todos estuvieran juntos. Pero eso apenas en un sueño. Aquí sí que está sauve porque puedo pensar en lo que yo quiera. Apenas estando uno sólo puede juntar a todos. (168)
> (I would like to see all those people together. And if I had long enough arms, I could hug them all at the same time. I would like to talk with all of them again, and have them all together. But that could happen only in a dream.)

"In a dream," or in a book, one might add. The last chapter of *tierra* expresses a desire to gather his people together and to immortalize their lives by telling their stories. This last chapter makes clear Rivera's consciousness of a vocation to write. He felt it strongly, deeply and emotionally, but historical circumstances and imperatives dictated a different direction for his life. How could he have known that he would not reach the age of our elders and then tell the stories that he was saving up?

The last paragraph contains the promise of a writer whose vocation was not favored by circumstances after he wrote the book. He represented a new generation of educated Chicanos, one of a small number, too much in demand to represent the collective body of our people. His vocation as writer had led him to a discovery nevertheless; he learned the value of synthesis. In reality he had lost nothing. On the contrary, "había encontrado. Encontrar y reencontrar y juntar. Relacionar esto con esto, eso con aquello, todo con todo. Eso era. Eso era todo". ("He had discovered something. To discover and rediscover and synthesize. To relate this entity with that entity, and that entity with still another, and finally relating everything with everything else. That was what he had to do, that was all," (169).

Another important dimension of the man is the historical destiny to which he was born by accident of time and place and which shaped the course of Rivera's life. At the memorial services after his death, held at the UCR campus on May 19, 1984, several people expressed admiration for the departed Chancellor: President David P. Gardner; Regent Vilma Martínez; Mexican Consul from San Bernardino, Emerciano Rodríguez Jobrail; Vice Chancellor Carlton Bovell, and others. The Mexican Consul spoke eloquently about Rivera's historical destiny. His words acknowledge the interplay of vocation, circumstances and accident. They make clear that historical imperatives dictated a different direction for the life of the witness and storyteller:

> There is a way of being immortal which is offered only to those who possess privileged spirits, those whose passage through life—short though it may be—always leaves a mark. This happens only with persons who believe in something, who live as if obsessed by it, and who are ready to die for it. Tomás Rivera, from an early age, understood his historical destiny, embraced it, and he gave himself up to it completely.[8]

Rivera, the Mexican Consul stated, identified the principal element missing in the Mexican-American population community: the lack of a middle class possessing a high degree of civic responsibility; and he praised Rivera for seeing clearly that the remedy rested upon the persevering insistence on a quality education.

Given the historical accidents of time and place, Tomás was a writer with the credentials and qualifications to be appointed Chancellor of UC Riverside. Consequently, following Ortega's insights, fortune placed Rivera the writer in circumstances which in part favored and in part impeded his vocation as writer. In the last five to ten years of his life, Tomás Rivera's historical destiny took precedence over his writing.

When historical destiny brought Tomás Rivera to UC Riverside, his record at that time attested to an excellent performance and achievement in a variety of areas. His record demonstrated leadership abilities, success in college and university administration, dedicated service to higher education in the classroom and at state and national levels, respect for the mission of the university, unwavering insistence on the highest standards of academic excellence, and sensitivity to minority education.

Now, when Rivera is receiving many well-deserved honors posthumously, it is comforting to know that he was also honored and recognized in his lifetime. This recognition is much to the credit of those who saw the value of the legacy which he was to bequeath. Early recognition came immediately on the occasion of his winning the first Quinto Sol Literary Award in 1971 for the best Chicano literary work of 1970, . . . *y no se lo tragó la tierra.*

Rivera's literary art reflects analytical, intuitive and intellectual powers. At the same time the novel tells us a great deal about the personal vision of the writer. Complexly structured fiction that brings to mind many twentieth-century writers, the novel reflects Rivera's grasp of modern narrative forms and techniques and a knowledge of international literature. The artistic merits of *tierra* were immediately recognized.

Herminio Ríos C. perceptively recognized in his "Introduction" to the first edition of *tierra*, the significance of Rivera as a pace-setting novelist:

> The work of Tomás Rivera is simultaneously a continuation of the past, a landmark in the present, and a point of departure into the future of our literary tradition. It is a continuation because it reflects the multiple experiences of Mexican American themes. The reflection of these experiences and the exploration of their related themes is from the point of view of an inside participant.

Ríos also underlined the importance of the first and the last chapters of *tierra*. The first chapter, called "El año perdido," says Rios, "serves as an introduction" to the entire novel, and "It serves also to introduce the fictional narrator who will reveal what he saw and heard . . . The last selection, 'Debajo de la casa,' is a recapitulation, a synthesis and at the same time an expansion of the thirteen anecdotes and the thirteen selections of the book" (xv-xvi). Rightly, Ríos recognized that the first and the last chapters unify the entire novel and that the two chapters "provide an artistic frame for the entire collection" (xvi).

About the last chapter, Ríos emphasized that it is a symbolic repository of possible themes which subsequent Chicano writers would be able to tap in many ways. The same can also be said of the penultimate selection, "Cuando lleguemos." "It is in this regard that Rivera's work is a point of departure for future creations" (xvi).

Herminio Ríos and other Chicano literary scholars such as Octavio I. Romano, Gustavo Segade, Frank Pino, Juan Rodríguez, Ralph Grajeda and Nicolás Kanellos, among many others, recognized the literary merits of Rivera's work, and they acknowledged his role as a pacesetter. Since its publication, Rivera's *tierra* has been the subject of countless articles, reviews, critical essays and doctoral dissertations. According to Juan Rodríguez, Rivera's novel and other works of the early seventies represented the opening of a new "florecimiento" of Chicano literature.

In a few short years after the publication of *tierra*, Rivera and many other writers, Anaya, Hinojosa, Méndez, Arias, Morales, Valdez, among them, established contemporary Chicano Literature as a progressive and distinct area of literary study and they made it a significant part of the educational curricula in American high schools, colleges and universities. Moreover, Chicano literature soon thereafter attracted the attention of literary scholars beyond our national borders, in Mexico, Brazil, other parts of South America, and in Spain, Germany, France, Czechoslavakia and other parts of Europe, as Juan Rodríguez, then the beacon of the Chicano literary world, reported long ago in his *Carta abierta*.[9]

Tierra, therefore, brought distinction to Rivera the writer. In addition to traits previously acknowledged, his work has several noteworthy characteristics that illustrate the role of the Chicano writer as witness and storyteller. The manner in which certain stories are told and scenes created implies the presence of an observer, the child-narrator-witness, who, being a child, is very likely taken for granted by adults and is probably not even present as far as some adults are concerned. He may seem passive to some readers, but one senses that he is actively seeing and preserving, that consequently his memory is the repository for future stories of seen and felt experiences.

Granted, the child is a witness but not a passive bystander; he feels with uncommon and intense sensitivity, as the selection "Es que duele" makes dramatically clear. The depiction of the child and the expression of his feelings over a series of profound humiliations at the school from which he has been expelled—the most anguishing among them—bring to mind complexly narrated parts of Joyce's *A Portrait of the Artist* and the Benjy section of *The Sound and the Fury*. The child is indeed both eye and heart.

This selection and two others, "El año perdido" and "Debajo de la casa" create a portrait of the child as an artist-to-be, as storyteller. Son of migrant workers, the child protagonist is introspective, a dreamer, a visionary. Like Borges' witness he is not always certain whether he is awake or dreaming. In "El año perdido" he hears someone calling, but "nunca podía acertar ni quien le llamaba ni por que . . . Pero sabía que él era a quien llamaban," and one day he realizes "que él mismo se había llamado" ("he could never find out who it was that was calling him, nor the reason why he was being called . . . He found out that he had been calling himself," 1).

These visions suggest that the child is aware of a mysterious, inexplicable calling, and that he himself has acknowledged it symbolically. In this and other sections of *tierra*, the child wrestles with fugitive impressions, with vague and sometimes recalcitrant memories. In the final selection, as already suggested, a child's vocation as witness and storyteller, his future as writer, and his longing to synthesize set him apart from his people among whom significant formative experiences take place and become engraved in his memory.

The child ponders with unusual sensitivity what he sees and hears, and what enters his mind and heart. Around him, there is much to lament and grieve. The migrant workers' world is summed up admirably in "Cuando lleguemos." Hardships, sorrows, intolerable living conditions, helplessness, suffering, discrimination, misunderstanding, and death—as in "Los niños no se aguantaron" and "Los quemaditos"—are part and parcel of daily life. Rivera's characters are anguished and saddened by undeserved humiliations. Standing up and crowded into a truck, about forty persons are being transported to Des Moines. The reader is permitted to enter into their consciousness and to hear their voices, expressing gentle feelings and hopeful dreams that are dramatized by contrast with a consciousness of biological needs.

The crowded truck is filled with dreams and aspirations, intense anger and overwhelming helplessness, discomfort and resentment, tender recollections and gentle emotions, love and hope. Rage. Surely the thoughts that pass through their minds have been overheard at one time or another by children and remembered in later years.

Rivera's characters feel deeply. They know love and they dream. But as victims of their circumstances they are helpless. Rivera the storyteller conveys their bewilderment, the awe and wonder they experience on migrant journeys to unfamiliar places like Utah and Minnesota; the disorientation that occurs when they are far from home, or even when a mother goes shopping for Christmas for her children in the very city where she lives, as in "La noche buena." They are victims of strangers far from home, of parasites among their own people, as in "El retrato," and of nuns and priests, as in "La primera comunión." They follow cultural traditions, believe in popular superstititions, and accept religion without question. Some of the people pray but God does not listen, for example, the mother whose son is missing in action in "Un rezo," an immensely moving selection. The prayer is a familiar one to those of us who have known mothers with sons in the military forces during the war.

Other people also pray, but god is indifferent to their prayers. The absence of god in the migrants' world of sorrows and sufferings is a dominant theme of *tierra*. In the section that gives the novel its title, the child narrator curses God for not listening to his mother's prayer to restore his father's and his little brother's health. He is astonished that the earth does not open and swallow him up.

The storytelling art of Tomás Rivera is characterized by *objectivity of observation* and *subjectivity of selection*. Scenes rendered with objectivity of observation place before the reader's eyes what can be seen or allow the reader to hear a conversation which is taking place. Rivera points no accusing fingers, does not judge or indict; the incidents or his characters' stories speak for themselves. The reader draws his own conclusions. Subjectivity of selection of scenes, stories, overheard conversations, however, permit the author to comment, to lament, to express compassion, in order to touch the reader's emotions and feelings.

Tierra is a novel about sorrow and sadness. This is true. But Rivera is not saying that all Chicanos live in an unfortunate world. The novel is also about a special kind of childhood—the childhood of the artist. *Tierra* is about a child's delicate feelings, about a child's waning innocence, about people's dreams and hopes, and about gentle transformations of the heart and soul. Even in those sections of the novel where the child protagonist is absent, his presence is strongly felt. Rivera has so subtly and skillfully established the child as the consciousness through which all things pass and acquire artistic form, that the reader assumes his presence. Often, therefore, the reader sees with the child's eyes, hears and *overhears* with his ears, feels with the child's heart, shares his emotional experiences, and his awe and wonder and curiosity about life. One feels the child's presence; since he is a writer-to-be, nothing escapes his eye, his mind, his feeling.

Rivera's storytelling gifts are much in evidence in . . . *y no se lo tragó la tierra*. His depiction of the migrant workers' world is realistic. For the most part this depiction is characterized by fidelity to his characters' way of life, objectivity of observation and directness of expression. There is no embellishment or aggrandizement, no protest or outrage. The absence of author or narrator commentary and the fact that the child is solitary should not be misinterpreted. Neither the child protagonist nor Rivera the writer have separated themselves from their people. Rivera's and the child protagonist's world of reflection, because of the writer's subjectivity of selection, never leaves any doubt about his compassion towards his fictional creations and the world they represent.

Rivera has not, of course, interpreted the whole of Chicano reality. The migrant workers' world is a significant single facet of the Chicano Experience. One can take any position, according to one's own disposition and inclinations, with respect to that world. But the fact remains that it is there, and whereas the reader's position may be in question, Rivera's never is. His subjectivity of selection reflects the writer's sensibility, a fascination with a particular kind of experience which reveals an unusual degree of human vulnerability, fundamental goodness and faith. Rivera exhibits in his work deep understanding, compassion and sensitivity to human feelings. Rivera's *tierra* may very well contain a message that one must give due credit to those experiences which shape our spirits and the whole direction of our lives.

In Rivera's art, consequently, many facets of a collective way of life pass through his perceptive and experienced eye, come together, coalesce and acquire an artistic configuration. Artistically, some of Rivera's prose is as compact, direct and powerful as that of Hemingway. As a novel of voices,[10] Rivera's work attests to his kinship with Faulkner and Juan Rulfo. The subject matter of some of the stories and the conversational quality of the style relate *tierra* to the traditional ballad form, to the Mexican *corrido*, and to the literature of childhood and the provinces. "La noche que se apagaron las luces" tells a well known story many times expressed in Mexican *corridos*, a story of unrequited love, drinking, jealousy, and tragedy based on misunderstanding. Through his art, then, Tomás Rivera has expressed in a remarkable way, the child's and the writer's joy in the discovery that art synthesizes, gives meaning and lasting form to diverse experiences.

Tomás Rivera—witness and storyteller—touched many lives with his own, as educator, administrator, writer, and man. In literature he opened up Chicano eyes to the rich storehouse of experiences among our people, to the beauty of our language and cultural inheritance. As a national leader and representative of Chicanos, he lived at a fast pace, with an admirable sense of mission. That he did not publish more requires no apology.

The accident—*el azar*—of his birth at a significant time in history placed him in *circunstancias* that did not favor his *vocación* as a writer. That he did not publish more is a positive sign of his double sacrifice. His historical mission made him a gregarious person; the artist was a solitary man in my judgment. He was a witness. Rivera was a socially conscious educator, a busy administrator, a fervent advocate of educational opportunities for Chicanos, a member of countless national organizations and committees. The inspiration and encouragement which Tomás brought into countless people's lives will always be remembered. His literary art and the naming of the campus library in his honor—the Tomás Rivera Library at the University of California Riverside—ensure for him a place of immortality in the world of books.

---

[1] José Ortega y Gasset, *Velázquez* (Madrid: Revista de Occidente, 1959 ed.). The epigraph and the passages quoted in the present essay are from Chapter II of this edition. All translations are my own and contain some paraphrasing.

[2] Pages in parenthesis in the text, from Yáñez's novel, refer to the Mexican edition (México: Editorial Porrúa, 1969 ed.) and the English translation by Ethen Brinton (*The Edge of the Storm*, Austin: University of Texas Press, 1963), respectively. For reasons of style and conceptual consistency in developing my theme of the writer as witness and storyteller, I have made my own translation of the Yáñez text.

[3] Tomás Rivera . . . *y no se lo tragó la tierra* (Berkeley: Quinto Sol Publication, 1971). The "Introduction" by Herminio Ríos C. in Spanish is on pages viii-xi. Quotations in English are from this edition.

[4] Ernestina Eger has advanced Chicano literary scholarship with her *A Bibliography of Criticism of Contemporary Chicano Literature* (Berkeley: University of California, Chicano Studies Library Publications, 1982). See the valuable index of topics, particularly pp. 267-269, for Mexican and Chicano literary connections. Her bibliography on criticism of Rivera's work is on pp. 161-167, and includes cross-references to other critical articles that deal with Rivera's work. See also the entry "Tomás Rivera," by Oscar Urquídez-Somosa, in Julio A. Martínez and Francisco A. Lomelí, eds. *Chicano Literature: A Reference Guide* (Westport: Greenwood Press, 1985), 332-46.

[5] The following works will be useful in establishing parallels and similarities between Chicano and Latin American literary works. Alejo Carpentier, *Tientos y diferencias* (Montevideo: ARCA, 1967), especially the first chapter, "La problemática de la actual novela latinoamericana," 9-60; Eliud Martínez, *The Art of Mariano Azuela* (Pittsburgh: Latin American Literary Review Press, 1980); Eliud

Martínez, "Ron Arias' *The Road to Tamazunchale:* Cultural Inheritance and Literary Expression," an introduction to a forthcoming edition of Arias' novel, to be published by the Bilingual Review Press.

[6] Jorge Luis Borges, "The Witness," *Labyrinths* (New York: New Directions, 1964), 243.

[7] See Tomás Rivera, "Recuerdo, descubrimiento y voluntad en el proceso imaginativo literario," *Atisbos: Journal of Chicano Research*, I (1975), 72, for a discussion of the shock produced in the Chicano child upon his exposure to the North American educational system and the cultural values it espouses.

[8] Parts of the Mexican Consul's statement appeared in the *University Bulletin*, UC, vol. 32 (May 28, 1984), 1.

[9] See Eger, op. cit. for a complete list of Juan Rodríguez's critical essays.

[10] Stephen M. Ross, " 'Voice' in Narrative Texts: The Example of *As I Lay Dying*," *PMLA* 94:2, 300-310, discusses two kinds of voice narrative methods. See also Joseph Warren Beach, "The Esthetics of Simplicity," in *American Fiction: 1920-1940* (New York: Atheneum, 1941, rpt. 1972), 97-119.

Language and Dialog in
. . . y no se lo tragó la tierra

Nicolás Kanellos

One of the most important contributions of Chicano literature can and must be the examination from within of a living culture that has survived, evolved and is now making its existence known with pride, despite having had to overcome a long history of intellectual and artistic neglect by a society and publishing industry dominated by Anglo-Saxon norms. The Chicano writers, as intellectuals, must try to analyze Mexican American culture from within as participant observers in order to bring the culture's values to the forefront and combat the too often repeated cliches and stereotypes that even the social scientists of the last three decades have legitimized with their "objective," but too often culture-bound methods and their dehumanizing jargon.[1] Where social scientists may succeed in isolating and analyzing one or another element of this culture, the Chicano artist can portray the full cultural experience as he sees it, revealing whole patterns of the tapestry for our perusal rather than a thread at a time. While a scientist may study "public language versus private language in Mexican Americans,"[2] the artist can reproduce that language in its social and cultural context.[3] An artist who fulfills this need to reveal Chicano life in all of its richness through literature is Tomás Rivera. His prize-winning novel, *. . . y no se lo tragó la tierra*, is a warm and sensitive portrayal of the Chicano experience in the agricultural fields of the Midwest and the barrios of Texas. It is an accomplished landmark of Chicano literature in that it permits the reader to hear the testimony of the Chicanos first-hand in their own language while interpreting experience from within their own culture.

The narrative structure of *. . . y no se lo tragó la tierra*, taken as a whole, along with the Chicano language that is faithfully, but artistically reproduced, helps to bring the reader into a world rarely ever depicted in the written literature of the Spanish language. As the narrative point of view shifts from the impersonal omniscient narrator to dialog, monolog and first person narration, the Chicano language becomes accordingly more intimate and emotive, opening up new realms of experience with an appropriately new literary vocabulary that is highly endowed with the phonology, neologisms, anglicisms and idioms of Chicano Spanish. The Chicano language, considered by some as a regional dialect of Spanish, is represented here in its most universal and artistic form, while exhibiting the flexibility and expressiveness to reproduce the argot called for in each social situation, whether it be a dialog between fieldhands, the impassioned litany of a mother beseeching her gods to protect a son in Korea or the thoughts of a confused child expelled from school.

The diverse narrative elements of . . . *y no se lo tragó la tierra* represent a collage of personal experiences, overheard conversations, and observations of a young boy who has lost his memory and, therefore, sets about reconstructing the past year of his life for himself. An impersonal omniscient narrator penetrates the innermost thoughts of the child from the start and almost immediately lessens the distance between himself and his subject by gradually mimicking the speech and thought patterns of the child, by adopting the viewpoint of the child and finally by turning the narration over to the child as a dramatic narrator. Both the omniscient narrator and the child as a dramatic narrator stop telling the story and incorporate whole dialogs by unidentified interlocutors who narrate and offer commentary through their dialogs in a more colloquial and informal, but, certainly, more immediate manner. One can see, then, that both monolog and dialog play an important role in the narrative structure and the style of . . . *y no se lo tragó la tierra*; through them the Chicano characters relate and interpret their own lives and the lives of their neighbors in the most dramatic manner with the most vivid and orally effective language. Thus, of the different narrative devices utilized in . . . *y no se lo tragó la tierra*, the one that most effectively and with the greatest impact communicates the life-style, worldview and culture of the Chicanos is dialog. That is, the testimony of the people themselves, with their most candid and humble voices, is the factor that makes this novel one of the most powerful pieces of Chicano art. We must remember, moreover, that it was the collective voice of the people that preserved the Hispanic tradition in the form of folklore through the lean years of the Chicano past. The following will be an examination of the use of dialog in . . . *y no se lo tragó la tierra*.

Narration Through Dialog

Tomás Rivera's . . . *y no se lo tragó la tierra* is haunted by the nameless Chicano masses whose nocturnal voices reflect on the events narrated and record them into the collective memory of the Chicano. Rivera, in reproducing the Chicano social milieu, allows the reader to eavesdrop on the candid, all-knowing and unguarded conversations of the unidentified interlocutors who represent the collective subconscience of the Chicanos. We see through them how Chicanos interpret reality. For the most part, these night-time speakers are not even circumstantially related to the plot; rather, they review for each other what they themselves have heard. It seems that they are one step from oral history and folklore, one step from immortalizing their subjects in a *corrido* or folktale. In one of the last sketches, there is a curious troubador by the name of Bartolo who performs a task similar to that of these voices when he makes the rounds each year to sell the poems he has written on the lives of his people. He prefers to have the poems read aloud, for he believes that the voice is "la semilla del amor en la oscuridad" ("the love seed in the dark")[4]. Indeed, much of our narration comes from loving nocturnal voices, the voices of the Chicano collective subconscience.

In "Los niños no se aguantaron" ("The Children Were Victims"), after hearing the tragic story of the boss who shot a child that was pausing from his labor to drink water, the voices of the anonymous chroniclers of Chicano life summarize the outcome of the story in dialog and reveal to the reader the impression that the incident has left on the Chicano collectivity. On the one hand, the Chicano feels that divine justice has intervened to plague the boss with guilt, poverty and drunkenness. This causes the Chicano to pity the murderer. But on the other hand, the Chicano remains somewhat silently skeptical and bitter because the boss has not been punished by the law:

—Pero no se mató, ¿verdad?
—Pos no.
—Ahí está. (7)
(But he didn't kill himself, right?—Well, no.—There you are.)

A similar case of narration through dialog also follows a tragedy involving children in "Los quemaditos" ("Little Children Burned"). Here too the tragedy basically derives from social injustice and ends with a note of bitter irony. A father has given his children boxing gloves, wishing them to learn the art of boxing to someday, perhaps, arise from their poverty through success in the ring. The children, who must be left at home while the parents work, accidently set the house on fire while they are playing at boxing and perish in the flames. The Chicano sensibility is quick to point to an ironic paradox:

—Pero, ¿por qué no se quemarían los guantes?
—Es que esta gente sabe hacer las cosas muy bien y no les entra ni la lumbre. (96)
(But I wonder why the gloves didn't burn.—The fact is that these people know how to make things so well that not even fire will touch them.)

That is, "these people" know how to make such things as boxing gloves last and withstand fire, but such things as children and houses are perishable. Ultimately, this idea points to a society that cares more about material goods than human beings.

In "La noche que se apagaron las luces," ("The Night of the Blackout"), this type of indirect narration is used most effectivly when combined with the dramatic dialogs in which Ramón and Juanita act out their feelings for one another. Here the situation of a love triangle reaches a violent climax when honor and love clash during a dance. This is one of the most well known and repeated themes in the oral as well as the written literature of Mexicans and Chicanos. In this literary version, the anonymous commentators narrate the tale as set against the background of migrant farmwork in Minnesota and Texas. The story of Ramón and Juanita, as presented here, seems one step from being assimilated into the repository of Chicano folklore, perhaps in the form of a *corrido* similar to "El Corrido de Rosita Alvírez."[5] Here, as in the *corrido*, the story culminates in tragedy; however, the senseless loss of life is somewhat underscored by one of the last paradoxical statements made by the nocturnal narrators:

—Es que se querían mucho, ¿no crees?
—No, pos sí. (109)
(They were very much in love, wouldn't you say?—Yes. Of course.)

Rivera has also used this type of narrative technique in the miniatures that are affixed to the stories. In the twelfth one, voices tell of the misfortune that befell a migrant worker named Figueroa. He was imprisoned in Texas for statutory rape, having brought back a seventeen-year-old Anglo girl with him from Wisconsin. To the narrators it seems that the reason that he was turned in and convicted was that she was an Anglo and thus out of bounds for a Mexican.

In summary, in the above dialogs carried on by unidentified voices that echo through the night, the tales of Chicano life are being recorded into the collective memory of the people. The language of the omnipresent witnesses is that of the common man passing on information to his neighbor. The social setting of such dialogs could be that of a street corner, a tavern, a front porch or any place where people pass the time together. The language is not as immediate and subjective as that of the direct dialogs that take place in the family setting nor as intimate as the language of the monologs and private thoughts of the other characters of the book, but it definitely is a more colloquial type of speech than that of the third person omniscient narrator.

Dialog as Drama

The language of . . . *y no se lo tragó la tierra* is basically the language of oral expression and, as such, can be very dramatic. But the language that is most dramatic and most authentic in its reproduction of Chicano Spanish is to be found in the dialogs of the characters who interact socially, as opposed to those who merely narrate. These dialogs are mimetic or representational in that they recreate the actions, language and attitudes of Chicanos in definite social situations rather than describe them. Moreover, some of the short, introductory sketches affixed to the longer narratives are complete dramatic vignettes that explore some facet of life in the *barrio* or in the field. They are made up entirely or mostly of dialog and are similar to Chicano theatre skits. In fact, in . . . *y no se lo tragó la tierra* and in lectures that he has given, Tomás Rivera has revealed himself to be not only familiar with, but an admirer of Chicano improvisational theatre and folkdrama. In "La noche estaba plateada" ("It Was a Silvery Night"), he makes reference to the traditional shepherds' play, the *pastorela*, and makes a study of the Devil, the principal character of the "Coloquio de los Pastores":

> Lo del diablo le había fascinado desde cuando no se acordaba. Aun ya cuando lo habían llevado a las pastorelas de su tía Pana tenía la curiosidad por lo que podría ser y cómo sería. Recordaba a don Rayos con la máscara de lámina negra y los cuernos rojos, y la capa negra. (55)
> (The thought of the devil had fascinated him ever since he could remember. Even when they took him to his aunt Pana's pastorals he was curious as to the devil's nature and how it might appear. He remembered don Rayos and his black tin mask that had the red horns on it, and his black cape.)

The most recent manifestation of the long tradition of Mexican folkdrama in the Southwest is *teatro chicano*, the traveling theater of improvised *actos* or skits which attempt to present "estampas de la vida del barrio" for the Chicano community. The *actos* are performed in Spanish, English or a combination of both, depending on the social situation depicted. *Teatro chicano*, reminiscent of the *commedia dell'arte* and Chicano vaudeville, attempts to recreate the bittersweet scenes of Chicano life through humorous, but true-to-life dialog. Satire, pathos, irony, humor and, at times, slapstick comedy are constants of this theater. On various occasions Rivera has referred to Chicano theater as "the most pure and committed" of Chicano art forms.[6] It is interesting to note that one of these theater groups, El Teatro del Piojo of Seattle, Washington, is planning to perform "Cuando Lleguemos" from . . . *y no se lo tragó la tierra*.[7] This curious fact more than underlines the kinship of Rivera's work to Chicano theater.

Some of the sketches or miniatures in . . . *y no se lo tragó la tierra* are similar in format, content and language to Chicano theater *actos*. They are dramatic capsules that present typical scenes and archetypal characters of Chicano life with humor, pathos and social satire. A good example of this type of dramatic miniature is the piece that humorously depicts the dilemma of the poor migrant worker who must travel to far away to unfamiliar regions at the mercy of the traditionally untrustworthy labor contractor, the "enganchista":[8]

—Comadre, ¿ustedes piensan ir para Iuta?
—No, compadre, si viera que no le tenemos confianza a ese viejo que anda contratando gente para . . . ¿cómo dice?
—Iuta. ¿Por qué, comadre?
—Porque se nos hace que no hay ese estado. A ver, ¿cuándo ha oído decir de ese lugar?
—Es que hay muchos estados. Y esta es la primera vez que contratan para ese rumbo.
—Pos sí, pero, a ver, ¿dónde queda?
—Pos nosotros nunca hemos ido pero dicen que queda cerca de Japón. (21)
(¿Comadre, are you planning to go to Utah?—No, compadre, you see, we don't trust that man who is signing up people to go to . . . what place is that?—Utah. Why, comadre?—Because we don't think such a state exists. Look, when did you ever hear of that place?—It's just that there are so many states. And this is the first time that they are signing up people for that area.—Well, yeah, but let's see, where is it?—Well, we've never been there ourselves, but they say it's close to Japan.)

This short dialog is bittersweet in that it satirizes a serious problem of Chicano life, the problem of migrant farmwork, through the humorous situation of the worker who is not too sure about the existence of the state of Utah. While one tends to smile at the innocence of such humble people, one also sees the injustice and hardship in their being transported like cattle to far off and unheard of regions to *camellar*, work, as the *corridos* put it.[9] The language is the everyday speech of the Chicanos who share the *compadrazco* relationship. As such, it is informal, relaxed and colloquial.

Another *teatro*-type miniature deals with the motivation of Chicano children to continue their education:

—¿Para qué van tanto a la escuela?
—El jefito dice que para prepararnos. Si algún día hay una oportunidad, dice que a lo mejor nos la dan a nosotros.
—N'ombre. Yo que ustedes ni me preocupara por eso. Que al cabo de jodido no pasa uno. Ya no puede uno estar más jodido, así que ni me preocupo. Los que sí tienen que jugársela chango son los que están arriba y tienen algo que perder. Pueden bajar a donde estamos nosotros. ¿Nosotros que? (37)
(Why do you go to school so much?—My father says that it's to prepare us. If some day there's an opportunity, he says that maybe they'll give us a chance.—Hell, man. If I were you I wouldn't even worry myself over that. The downtrodden will always be downtrodden. Things can't get any worse, so I don't have to worry about it. The guys who really have to play it smart are the people who have something to lose. They could come down to where we are. And then what about us?)

Here, in the form of folk wisdom, someone dissuades a child from studying too much because there is no opportunity for educated Chicanos and, at least, there is security in the knowledge that you are at the bottom of the social ladder. While the speech patterns of the philosopher who is expressing his frustration may evoke humor, underlying his words is defeat, defeat accepted and rationalized.

An equally pathetic scene which is developed in dialog is that of the mother who consults the *espiritista* to see if her son has died in Korea, as the missing-in-action telegram warns. She is greatly relieved after a possessed body tells her that her son is safe and sound. In this *acto*, as in the other two, the characters remain nameless, their only identification being their social role. This too is a characteristic shared with *teatro chicano* where the characters will go to the extent of wearing signs which declare their relationship to one another: "La Mamá," "El Compadre," "El Patroncito," "La Gringuita," etc.

Dramatic dialog is also very important in the longer stories. In "Cuando lleguemos" ("When We Arrive"), it is used almost exclusively, there being only a short prose paragraph at the beginning and another at the end serving as introduction and conclusion. It is noteworthy that *teatro chicano* skits are also preceded by an explanation or introduction by a member of the troupe, usually the leader, who serves as a master of ceremonies. "Cuando lleguemos" is a dramatization of the frustrating life of the migrant worker who, in this instance, has to endure the further burden of the truck breaking down. The people are tired and disgusted and some voice their resolutions to stay up north and look for work in the city. One of the more serious intentions of this selection, however, is the depiction of the motivations, trials and histories of migrant workers. The entrapment of the workers into debt and dependence by the ranchers is illustrated here, for example, as is the increasing migration of Chicanos to Midwestern cities. In "Cuando lleguemos" the humor derives from situation and somewhat from language, this time the language of vituperation. A very earthy comic incident occurs when a mother riding in the cab of the truck shakes out her child's soiled diapers. The excrement gets caught by the wind and flies back into the faces of the workers riding in the rear. Language in "Cuando lleguemos," as in Chicano theater, is identified with social reality and does not, therefore, shy away from the earthy, as can be seen time and again in this selection. In this concern for realism, passages in English are introduced here, as in "La Noche Buena" ("Christmas Eve") and "Es que duele" ("It is Painful"), when a non-Spanish-speaker talks. There is no attempt to translate his words into Spanish to create a linguistic unity in the book; this would not be true to life. Moreover, this may imply that the book's intended audience is bilingual.

In some of the selections of . . . *y no se lo tragó la tierra*, dramatic dialog is combined with other narrative devices. The dialogs serve to bring to life characters who, up to this point in the narration, may have been described in the third person. The reader gets an opportunity to hear them speak for themselves with their own characteristic speech habits. Through the dialogs of these characters, the reader also gets acquainted with a whole gallery of Chicano archetypes. This is possible because each slot in the society reveals itself through its own special argot and the deference it shows to the other stations of that society. In "Los niños no se aguantaron," the respect that a son has for his father is seen in the son's use of the third person singular when addressing the head of the family. The conversations in the family setting demonstrate the intimacy and warmth of the Chicano hearth. In the following excerpt we have a son coaxing his father in the nicest language possible and the father affectionately exorting his wife:

—Apá. ¿Por qué no deja la puerta abierta? Que al cabo ni hay zancudos.
—Sí, pero ¿si se mete un animal? Ya vites como se les metió el tejón aquel a los Flores.
—Pero si eso fue hace dos años. Andele, déjela abierta. Hace mucho calor. No se mete nada. En esta mota lo único que queda son los cuervos y esos no buscan las casas. Andale, fíjese como las demás gentes dejan las puertas abiertas.
—Sí, pero siquiera tienen telas.
—No todas, ándele, mire que bonita se ve la luna. Todo en paz.
—Bueno . . . . N'ombre, vieja, no se mete nada. Tú siempre con el miedo. (54)
(Father, why don't you leave the door open? There aren't even any mosquitos anyway.—Sure, but if some animal should crawl in? You remember how that badger got into the Flores' house.—But that was almost two years ago. Come on, leave it open. It's very hot. Nothing will crawl in. In this growth of trees the only things left are the crows, and they don't go around looking for houses. Come on, look at how the people leave their doors open.—Yeah, but at least they have screens.—Not all of them. Come on, look at how pretty the moon is. Everything so peaceful.—Well . . . Look, vieja, nothing is going to come in. You and your fear.)

In "Es que duele" we see the shyness of the child and the pride of the father through a *teatro*-type vignette. This piece shows that the parents have high expectations for their child; they wish him to study hard and do well in school so that someday he can become a telephone operator. Within the context of available opportunities for Chicanos, this seems to them to be a great goal for their son. Ironically, this point of view is corroborated for the father when the boss laughs at the idea:

—Sí, compadre, está muy empeñado m'ijo en ser eso, si viera. Cada vez que le preguntamos dice que quiere ser operador. Yo creo que les pagan bien. Le dije al viejo el otro día y se rió. Yo creo que cree que m'ijo no puede, pero es que no lo conoce, es más vivo que nada. Nomás le pido a Diosito que le ayude a terminar la escuela y que se haga operador. (26)

(Yes, compadre, you wouldn't believe it but my son is really set on that. Everytime we ask him he says he wants to be a telephone operator. I think they're well paid. I told my boss about it the other day and he laughed. He probably thinks that my son can't do it, but the fact is that he doesn't know him, he's smarter than anything. I just pray that God helps him finish school and that he becomes one.)

In the same story, the reader gets a sampling of an Anglo principal's language and the attitudes that it embodies.

The specialized language of the fields and farmwork is shown in the title story ". . . y no se lo tragó la tierra" as the workers discuss their strategy for dealing with the ungodly heat:

—Cuando vean oscuro, muchachos, párenle de trabajar o denle más depacio. Cuando lleguemos a la orilla descansamos un rato para coger fuerzas. Va a estar caliente hoy. Que se quedara nubladito así como en la mañana, ni quién dijera nada. Pero nada, ya aplanándose el sol ni una nubita se le aparece de puro miedo. Para acabarla de fregar aquí acabamos para las dos y luego tenemos que irnos a aquella labor que tiene puro lomerío. Arriba está bueno pero cuando estemos en las bajadas se pone bien sofocado. Ahí no ventea nada de aire. Casi ni entra el aire. ¿Se acuerdan? (69)

(When you kids see blurry, stop working or slow down. When we get to the end of the rows we'll rest awhile to regain our strength. It's going to be hot today. I wish it would stay cloudy, as it was this morning. No one would complain then. But no, once the sun bears down not even a tiny cloud dares show itself out of sheer fright. The hell of it is, we'll be finished here by two and then we have to go to that field that is nothing but hills. It's ok on the top of the hill but when we're in the low parts it's suffocating. Not even the slightest breeze blows through there. Air almost doesn't enter. Remember?)

"La Primera Comunión" studies an important institution of the Chicano environment through its depiction of the indoctrination of children by the Catholic Church. Nuns are among the most important people in this process. It is through them that the children acquire many of their concepts of religion and morality. "La Primera Comunión" presents a nun who is obsessed with sex and somehow transfers her obsessions or fears to the children through the emphasis she places on sins of the flesh. Her admonishingly authoritarian language tries to sweeten itself when talking down to the children by spicing her speech liberally with diminutives.

In all of the above instances and in other places throughout . . . *y no se lo tragó la tierra*, Tomás Rivera presents certain Chicano archetypes who, through language that is typical to them and their social status, enlighten the reader as to how Chicanos live and relate to each other. The Chicano is seen at home, at work, at play and at church. In short, he is seen within the context of his environment, physical and social.

The Dramatic Monolog

Many of the stories of . . . *y no se lo tragó la tierra* are told by the child protagonist to himself in his attempt to reconstruct the past year of his life. The narration for the most part is the language of oral expression: the child as a dramatic narrator talks to himself and, in some cases, even sees himself taking part in the action. Such phrases as "te acuerdas," "te imaginas," and "yo siempre recordaré aquel día de mi vida" remind the reader of this perspective. But the most intimate level of narration is represented in the child's reminiscences of his state of mind during some specific episode of the past; the state of mind is reproduced through the presentation of the monolog that was uttered or thought at the time. The monologs of other characters are reproduced as well in the stories. Through these monologs or dialogs with themselves they express the fear, frustration and hope that they may not be willing to voice in the company of others. Thus, this is one of the more important narrative devices that the author uses for the penetration into the psychology of his characters. The reader, already acquainted with the characters within their physical and social environment, can now approach the characters in their most private moments.

"Es que duele" is the lengthy interior monolog which expresses the shame and perplexity of the child who has been suspended from a northern school during his parents migratory tour of duty. Rivera recreates the indignities and insults that the small boy experiences at the hands of the northerners. The deft treatment of the problem illicits the reader's sympathies precisely because of the perspective adopted, that of the innocent child reacting to the role of inferiority that the society through the schools is casting upon him. Upon reporting for school, the child is first inspected and dusted for lice. When finally admitted to the classroom, he is kept apart from the other students:

> Siempre es lo mismo en estas escuelas del norte. Todos nomás mirándote de arriba a abajo. Y luego se ríen de uno y la maestra con el palito de paleta o de esquimo pie buscándote piojos en la cabeza. Da vergüenza. Y luego cuando arriscan las narices. Da coraje. (22)
> (It's always the same in these northern schools. Everyone just stares at

you up and down. Then they laugh at you, and the teacher with that popsicle or eskimo pie stick trying to find lice on your head. You feel ashamed. And when they turn up their noses, you get angry.)

The high regard that his parents hold for school and teachers causes the child to feel guilty and ashamed for having been expelled:

¿Qué les voy a decir? Me han dicho muchas veces que los maestros de uno son los segundos padres . . . y ahora? Cuando regresemos a Tejas también lo va a saber toda la gente. Mamá y papá se van a enojar; a lo mejor me hacen más que fajearme. Y luego se va a dar cuenta mi tío y güelito también. (25)
(What am I going to tell them? I've been told so many times that one's teachers are like second parents . . . and now? When we return to Texas everyone will know about it too. Mother and father will be angry; maybe they'll do more than just spank me. And then my uncle and grandfather will also find out.)

But the most pathetic element of the monolog is the recurring thought that perhaps he was not expelled from school, that is, because of the language barrier, the child is not even sure that he has been expelled. It is no wonder that many a Chicano child drops out from school when he has to face such trauma daily. The child comes to this conclusion: "Yo creo que es mejor estarse uno acá en el rancho, aquí en la mota con sus gallineros, o en la labor se siente uno a lo menos más libre, más a gusto" ("I think it's better to stay here in the ranch, here among the trees and chicken coops; or out in the field where you at least feel free, more at ease," 22).

Rivera creates the archetype of the mother in "Un Rezo" ("A Prayer") through a dramatic illustration of the maternal instinct. In a long sentimental monolog she prays to her gods for the protection of her son in Korea. She even offers to sacrifice her own life, her heart, for her son's: "Aquí está mi corazón por el de él. Aquí lo tiene. Aquí está en mi pecho, palpitante, arránquenmelo a mí" ("I offer my heart for his. Here it is. I offer you my throbbing heart; tear it from me," 15). The prayer is intensely emotional in its poetic plea for supernatural intervention. Her humility and naivete bring the reader closer to her suffering and heroic attempt to control the cosmic forces that have victimized her son. Quite characteristically, she still thinks of her son as a child and identifies him with his old toys in the loving language of familiar things called by their everyday Chicano names: *la troquita*, little truck, *la güila*, kite, *los fonis*, the funny books. Believing in his boyish innocence, the mother does not seem to be aware that her son, a soldier, is being transformed into a killer of other mothers' children: "Es muy inocente, protégelo, él no quiere hacerle mal a nadie, es muy noble, es muy bueno, que no le traspase una bala al corazón" ("He's very innocent, protect him, he doesn't want to harm anyone; he's of noble spirit; he is very kind; don't let a bullet pierce his heart," 14). The mother's exhortation for the protection of her son is made in the language with which she is familiar, the language of the home. She asks the Virgin Mother to directly and physically intervene on her son's behalf in terms that reflect her sphere of knowledge: "Por favor, Vírgen María, tú también cobíjalo. Cúbrele su cuerpo, tápale la cabeza, tápale los ojos a los comunistas y a los coreanos y a los chinos para que no lo maten" ("Please, Virgin Mary, you protect him too. Shelter his body, cover his head, blind the Communists' eyes, the Koreans' and the Chinese's so that they won't see him, so they won't kill him," 14).

Thus, through monolog, Tomás Rivera has taken the reader to the most private and intimate realms of the Chicano mind. He has allowed the reader to hear the Chicano when he is alone with his thoughts and when he is alone with his gods.

Tomas Rivera's . . . *y no se lo tragó la tierra* is a novel that examines the Chicano in the agricultural fields of the North and the *barrios* of Texas. The Chicano culture is depicted from within through the voices of a cross-section of the Chicano community in question. As the narrative point of view shifts and as the medium changes from descriptive narrative to dialog and then monolog, so does the distance between the reader and the characters. The reader is furthest away from the subjects with the third person omniscient narration and closest to them through their monologs. Accordingly, the language becomes more colloquial, subjective and intimate as the point of view passes from the exterior to the interior, from a vista of the greater society to the family and then to the individual psyche. The composite of all three levels is a view of the total culture of Chicano migrant workers. The mind of the child is what gives unity to this broad vision. In this process of interiorization, the oral language of dialog and monolog assumes important artistic and sociological functions. Dialog is used, from the perspective of the Chicano collectivity, to narrate. It also adopts a format similar to Chicano theater in order to portray a social reality. In combination with other narrative devices, dialog is used for characterization, for, through the idiosyncracies of speech, characters become more vivid and individualized. Finally, through monolog, the characters' interior fears and hopes are revealed. Thus, the examination of this migratory Chicano society is complete. The reader has been able to progress from the exterior physical and social environment to the interior psychology of the Chicano through a reproduction of the oral language of the Chicano.

[1]See Joseph Sommers, "Critical Approaches to Chicano Literature," *Modern Chicano Writers*, Joseph Sommers & Tomás Ybarra-Frausto, eds. (Englewood Cliffs, N.J.: Prentice-Hall, Inc., 1979), 31-40.

²See Thomas J. Schell, "Changes in Public and Private Language Among the Spanish-Speaking Migrants to an Industrial City," *International Migration*, III (1965), 78-85.

³This text was presented as a paper in 1973 at the symposium entitled, "Tomás Rivera and Chicano Literature," at Indiana University-Bloomington. Had the paper been drafted today, I would have commented on Richard Rodríguez' failure in *Hunger of Memory* (Boston: David Godine, 1982), to artistically render Mexican American language in its social and cultural context, and I would have criticized his development of a sociological thesis without the social scientist's methodology or credentials.

⁴Tomás Rivera, . . . *y no se lo tragó la tierra* (Berkeley: Quinto Sol, 1971), 163. Subsequent references will appear in the text and will be to the page numbers of this edition.

⁵See Arthur León Campa, *Spanish Folk Poetry in New Mexico* (Albuquerque, 1946), 99.

⁶Tomás Rivera, "Literature chicana: Vida en busca de forma," an unpublished paper read at the "Fifty-Third Annual Meeting of the AATSP" (Chicago, 1971).

⁷Since 1973, when this paper was presented, many of Rivera's stories have been performed on stage.

⁸See Manuel Gamio, *Mexican Immigration to the United States* (Chicago, 1930), 84-85.

⁹See J. Frank Dobie, *Puro Mexicano* (Austin, 1935), 225-227.

The Search for Being, Identity and Form in the Work of Tomás Rivera

Julián Olivares

Tomás Rivera's . . . *y no se lo tragó la tierra* is a landmark of Chicano creative expression. Published in 1971, this prize-winning novel gave impetus to the literary efforts of Chicano writers and brought wide recognition to the Hispanic creative presence in the United States. Rivera also produced a small but valuable corpus of poetry, in which we note much of the themes that inform his novel.[1] Rivera is also highly regarded for a literary criticism which has been instrumental in the esthetic and ethical appreciation of Chicano literature. Three significant contributions in this regard are "Into the Labyrinth: The Chicano in Literature," "Chicano Literature: Fiesta of the Living," and "Recuerdo, descubrimiento y voluntad en el proceso imaginativo literario."[2] They are especially important in the interpretation and appreciation of Rivera's own literary production.

In "Into the Labyrinth: The Chicano in Literature," Rivera reminds us that the *search* is the essential characteristic of both labyrinth and life: "We need to make the analogy between the Greek myth of Daedelus and Minos and our own lives . . . the labyrinth . . . is a man-made structure full of intricate passageways . . . the important element here is that the labyrinth provided a setting for a search . . . toward the exterior or the interior. In either case, the setting provided not only a setting for a search but also a setting for tension " (18). Consequently, the labyrinth, "a man-made structure," and literature, man's artifice, share a preoccupation for the search:

> Literature, and fiction, provide tension. Literature represents man's life, it also reflects his inner search and his outward search. It is in a sense an intricate maze to provide either exteriorization or internalization of the human involvement and evolvement . . . And the search can only exist if there is an impulse into the labyrinth of the human totality of conditions. Thus, the search and labyrinth complement each other to bring forth a vicarious sensibility to the perceiver. (18)

For Rivera, the labyrinth is also the means by which one searches for one's *alter ego*, the 'other': "It is a vicarious notion of humanity, or man, to attempt to search for the other 'alter ego' in order to better comprehend himself . . . the labyrinth . . . is a mold wherein he can place his life. In essence, is it not life in search of form—a conquest, a labyrinth in which to reflect his human condition?" (18). In the search for the form in which to mold the Chicano experience, the Chicano, newly arrived to this enterprise, invents his own labyrinth:

> This brings us to the Chicano . . . who also wishes to create a labyrinth, who wishes to invent himself in the labyrinth . . . where he can vicariously live his total human condition. However, since he has perceived continually the development of the North American and the Mexican literatures, literatures which have reached great heights of intricateness and sophistication for their counterparts, more stress is given to finding form or forms for expression. So we find Chicano literature and the Chicanos in fiction as simply life in search of form. (19)

Rivera develops the concept of the *other* in "Chicano Literature: Fiesta of the Living." Here Rivera affirms, "for me the literary experience is one of total communion, an awesome awareness of the 'other,' of one's potential self. I have come to recognize my 'other' in Chicano literature."[3] The search for the other represents "An exact, pure desire to transform what is isolated in the mind into an external form" (439), so that the creative process is "A personal ritual, a constant means of establishing contact with humanity and with one's origins" (452). The 'other,' then, is humanity, the recognition of one's people, *pueblo*, and its collective experience.

Implied in these discussions are the assertions of Rivera's third article, "Recuerdo, descubrimiento y voluntad en el proceso imaginativo literario."[4] Through memory the Chicano recuperates the past, discovers his history and affirms his own singular being and his identity as a collective person. With this cultural awareness, he applies his volition in the quest for intellectual and spiritual development. In the realm of creative expression, volition is indispensable for literary invention, crucial for the quest for a form in which to express his being and identity. I will now apply these concepts of labyrinth, 'other' and memory, discovery and volition in the search for being, identity and form in the fiction and epic poetry of Tomás Rivera.[5]

. . . *y no se lo tragó la tierra* begins with a brief narrative, "El año perdido" ("The Lost Year"),[6] in which we note the psychological drama of an alienated child protagonist who struggles to recall the events of the preceding year, of which he has no memory: "Aquel año se le perdió." Within the mind of this confused boy, we perceive a struggle whose ultimate resolution depends on his capacity to discover and give *form* to his past by means of words, but which dissipate at the point where the past begins to become clear: "A veces trataba de recordar y para cuando creía que se estaba aclarando un poco se le perdían las palabras." The lack of self-expression has caused him to lose himself; he is unable, therefore, to recover his history and to encounter his being and identity. Nonetheless, his 'other' calls him, urging the child to search for him, to search for himself: "Siempre empezaba todo cuando oía que alguien le llamaba por su nombre . . . Se dio cuenta de que él mismo se había llamado." The 'other' reveals himself in the perception, barely glimpsed by the protagonist, of the collective conscious of the people that he carries within his own as yet unconscious. Within the child, the collective conscious and experience struggle for their recognition. This protagonist, who cannot escape from the whirlwind of his thoughts, now finds himself on the threshold of the labyrinth in search of his authentic history and being.

"El año perdido" is followed by twelve stories and thirteen vignettes which portray the life of migrant workers, each story representing a month of the lost year.[7] The book closes with an additional narrative, "Debajo de la casa" ("Beneath the House"), whose young protagonist, we discover, is the same child of "El año perdido." The twelve sections constitute the past of a character who functions as the central conscious of the work. His experience is not limited to what he has seen or personally experienced, but includes what he has heard from his father—who "le contaba cuentos" ("told him stories," 165)—from his mother, grandparents, relatives, from the troubadour Bartolo and all the workers on the roads and fields of the migratory life, each contributing from his own harvest of wisdom and experience to the maturation process and epiphany of the protagonist. By means of this unique narrative framework, the limits of time and space are transcended. The collective conscious, at first scarcely perceived in the depths of the protagonist's being, now comes to the surface of his conscious. In the final story, this character declares in an interior monologue:

> Quisiera ver a toda esa gente junta. Y luego si tuviera unos brazos bien grandes los podría abrazar a todos. Quisiera poder platicar con todos otra vez, pero que todos estuvieran juntos. Pero eso apenas es un sueño. Aquí sí que está suave porque puedo pensar en lo que yo quiera. Apenas estando uno solo puede juntar a todos. Yo creo que es lo que necesitaba más que todo. Necesitaba esconderme para poder comprender muchas cosas. De aquí en adelante todo lo que tengo que hacer es venirme aquí, en lo oscuro, y pensar en ellos. Y tengo en tanto que pensar y me faltan tantos años. Yo creo que hoy quería recordar este año pasado. Y es nomás uno. Tendré que venir aquí para recordar los demás.[8]
> (I would like to see all those people together. And if I had long enough arms, I could hug them all at the same time. I would like to talk with all of them again, and have them all together. But that could happen only in a dream. This is a good place because I can think about anything I want. One has to be alone in order to bring everyone together. I think that this is what I needed more than anything. I needed to isolate myself in order to understand many things. From here on all I have to do is come back here in the dark and think about

them. And I have so much to think about, and so many years to catch up on. I think that today I wanted to remember this past year. But that's just one year, I'll have to come here to remember all the others.)

This narrative and the book close with the voice of the omniscient narrator:

> Había encontrado. Encontrar y reencontrar y juntar. Relacionar esto con esto, eso con aquello, todo con todo. Eso era. Eso era todo. Y le dio más gusto. Luego cuando llegó a la casa se fue al árbol que estaba en el solar. Se subió. En el horizonte encontró una palma y se imaginó que ahí estaba alguien trepado viendolo a él. Y hasta levantó el brazo y lo movió para atrás y para adelante para que viera que él sabía que estaba allí. (169)
> (He had discovered something. To discover and to rediscover and synthesize. To relate this entity with that entity, and that entity with still another, and finally relating everything with everything else. That was what he had to do, that was all. And he became even happier. Later, when he arrived at home, he went to the tree that was in the yard. He climbed it. On the horizon he saw a palm tree and he imagined that someone was on top looking at him. He even raised his arm and waved it back and forth so that the other person could see that he knew that he was there.)

In the final story, through memory, the fragments of the lost year coalesce in the protagonist's mind, and he comes to discover the 'other,' that is, he discovers that humanity and collective conscious that he carried within himself, and that is symbolically represented in the form of another youngster whom he discovers looking at him from a palm tree. This protagonist arrives at the realization of his own being by virtue of the experiences that, little by little, he threads together. And with this thread, like that of Daedelus, he emerges from the labyrinth with his being and identity. He becomes one with his people.

For a greater appreciation of the formal and symbolic originality of *. . . y no se lo tragó la tierra*, we first return to Rivera, where he says he has "a desire to transform what is isolated in the mind into an external form." The context is the following: "to perceive what people have done through this process and to come to realize that one's own family group or clan is not represented in literature is a serious and saddening realization" ("Fiesta," 439). The *raza's* experiences remained isolated, retained in the collective conscience of its people, preserved to be sure in its oral literature, yet it had not encountered its external form, a form forged in a written literature. Rivera in this work externalizes the images isolated in the mind—in his own as well as in the protagonists's—and he gives them coherence in the form of a young boy in search of his own being. We venture to add that this being is, in turn, the 'other' that Rivera himself encounters; he is also the central conscious through which the author relives—and we arrive at—the Chicano experience. The youngster, on the narrative level, strings together the histories which make up a year of his life, but which, essentially, because of the *forms* preserved, are *all* his life and *all* the life of his people.[8] Structurally, this gives unity to the stories, and the work is resolved thematically in the protagonist's epiphany when he discovers himself. On an allegorical level, the youngster symbolizes the struggles and efforts of the creative process, and the unity to which this process leads.

The boy is beneath the house: "De donde estaba nada más se veía una línea blanca de luz todo alrededor" ("From his hiding place he could only make out a white band of light all around the house," 164). This dark and literal place serves as a concrete projection of the character's psychological state. It is within the dark solitude of the mind that the protagonist enters the labyrinth of self-discovery: "Aquí no está mal. Me podré venir aquí todos los días. Yo creo que esto es lo que hacen los que corren la venada. Aquí ni quien me diga nada. Puedo pensar a gusto" ("It's not at all bad here. I could come here every day. I think that this is what the kids do when they play hooky. No one can tell me anything under here. I can think in peace," 165). It is in this concrete and psychological space that the protagonist finds his way and recovers the fragments of the lost year; and, upon discovering the links that unite him with his people, he arrives at self-discovery. Symbolically, the protagonist's revelation points to that unity that Rivera himself searches for in the creative process. The author creates a character who, in turn, is a creator. Upon recreating the experiences of his people, the youngster creates himself in his own discovery. He arrives at a communion with the 'other' which is the collective humanity of his people. The youngster's *I* grows larger than himself, leaving behind the solitary self and becoming a collective personality. In addition to symbolizing the creative process, the youngster represents the 'other' for whom Rivera, the author, searches. Upon creating him, Rivera also encounters himself. In the search and encounter of the 'other,' both the author and his creation emerge from the labyrinth.

Rivera comments on his protagonist's epiphany and its effect:

> In the final story of my work . . . *y no se lo tragó la tierra*, "Debajo de la casa," the child remembers and discovers. He remembers the child of before. But he also remembers that other years exist. Furthermore, he discovers that existence is, in short, a relationship between memory and constant discovery. But he goes even further. He invents. He invents himself. Arriving home, he climbs a tree. In the horizon he sees a palm tree. He imagines that someone is there looking at him, and that is why he greets him moving his arm back and forth . . . I believe that whoever proposes to discover his own life

through memory will find the volitive strength to invent himself continuously as desiring love for all men on earth ("Recuerdo," 75).

Volition, here, refers to a will to discovery and self-discovery that affirms a love for mankind, but in the "literary imaginative process" it refers to the will to express this love in literature, to give it a form. This last process is implied in the protagonist's self-invention. Memory has led to discovery, self-discovery and the encounter of the 'other.' Although the structure of the novel is circular, it is open-ended. At the novel's conclusion, it remains that this boy give a literary invention to his experience. The boy, thus, represents an author *en potencia*. Through memory, he can recreate these experiences as an adult and immortalize them in literary form.[9]

The encounter of one's self, the 'other,' and the realization of form gives rise to that exaltation that Rivera calls "The fiesta of the living." Rivera recounts how in his youth he used to listen to Bartolo, the jongleur of South Texas, recite his poetry in which young Tomás heard the names of the people of his community and neighboring areas. He says that he experienced "an exaltation brought on by the sudden sensation that my own life had relationships, that my own family had relationships, that the people I lived with had connections beyond those at the conscious level" ("Fiesta," 440).

Giving literary form to this experience, the vignette that precedes the section of "Debajo de la casa" says:

Bartolo pasaba por el pueblo por aquello de diciembre cuando tanteaba que la mayor parte de la gente había regresado de los trabajos. Siempre venía vendiendo sus poemas. Se le acababan casi para el primer día porque en los poemas se encontraban los nombres de la gente del pueblo. Y cuando los leía en voz alta era algo emocionante y serio. Recuerdo que una vez le dijo a la raza que leyeran los poemas en voz alta porque la voz era la semilla del amor en la oscuridad. (162)

("Bartolo always came through town around December, when he felt that most of the people had returned from work in other states. He always sold his poems. They were almost completely sold out by the end of the first day because they mentioned the names of the people in town. And when he read the poems out loud, it was a serious and an emotional experience. I remember once he told the people to read his poems out loud because the voice was the love seed in the dark.)

We ask ourselves whose voice this is? Speaking immediately before the narrative of the young protagonist and seen in light of the symbolic action of the work, this voice could well belong to the youngster. We know, from Rivera himself, that this Bartolo is related to the author's own experience.

Consequently, it may be that the narrator is the author-Rivera symbolically disguised and speaking in character, mediated by the latter's eyes and ears. Which brings us to pursue this symbolic action, this narrative strategy: in the book Bartolo is to the child what the author is to the reader. The ballads that Bartolo recites are to the boy what the stories the author tells are to the reader. Furthermore, Bartolo plants the seed of love in the mind of the boy, and in that darkness it grows and, in the light of discovery, it flowers in the character's love for all his people and forms of life. And the author plants that same seed in the mind of the reader.

The recreation of the Chicano experience through the word, the seed, is a ritual that immortalizes *la raza*.

> Is it not . . . that we sense that we are a part of the same ritual? Perhaps this is the case: a bond that comes from a sense of destiny. Yes, we sense a prophecy, and we sense a fulfillment of this prophecy. We have been alive since time began. We are not just living; we have been living for centuries. We must ritualize our existence through words. To me there is no greater joy than reading a creative work by a Chicano. I like to see my students come to feel this bond and to savor moments of immortality, of the total experience ("Fiesta," 440).

It is this sensation of immortality that the youth experiences when he emerges from the darkness beneath the house:"Quisiera ver a toda esa gente junta. Y luego si tuviera unos brazos bien grandes los podría abrazar a todos."

Rivera gives a singular literary form to the uniqueness of his people. If, by means of the labyrinth, one searches and encounters one's being and identity, the latter conceived as union with the 'other'—that is, with one's people—, a singular form is also searched for and realized. . . . *y no se lo tragó la tierra* is remarkable for the originality of its literary form. It is original in the true sense; it is an initial work, an inaugural event, of a culture that, like the *Lazarillo de Tormes*, emerges from folklore. . . . *y no se lo tragó la tierra* is characterized by being, at once, novel and story, the product of an oral literary tradition based on memory. "Memory," says Rivera, "is a narrative method used by the people. That is, I remember what they remembered and the way they narrated . . . in the migratory fields an oral literature was invented. The people sought refuge not only in church or with their brothers, but also sitting in a circle and listening and narrating, and by means of words escaping to other worlds, by inventing themselves as well."[10]

We have noted that the concepts of labyrinth, 'other' and memory, discovery and volition are indispensable in the search and encounter of being, identity and form in Rivera's novel. With regard to form, we add that this search culminates in the realization of three *modes* of form: 1) the formation of the protagonist; 2) the preservation or documentation of forms of life, the migrant workers, without whose documentation these forms would be lost; and 3) a literary form that, as we shall see, takes it place in the American grain.

If, on the one hand, Rivera wrote with the aim, as he declares, to "document" the condition of the migrant worker—the life that he knew—, on the other hand, he conceived this literary documentation as part of a long American tradition. Rivera saw in his people that same spiritual nobility on which our country and continents were founded. Rivera affirms:

> I think of the whole American scene—both continents—and the fact that we have transplanted cultures from Europe, and the fact of the indigenous cultures still being here. I wanted to document that, but I also wanted to throw light on the spiritual strength, on the concept of justice so important for the American continents. I wanted to treat the idea of mental and intellectual liberation and where it fits into the spectrum of the Americas. Can it be achieved here, and if so, can it be done? . . . creo que aquí tenemos la capacidad y la posibilidad de una emancipación intelectual mucho más fuerte y total (I think that here we have the capacity and possibility of a much stronger and complete intellectual emancipation). Within those migrants I saw that strength. They may be economically deprived, politically deprived, socially deprived, but they kept moving, never staying in one place to suffer or be subdued, sino siempre buscaban trabajo (but always searching for work). Siempre andaban buscando (they always kept searching); that's why they were "migrant" workers. La palabra *trabajador* está muy implícita allí (The word *worker* is very implicit there); they were travelers. If they stayed where there was no work se morían (they would die), y no se murieron (and they didn't die). I see that same sense of movement in the Europeans who came here, and that concept of justicia espiritual también (spiritual justice, too). It was there. And the migrant workers still have that role: to be searchers. I've written a poem called "The Searchers." Para mí era gente que buscaba (To me they were people who searched), and that's an important metaphor in the Americas. My grandfather was a searcher; my father was a searcher; I hope I can also be a searcher. That's the spirit I seek.[11]

"The Searchers" is an epic and, like all epics, it is structured on the motif of the search—an odyssey—and it expresses the collective sentiment of a people, *la raza*.

> How long
> how long
> have we been searchers?

> We have been
> behind the door
> Always
> behind screens and eyes
> of other eyes
> We longed to search
> Always
> longed to search (24)

The parallel with the young protagonist of "el año perdido"—"A veces trataba de recordar y ya para cuando creía que se estaba aaclarando un poco, se le perdían las palabras"—becomes evident in these lines:

> We searched through
> our own voices
> and through
> our own minds
> We sought with our words (24)

Here we note an allusion to the labyrinth in which the quest for being and identity parallels the search and discovery of form.

The epic contains multiple levels. While the narrative level sets forth the search for full existence, the Chicano's rightful place in society—the social theme, the allegorical level expresses the search for form.

> From within came
> the passions to create
> of every clod and stone
> a new life
> a new dream
> each day
> In these very things
> we searched
> as we crumbled
> dust, our very own
> imaginary beings (. . .)
> A terrón lighted our eyes
> and we watered it and made
> mud-clay
> to create others in (25)

After affirming the persistence of the search over many years, "only to feel the loneliness of centuries," the poet utilizes the Spanish folkloric tradition in order to express the feeling of loss and loneliness:

> Una noche caminando
> una sombra negra vi

> Yo me separaba de ella
> y ella se acercaba a mí.
> ¿Qué anda haciendo caballero?
> ¿Qué anda haciendo por aquí?
> Ando en busca de mi esposa
> que se separó de mí.
>
> Su esposa ya no está aquí,
> su esposa ya se murió
> Cuatro candeleros blancos
> son los que alumbran allí. (26)

While the lines in English allegorically express the search for form, the poem embeds lines in Spanish that achieved their form centuries ago and are readily recognizable as *poesía popular* with lines in *arte menor*, octosyllables or less. Hence, we note in the poem the integration of this traditional form in a search of a more comprehensive form, and one that will express the bicultural and bilingual components of the Chicano artist.

A fundamental theme of this epic is the rescue of the dead and the salvation of the living, as the youth achieved at the conclusion of *tierra*. The rescue is realized by an odyssey through the zone of death:

> Death
> We searched in Death
> We contemplated the original
> and searched
> and savored it
> only to find profound
> beckoning
> A source that continued the search
> beyond creation and death
> The mystery
> The mystery of our eyes
> The eyes we have as
> spiritual reflection
> and we found we were
> not alone (26)

The search in death brings us to the depths of our solitude where we encounter our 'other,' for it is in the creative space of solitude that we become linked with our dead and our history:

> In our solitude
> we found our very being
> We moved into each other's
> almost carefully, deliberately

> Had we been here before? (. . .)
> We found ourselves in ourselves
> and while touching
> we found other mysteries
> that lay beneath
> every layer of truth
> unwinding each finding
> another lonely vigil
> another want, desire
> to find
> to find what?
> What we always had?
> Did anyone know that we
> were searching?
> That every look toward the earth
> was a penetrating search that
> had lasted for years
> the mystery of time halted
> and unknown without
> itself discovery (26-7)

Like the youth in *tierra*, we find that "It is from the past that we are able to perceive, create and give life of our ritual; it is from this that we derive strength, that we can recognize our existence as human beings" ("Fiesta," 440). Through memory we encounter our own salvation. We discover that "we are not alone," but that, rather, we carry in ourselves the history of all our people, our collective experience. Rivera declares here the quest, maintained for centuries, for our full existence. The dead give us their shoulders, and together we withstand the burden of injustice:

> We are not alone
> if we remember and
> recollect our passions
> through the years
> the giving of hands and backs
> "dale los hombros a tus hijos"
>
> We are not alone
> Our eyes still meet with the passion
> of continuity and prophecy
>
> We are not alone
> when we were whipped
> . . . for speaking Spanish
> on the school grounds

> or
> when Chona
> dear Chona
> a mythic Chicana,
> died in the sugar beet fields
> with her eight month
> child
> buried deep within her
> still
> or
> when that truck
> filled with us
> went off the mountain road
> in Utah with screams
> eternally etched among
> the mountain snows
> We were not alone. (28)

The *estribillo*, "We are not alone," is now posited in the past, "We were not alone." The effect is to nullify time and to make contemporaneous the living and the dead; we live together in our collective conscious. Through memory, we rescue the dead and achieve our own salvation in the affirmation of our being and identity:

> We were not alone in Iowa
> When we slept in wet ditches
> frightened by salamanders (. . .)
> or
> in San Angelo
> when we visited the dessicated
> tubercular bodies of
> aunts and uncles
> friends and lovers
>
> We were not alone
> when we created children
> and looked into their eyes
> and searched for perfection
> We were not alone
> murmuring the novenas,
> los rosarios, each night,
> los rosarios we hoped
> would bring joy and lasting peace
> for Kiko
> killed and buried in Italy in 1943 (29)

"The Searchers" is Rivera's poetic complement to his . . . *y no se lo tragó la tierra*, and has three principal intentions which we can deduce as well for his novel. First, the affirmation of a spiritual nobility that is manifested in the persistent search for justice and the realization of our potential existence. Second, the search oriented toward the past where we unite with the dead, and so rescue their dreams from oblivion and carry them within ourselves in the search in the future for the realization of our prophecy:

>We are not alone
>after many centuries
>How could we be alone
>We were seekers
>We are searchers
>and we will continue
>to search
>because our eyes
>still have
>the passion of prophecy. (30)

But it is the third, the search and discovery of literary form, that makes possible the rescue of the dead, the recuperation of the spirit of the search and the salvation of the living. "Chicano writing," declares Rivera, "is a ritual of immortality, of awe in the face of the other . . . a ritual of the living . . . a fiesta of the living." By virtue of literary creation, we realize that the living are all of us from the beginning: "We have been alive since time began."

By pursuing this labyrinth called literary creation, we continually discover the forms of Chicano existence; and in this way—represented in literature—the Chicano finds his place in the modern world:

>as the Chicano invents himself as a total human being he not only gains complete psychological control over his world and gives thrust to his will but also, and perhaps most important, he condemns himself to liberty and in so doing joins the twentieth century family of man. Into the labyrinth goes the Chicano, condemned by himself to search for intellectual emancipation, and to internalize his life to make it more complete. The labyrinth is not a provider of great truths but a reflector of great questions. This is what the Chicano will find. He could not find these if he himself had not gotten into the labyrinth, and thus Chicano literature is an actuality. ("Labyrinth," 25)

I would like to conclude with a brief poem that appears in a modest collection of Rivera's poetry titled *Always and Other Poems*. The poem is called "Soundless Words":

>Words without sound

> how terribly deaf
> What if I were to remain
> here
> in the words
> forever?

I can assure you, amigo Tomás, that your words will resound with their "semilla de amor." Through our continual search, *te rescatamos del olvido y vives con nosotros*.

---

[1] Rivera's poetry is found in the inaugural issue of *Revista Chicano-Riqueña*, 1:1 (1972); in *El grito*, 3 (1969); in a chapbook, *Always and Other Poems* (Sisterdale, Texas: Sisterdale Press, 1973); and includes his epic poem "The Searchers," in *Ethnic Literature since 1776: The Many Voices of America*, 2 vols. (Lubbock: Texas Tech Comparative Studies, 1977), I, 24-30; his poetry is also included in various anthologies.

[2] "Into the Labyrinth: The Chicano in Literature," *New Voices in Literature: The Mexican American, a Symposium* (Edinburg, Texas: Pan American University, 1971), 18-25; "Chicano Literature: Fiesta of the Living," *Books Abroad*, 49:3 (1975), 439-52; "Recuerdo, descubrimiento y voluntad en el proceso imaginativo literario"/"Remembering, Discovery and Volition in the Literary Imaginative Process," *Atisbos, Journal of Chicano Research*, 1 (1975), 66-76.

[3] "Fiesta," 439. Other themes in Rivera's article are the concepts of *casa*, *barrio* and *lucha*. For a discussion of these concepts, see Luis Leal's article in this same collection, and my "Seeing and Becoming: Evangelina Vigil, 'Thirty an' Seen a Lot,' " *The Chicano Struggle* (State University of New York at Binghamton: Bilingual Press/Editorial Bilingüe, 1984), 152-65.

[4] This was first a paper presented at a symposium on "Tomás Rivera and Chicano Literature," Indiana University, Bloomington, April 14-15, and repeated at the Chicano Writers Workshop, Merritt College, Oakland, CA. Portions of it are cited in his "Fiesta."

[5] See also Juan Rodríguez, "La búsqueda de identidad y sus motivos en la literatura chicana," in *The Identification and Analysis of Chicano Literature*, Francisco Jiménez, ed. (New York: Bilingual Press, 1979), 170-78.

[6] *. . . y no se lo tragó la tierra / . . . and the earth did not part* (Berkeley: Publicaciones Quinto Sol, S.A., 1971), 1.

[7] Rolando Hinojosa has told me that in the original manuscript of *tierra*, the twelve stories had months for titles.

[8] *tierra*, 168. Hinojosa told me that this concluding story was originally titled "El año encontrado."

[9] Upon completion of this essay, I read José D. Saldívar's article, "The Ideological and the Utopian in Tomás Rivera's *. . . y no se lo tragó la tierra* and Ron Arias' *The Road to Tamazunchale*," *Crítica*, 1:2 (1985), in which he notes, "*Tierra* . . . is about this dawning sense of solidarity of migrant farmworkers with other members of their class and race. Class consciousness, as such, in *tierra*, is utopian insofar as it expresses the unity of a collectivity; yet it must be stressed that this proposition is an allegorical one," 103.

[10] Inasmuch as there is a biographical basis to various of the stories that Rivera relates, it is not improbable that he was the boy under the house; see James H. Abbott's article.

[11] "Recuerdo," 70. Because the migrant workers shared the same experiences, they collectively possessed what Rivera calls, an "intrasensibilidad." And the stories that emanated from this collective effort were products of their "intrainventividad": "El recuerdo cada vez untado de imaginación fue capaz de proyectar esta intrasensibilidad. Al recordar y al contar y al recontar, el elemento imaginativo y la sensibilidad se elaboraron, se prepararon y se inventaron. Así, fue esto no solamente intrasensibilidad sino intrainventividad," 70; cited in "Fiesta," 441.

[12] Juan Bruce-Novoa, "Tomás Rivera," *Chicano Authors: Inquiry by Interview* (Austin: University of Texas Press, 1980), 151.

Invisible Women in the Narrative of Tomás Rivera

Patricia de la Fuente

Some years ago, in an essay entitled "The Image of Woman in Chicano Literature,"[1] Judy Salinas pointed out, with a certain guarded optimism, the increasing use of realism in the development of female characters by some Chicano authors. Salinas specifically mentioned several well-known authors, including Rolando Hinojosa and Estela Portillo, who have to some degree freed themselves from the conventionalism inherent in the traditional stereotyping of Hispanic women, both socially and in literature. According to Salinas:

> The cultural and traditional roles and stereotypes of women and the Hispanic woman in particular as depicted in literature have been perpetuated through the centuries by authors reflecting their societies' majority views—male and female alike. There are two main categories or images of woman . . . the "good" woman, symbolized by the Virgin Mary, who can think no evil, do no evil, is pure, innocent, understanding, kind, weak, passive, needs to be protected, but yet has an inner strength which God granted her, a capacity for endurance and suffering, an inner strength which she passes on to her children, the procreation of which is her task in this world, or ought to be, along with that of making her man happy and satisfied with a minimum of nagging and complaints. . . . Second, there is the "bad" woman, symbolized by Eve, who is temptress and seductress, representing evil through love and the perversion and excesses of its passions . . . her sole purpose is to entrap, confuse, entice, manipulate and weaken man by means of all her magical and mysterious powers. (2)

This dichotomy between an absurd idealization and an irrational, even neurotic stigmatization of feminine reality has a long and tedious history in Western "civilization," which endures despite the intellectual and technical enlightenment in other areas. Such an approach to female characterization, long the rule rather than the exception among Chicano authors, borders on the simplistic by reducing the rainbow of psychological complexities which constitutes the female personality to a one-dimensional shadow draped in black or white.

As Salinas points out, this myopic perspective persists in Chicano literature, and many Chicano authors of both sexes, including some of the most successful, clearly prefer to project this partial or distorted vision of reality in their creative work. One of the most prominent of such authors is Tomás Rivera, who has been brought to task for adopting this point of view in his novel . . . *y no se lo tragó la tierra*.

In his article "Interpreting Tomás Rivera," Joseph Sommers identifies this narrative characteristic as a flaw in Rivera's novelistic structure:

> A final limitation, also tending to counter the novel's value system as a whole, lies in its treatment of female characters. With the noteworthy exception . . . of critical awareness on the part of the boy's mother, women tend to be presented either as passive prisoners of traditional culture in its most static form, or as tempters whose charms provoke men to tragedy. . . . As a consequence, the novel lacks depth which might have been created had there been more sharing by women, even on a secondary level, of the boy's experiential process. (3)

Undoubtedly, at first glance, Sommers is correct. Rivera's female characters are, with rare exceptions, stereotypical, totemic women, even caricatures, and contribute a muted, often inconsequential background to the male experience. Their humanity is arbitrarily submerged and at times trivialized. These women function as theatrical props, reduced to a role that Sommers has aptly qualified as less than secondary. They are, in a sense, practically invisible.

On the other hand, Salinas is also correct in pointing out that the literature of any age will necessarily reflect, consciously or unconsciously, favorably or unfavorably, the influence of the predominant values of that age. Therefore, it might also be argued that, if Rivera's female characters appear as only secondary, tertiary or even invisible presences, it is because the author has chosen for his theme a purely masculine psychological reality. Such a point of view is no less valid in depicting women in unflattering or static roles since there are undoubtedly men for whom women do indeed occupy such roles. To suggest otherwise is to impose inadmissible restrictions on the author by questioning the honesty of his perception of reality. It might be more accurate, therefore, to say that the female characters in Rivera's novel do not represent, nor should we assume they were created to represent, a feminine perspective, since such a perspective does not exist in the novel. It is more consistent with the structure of this narrative to interpret the femal characters as psychological extensions of the male characters, especially of the narrator. The recurrence of semi-invisible women in the novel may function as a mirror effect, a narrative reflection of the spiritual and psychological limitations and values of the male characters, and to reinforce, perhaps even to criticize, this unilateral male perspective.

If this were so, there would be no point in criticizing the author, as Sommers does directly and Salinas indirectly, for not developing in more depth the feminine perspective within the narrative. Such an inclusion of female values, while certainly adding depth to what Sommers calls "the novel's value system as a whole," would consequently have produced a very different novel. But if this deliberate absence of feminine characterization can be identified, not as a flaw, either structural or philosophical, but as evidence of a creative force operating within certain limits imposed by the author to achieve his artistic purpose, then the narrative phenomenon of Rivera's invisible women must be considered in a different light.

If indeed the narrative function of Rivera's female characterization is an index of a male psychological reality, the male characters immediately acquire an additional dimension and the host of semi-invisible, seemingly marginal women who flit through the novel demand a much closer examination than they have received from the critics. This is especially true since such a study would reveal, not a clearer understanding of feminine point of view—which is simply not there—but an intimate psychological exposé of the masculine characters, especially that of the young narrator whose maturation the novel explores.

One of the first observations to be made about the invisible women in . . . *y no se lo tragó la tierra* is that they do indeed fall into the two traditional categories of "good" and "bad" mentioned by Salinas. Such a broad generalization contributes little to the projection of the male characters, however. What is needed is a specific classification of the types of women Rivera has included and the role their "goodness" or "badness" plays in the narrative creation of the predominantly masculine world of the novel.

It is also evident that the women in the novel differ not only in degrees of "goodness" or "badness" but also in occupation, such as teachers/nuns/housewives; in marital status: single/married/divorced/widowed; in age: old/young; and in culture: Chicanas/Anglos. Although some of these variants are probably inconsequential, others definitely are not, and should be taken into account in any valid classification of Rivera's female characters.

One such classification might include the following categories:

1. mothers or surrogate mothers
2. wives
3. girl-friends or young single women
4. comadres or older women

Each of these categories includes examples of the basic "good" and "bad" stereotypes, but there are others who are neither good nor bad, but who fall into that gray zone which Judy Salinas identified as a synthesis representing different degrees of realism within individual characters (Salinas, 139). Furthermore, of all the possible variants, the Chicana/Anglo dichotomy appears to be the most significant and offers certain important insights into the narrator's sytem of values.

Mothers

The largest and most significant category is that of mothers and their surrogates. The narrator's mother falls into this group and is repeatedly stereotyped as one of the "good" women, protected but ignorant. The first of the many vignettes which separate the main episodes of the narrative offers a typical example of the author's indirect characterization of a woman who is not physically present: "Lo que nunca supo su madre fue que todas las noches se tomaba el vaso de agua que ella les ponía a los espíritus debajo de la cama" ("One thing his mother never found out was that every night he would drink the glass of water that she had placed under the bed for the spirits," 3). This incident displays a deliberate focusing on the mental landscape of Rivera's principal protagonist. The narrator might well have chosen any number of more tender or flattering memories of his mother, but he chooses one that brands her as ignorant, superstitious and easily gullible. Through this deliberate choice, the narrator reveals, indirectly but irrevocably, a blind faith in his male superiority and that arrogance of the man who manipulates and controls a woman's potential by denying her access to the truth: "El le iba a decir una vez pero luego pensó que mejor lo haría cuando ya estuviera grande" ("Once he was about to tell her, but then he thought he would do it later when he had grown up," 3). This male child already perceives his world as a place dominated by men, but he is smart enough to realize that to confront his mother openly, he must wait until he is one.

Through this brief glance at the narrator's memories of his relationship with his mother, Rivera reveals a vital dimension of that masculine psychological reality, limited and one-sided as it undoubtedly is, that constitutes the central theme of the novel. If the characterization of the mother and all future impressions of her, filtered through the consciousness of the protagonist, appear as strictly one-dimensional, surely it is because her son—rather than the author—perceives her in this light.

The novel provides many such examples, in which the main character reveals his personality through memories of his mother. For example, when his uncle and aunt contract tuberculosis, "fue cuando vio llorar a su madre (a) cada rato" ("he saw his mother crying all the time," 46) clamoring for the mercy of God and lighting candles. In criticizing the ignorance and religious faith of his mother: "¿Qué se gana, mamá, con andar haciendo eso?" ("What do you gain, Mother, by doing that?" 48), the child confirms his own incipient cynicism and assumption of superior knowledge. Memories of his first communion emphasize this attitude in his easy acceptance of the master-servant stereotype: "Andele, mamá, arrégleme los pantalones, yo creía que ya lo había hecho anoche." ("Hurry, mother, iron my pants; I thought you had done that last night," 60).

At the other extreme of these self-sacrificing, long-suffering mothers there are others who leave much to be desired. The most patently "evil" is doña Bone, the narrator's substitute or surrogate mother, who feeds him rotten meat and forces him into the role of accomplice in her depraved and criminal life. It is no coincidence that doña Bone is one of the few women in the novel who has a vigorous and distinctive personality. Although she is perceived by the narrator as a traditionally evil, witch-like female, in actuality both she and her husband, don Laíto, are merely petty thieves and exploiters, and belong to that grey zone of realism between the two extremes of good and evil. In spite of being a witness to their villainy, the narrator does not condemn them but rather reveals his own immaturity in his deeply ingrained, irrational acceptance of the traditional concept of the "good" mother:

> Era verdad lo que decían de ellos cuando no estaban presentes. De como hacían el pan, los molletes, de como a veces robaban . . . Yo lo vi todo. De todos modos eran buenas gentes . . . (27).
> (It was true what people said about them when they weren't around. The way they made bread and bread rolls, how they sometimes stole . . . I saw it all. Anyway, they were good people . . .)

It is almost as though the narrator were reluctant to accept this surrogate mother-figure in any but the traditional "good" role. By defining doña Bone with cliches, he sublimates the threat to his masculinity posed by this non-traditional woman.

Wives

A noticeable characteristic of the novel is that all mother-characters are Chicanas, some of whom also appear as wives. These wives belong, as do most of the mothers, to the category of "good" women. A typical example of this characterization of the long-suffering female is the mother/wife whose main concern is the well-being of her husband, an attitude which indirectly defines the centrality of the male figure in her life and her own sense of guilt at her failure to fulfill her "obligations":

> pobre viejo ha de venir bien cansado ya, parado todo el viaje. Hace rato lo vi que iba cabeceando. Y ni cómo ayudarle con estos dos que llevo en los brazos . . . Comoquiera le voy a hacer la lucha para ayudarlo . . . Ojalá y le pueda ayudar. Dios quiera y le pueda ayudar. (112)
> (My poor husband, he must be very tired by now, standing all the way. And there's no way I can help him, burdened as I am with the two children I'm holding . . . But I'll do my best to help him . . . I hope I can help him. May God grant that I be able to help him.)

On the other hand, the Anglo wives in the novel clearly belong at the opposite end of the spectrum and their actions perhaps suggest, from the narrator's point of view, a fatal independence from masculine domination. One of them provokes an accident which causes sixteen deaths:

> Dicen que la americana que iba en el carro era de un condado seco y que había estado tomando en una cantina de puro pesar que le había dejado su esposo. Fueron diez y seis muertos. (83).
> (They say that the Anglo woman who was driving the car lived in a dry county, and she had been drinking in a bar out of sadness because her husband had left her. Sixteen people were killed.)

In this incident, not only does the "bad" Anglo wife commit a criminal action, but she also gets drunk and is abandoned by her husband. This brief vignette clearly suggests that the rejected or "fallen" woman leads a disordered life and is both culturally and socially excluded from the narrator's value system.

A second example illustrates a similar pattern of negative characterization. A protestant minister promises the townsmen that a carpenter will come to teach them manual skills:

> El fulano vino como a las dos semanas en una camioneta y con una trailer. Traía de ayudante a la esposa del ministro para que le interpretara. Pero nunca les enseñaron nada. Se pasaban todo el día dentro de la trailer. A la semana se fueron sin decir una palabra. Supieron después que le había quitado la esposa al ministro. (45)
> (Two weeks later the young fellow came in a pickup truck and a house trailer. He brought with him the minister's wife. She was to be his assistant as an interpreter. But they never taught them anything. They spent day after day inside the trailer. A week later they both left without having said a word. Later the men found out that he had run off with the minister's wife.)

The narrator's criticism of the minister's wife, presumably though not explicitly Anglo, is implicit in this passage. She fits the traditional mold of temptress who manipulates and exploits men through passion. Her evil influence in this instance is operative on three levels: a husband ridiculed, a carpenter deflected from his job, and a group of workmen cheated out of the opportunity to learn a new trade. Unlike the case of Doña Bone, there are no extenuating circumstances invoked to soften the negative impression of this wayward wife.

Girl-friends

Perhaps the most interesting category of female characters in terms of narrative technique is that comprised of girlfriends or younger women. As with the wives, this category includes both Chicanas and Anglos.

The most important episode illustrating this category is called "La noche que se apagaron las luces" ("The Night of the Blackout"), in which Ramón, feeling betrayed by his girlfriend Juanita, commits suicide by throwing himself into the electric generating plant. In this incident, masculine perspective manifests itself as soon as the lovers meet after a prolonged separation. Ramón immediately confronts Juanita with her betrayal, while she tries to establish her independence in an identity separate from the dominating male:

J. —Tú sabes lo que haces.
R. —Claro. Yo sé lo que hago.
J. —¿Pierdes conmigo?
R. —Sí, y a la noche si vas al baile más vale que no vayas a bailar con nadie.
J. —¿Va, y por qué? Si ya no somos novios. Ya perdimos.
R. —A mí no me importa si hemos perdido o no. (78-80)
(J. —You may do whatever you like.
R. —Sure. I know what I'm doing.
J. —Do you want to break up with me?
R. —Yes, and if you go to the dance tonight you'd better not dance with anyone else.
J. —And why can't I? We're not going together anymore. We broke up. You don't own me.
R. —I don't care if we've broken up or not.)

The significance of this incident is not the characterization of Juanita, the stereotyped flirtatious, faithless woman, but the reaction of the narrator who witnesses this encounter between the quarrelling lovers. He is evidently a good friend of Ramón's, privy to the step-by-step development of the ill-fated romance and avid listener to the gossip filtering down from the North where Juanita was having her little fling. While it is entirely natural for the narrator to side with his friend, his laconic epilogue to the affair after Ramón's suicide reveals a highly simplistic reaction to a complex psychological male-female confrontation:—"Es que se querían mucho, ¿no crees?—No, pos sí." (—"They were very much in love, wouldn't you say?"—"Yes. Of course," 80). By attempting to explain away the situation with a traditional, romanticized cliche, the narrator defines his own inability or unwillingness to accept Ramón's action for what it is: an irrational display of macho bravado and pride, and a protest against female independence. As in the case of doña Bone, the narrator repeats conventional platitudes to avoid passing unfavorable judgment on a traditionally "good" character.

87

Anglo girls in the novel are equally destructive. One vignette gives us a glimpse of Figueroa, who is jailed because of "la bolilla (de diez y siete años) que se trajo de Wisconsin" ("The (17-year-old) Anglo girl he brought back with him from Wisconsin," 105). The implication is that this temptress is the cause of Figueroa's bad luck, both his prison record and the sickness he contracted in jail: "dicen que tiene una enfermedad muy rara" ("They say he has a very strange disease"). In fact the general feeling is that Figueroa will die within the year.

Comadres

This category includes both Anglo and Chicano women, all of them ignorant. In the former, ignorance takes the form of vicious prejudice, while in the latter it is revealed as gullibility and superstition. When two Chicanas talk of going to Utah, for example, one of them refuses to go: "Porque se nos hace que no hay ese estado. A ver, ¿cuando ha oido decir de ese lugar? ("Because we don't think there is such a state. Look, when did you ever hear of that place?" 18). The other replies, with appalling innocence: "nunca hemos ido pero dicen que queda cerca del Japón" ("we've never been there ourselves, but they say it's close to Japan.")

The few older Anglos are stereotyped as aggressively prejudiced. The narrator has to listen to his Anglo playmate tell him candidly that "some old ladies told mamá that Mexicans steal and now mamá says not to bring you home anymore" (121), while he remembers Texas teachers as "puras viejitas con la tabla en la mano cuidando que no perdiera uno el lugar en el libro" ("old hags with a board held in their hands just waiting for you to lose your place in the book," 123)

Although Sommers is certainly correct in his evaluation of the female characters in . . . *y no se lo tragó la tierra* as conventional, one-dimensional creatures, he has overlooked the possibility that this de-emphasis of the female presence in the novel may well be a deliberate narrative technique rather than an unconscious flaw. Rivera seems to have used these semi-invisible figures as stage props to create a series of emotional conflicts for his male narrator, in whose world women are necessary though clearly peripheral figures. One way to centralize this narrative focus on the unfolding awareness and spiritual maturation of his male protagonist is to maintain female characterization at the perceptive level of that protagonist rather than to allow the female figures to develop as separate individuals. If such is the case, it is not surprising that Rivera's female characters, deprived of any significance within the value system of the narrator, appear as insubstantial shadows in a clouded mirror, lifeless and for all intents and purposes, invisible.[4]

[1]Judy Salinas, "The Image of Woman in Chicano Literature," *Revista Chicano-Riqueña*, 4:4 (1976), 139-148.

²Joseph Sommers, "Interpreting Tomás Rivera," *Twentieth Century Views: Modern Chicano Writers*, ed. Joseph Sommers and Tomás Ybarra-Frausto (Englewood Cliffs, NJ: Prentice-Hall, 1979), 94-107

³Tomás Rivera, *. . . y no se lo tragó la tierra* (Berkeley, CA: Editorial Justa Publications, 1976. All textual references are taken from this edition.

⁴A shorter version of this paper was presented in Spanish at the Louisiana Conference for Hispanic Languages and Literature, Tulane University, New Orleans, on February 14-16, 1985.

The Patriarchal Ideology in "La noche que se apagaron las luces"

Sylvia S. Lizárraga

It is well known that interpretations of social conventions in literature are artistic representations of the author's perspective and his interpretation of the conventions of his own society. In Chicano literature, in general, the treatment of the image of women differs little from that of any other literature.[1] Therefore, it is not common to encounter in fiction a woman who breaks radically with the existing social conventions and relationship between the sexes and does not pay for the transgression with her life.[2]

Just such an exception, a variant treatment of women in literature, is found in Tomás Rivera's novel, *. . . y no se lo tragó la tierra*, in the section entitled "La noche que se apagaron las luces." Here, the female protagonist's break with the social conventions of her milieu can be seen by looking at the history and cultural background of the characters in this novel. Although the situation portrayed here could fit the situation of women in any other geographic location, this study will analyze its specific context following some general statements regarding the social perspective that influences it, as well as the origins, tradition and culture of the characters.

All of us, women and men alike, are conditioned to see reality through a lens. This lens can at times be like a mirror that distorts our vision to different degrees, according to our culture (tradition, customs, upbringing). One of the most powerful of such distortions is the sexism that legalizes and naturalizes before our eyes the actions of men; we see them as correct and consider our customs to be proof of our civilized culture.

In recent times, from a different perspective, the historical situation of women has been under investigation, and the results never fail to surprise. The research that has focused on Mexico has revealed that the history of Mexican women has been a history of repression. In the Aztec civilization as well as in the colonial period, the woman was always subject to the mandate of the male. The double standard was always applied in questions of morality and social and legal justice.[4]

The role reserved to women among the Aztecs was one of subordination and servility.[5] These customs did not enter in contradiction with those of the conquering Spaniards, who also practiced them. The only change was that racism was added to the existing sexism. The viceroyalty established supremacy and privilege for one class, and for only one sex within that class. The moral and political repression implanted by this system continues to the present in spite of the new stirrings of the Mexican feminist movement.

There have been transgressions of the established customs in all periods and many times they have been used as contradictory examples. But history reveals that, in general, the actions of women have always been well received when their purpose is to please their lords and masters. For example, the contribution of Mexican women during the war for Independence, the war against French intervention and the Revolution of 1910 has been exalted because it was directed to the support of the "common" causes initiated by the men. But much remains to be investigated with regard to the price these women paid for their contribution. Did the price of pain, suffering, sacrifice and work exceed that paid by the men? Were the rewards equitably distributed?[7]

The answers resulting from such investigations might apply to the actions of women so far as public life is concerned, but in the daily relations between the sexes transgressions are not so common. For the woman, the foremost requirement was and still is *obediencia* "ante cualquier situación y donde las nociones de honra y virtud se integran como respuestas sociales y políticas."[8]

Given this primary requirement, and the fact that the characters in Rivera's novel are of Mexican descent, our attention is drawn to the behavior of the young female protagonist who departs from the established social conventions. The story deals with two adolescents in love, Ramón and Juanita, who for economic reasons have to be separated for four months. She has to leave Texas and go with her parents, migrant farm laborers, to work in the fields of Minnesota. Once there, she meets and is attracted to Ramiro, another young man, with whom she dances and talks. Some "friends" of Ramón immediately accuse her of infidelity and inform him about it. When Juanita returns, she has already been judged by the community and the unexpected outcome of the story is Ramón's suicide.

The preference shown to one sex by the sexist tradition that rules in the community can be seen in the comments that definitively blame Juanita for the suicide:

> Pero a ella yo creo que le gustaba el borlote también, si no, no le hubiera sido infiel. (107)
> *Dicen* que empezó a bailar todo el baile con Ramiro solamente . . . *dicen* que se prometieron verse acá. Yo creo que en ese momentito ni se acordaba ella de Ramón. (108, emphasis added)
> (But she must have liked to fool around, otherwise she wouldn't have been unfaithful [. . .] They say that that was the first time she had danced with Ramiro for the entire evening . . . they promised to see each other over here. I think at that moment she didn't even remember Ramón.)

Also within the custom, and this is both implicit and explicit in the narration, there is an emphasis on the aspect of domination on the part of the men in the personal interrelation of the sexes. But something out of the ordinary happens in the case of this couple. She reverses the relationship.

It is well understood that in concrete reality a deep and intimate transformation takes place in the great majority of women. This transformation results from the conditioning to obedience from infancy, and to woman's role established and practiced by society, which relegates her to remain second class and declares her inferior. This fictitious inferiority, declared and accepted by society (any society), becomes real inferiority. This inferiority is continually reinforced by statements that bombard women every day of their lives through the communications media—commercials, television scripts, etc.—by the socialization in the home from infancy, by institutionalized education, and by the daily relations between the sexes. These influences "naturalize" that inferiority and make its transgression more difficult.

In Rivera's story, that "real inferiority," which rules within the custom, is altered by the adolescent girl who refuses to obey the orders of the *macho*.

Juanita also changes the definition of femininity. As we know, sexism has divided the world into two roles: masculine and feminine. The young girl alters the "natural" and "instinctive" characteristics of her femininity. The shyness, the docility, the prudence, the sweetness, the patience, the abnegation, the integral passivity, the lack of initiative, all go by the board when she decides not to obey.

What is unusual in the situation Rivera develops is that Juanita appears to have escaped the conditioning, the internalized psychology that postulates patriarchal ideology as an irrevocable law that must be respected. With her actions she demonstrates that a possibility of equality also exists. A feminine ego exists. An ego that demands its own satisfaction and self affirmation separate from that accepted by tradition. A manner of behaving which goes beyond the sole conventional function of living to please the male. A life of one's own!

But as we have said, the community accuses Juanita of "infidelity." It becomes apparent in the narration that what she betrays is not her love for Ramón but the *customs*, the *tradition*. Within the tradition of the community, a girl who is engaged dances with nobody but her sweetheart. In this case the infidelity consists of dancing and talking with another young man.

We learn through Juanita's interior monologue that she does love Ramón, that she does not want to break off with him, that she wants to see him:

> No, no voy a perder con Ramón. Además, qué hay de mal con sólo hablar. Yo no quiero hacerle caso a éste, le prometí a Ramón . . .

pero me sigue, me sigue y me sigue. Yo no quiero hacerle caso . . . No necesito perder con Ramón, no voy a andar con éste. Nomás conque me siga para que se queden picadas las demás, las otras. No, no pierdo con Ramón porque de veras lo quiero mucho. Ya no falta mucho para vernos otra vez. (108)

(No, I'm not going to break up with Ramón. Furthermore, what is wrong with just talking with him? I don't want to get involved with this guy, I promised Ramón . . . but he keeps following me around. I don't want to get involved with him . . . I don't have to break up with Ramón, I'm not going to go around with this guy. All I want him to do is notice me so that the other girls will be jealous.)

It is also obvious that she feels flattered by the attentions of Ramiro and the letters he sends her, especially since she knows she is envied by other girls because he prefers her. This undoubtedly influenced her decision to go to the dance, which gave rise to the accusations by the community. Her rebellion against custom is also evidenced when she says "qué hay de mal con sólo hablar?" But custom will not tolerate this behavior in a woman; the double standard does not permit it. Before she returns, she has been accused of infidelity by the community.

In the development of this narrative, it seems that Rivera condemns the patriarchal ideology for the damage it causes to both sexes. The denouément of the story so indicates. In the fixation of the roles perpetuated by sexism, the male also is harmed. He must suitably adjust to the dominant role. He must cultivate in himself the necessary characteristics for the exercise of power. And this is what happens in the story. Ramón puts into practice all the mechanisms of domination according to the dictates he has learned from his culture:

—¿Pierdes conmigo?
—Sí, y a la noche si vas al baile más vale que no vayas a bailar con nadie.
—Va, y ¿por qué? Si ya no somos novios. Ya perdimos. Tú no me mandas.
—A mí no me importa si hemos perdido o no. Me lo vas a pagar. Ahora vas a hacer lo que yo te diga cuando yo quiera hasta cuando yo quiera. De mí no se burla nadie. Así que me las vas a pagar por la buena o por la mala.
—Tú no me mandas.
—Vas a hacer lo que yo te diga, y si no bailas conmigo, no bailas con nadie. Y todo el baile. (108-109)

(Do you want to break up with me?—Yes, and if you go to the dance tonight you'd better not dance with anyone else.—And why can't I? We're not going together anymore. We broke up. You don't own me.—I don't care if we're broken up or not. You'll be sorry for this. From now on you're going to do whatever I say, when I say, and as long as I say. Nobody is going to laugh at my expense. I'll make you pay for this one way or another.—You can't boss me around.—You'll do whatever I say, and if you don't dance with me, I won't let you dance with anyone else. You'll dance with me the entire evening.)

However, when the woman does not act according to those dictates, a situation results that is difficult to resolve.

Ramón is totally confused when Juanita refuses to obey. When the known mechanisms fail, he does not know what to do. When threats also fail it is clear that he feels obligated to do something. He solves his confusion by committing suicide. Through this act he reveals that he could not handle an alteration of the conventional patterns. In this tragic manner he ends his problem. Upon losing his position of dominance, his manliness, which signifies his being, his reason for existing, he cannot find other solutions but death. He could not continue existing without being the dominator.

This theme, of a man who chooses suicide as the solution to a situation in which his demands are not met, and the woman is blamed for his death, is also found in the unforgettable anecdote of the peasants Grisóstomo and Marcela in Don Miguel de Cervantes' masterpiece, *El ingenioso hidalgo Don Quijote de la Mancha*.[9] Marcela defends herself against the attacks of those who accuse her of cruelty and murder because she did not return Grisóstomo's love. Her defense is based on a desire to be honest with herself (if she does not love him, why must she accept him?). At the same time she wishes to assert herself, according to the dictates of her own conscience and not in conformity with the customs of the community. Marcela says to Grisóstomo's friends: "Porfió desengañado, desesperó sin ser aborrecido: mirad ahora si será razón que de sus penas se me dé a mí la culpa," and explains further that his impatience and rash desire killed him. She adds that she is "emancipated" and does not want to subject herself to anyone.

There is a similarity between the specific causes cited by Marcela and the implicit ones of Juanita, the girl in Rivera's story. They both refuse to be dominated and resist obeying the dictates of the patriarchal ideology. Each in her own way changes the conventional patterns and is therefore blamed by the community for the tragedy. Although in Rivera's narrative there is no direct accusation of murder by the suicide's friends, as there is in Cervantes', it can be found implicitly in the dialogue, especially the last one:—"Es que se querían mucho, ¿no crees?—No, pos sí." ("They were very much in love, wouldn't you say?"—"Yes. Of course.")

Tomás Rivera, in constructing this narrative, condemns the sexism that dominates the relationship between the sexes in the Chicano community. His presentation of the conflict that results from an alteration of the dictates of the patriarchal ideology and its unexpected solution indicates his desire for a change in these customs that are so damaging and regressive for both sexes.

[1] Whenever it deals with the representation of women of the same race as the author.
[2] Speaking of American literature, Elizabeth Ermarth says that heroines who do not follow these conventions or who fight them are subtly eliminated by the authors. However, men to whom this happens do not die; they change and develop, but rarely are they punished by death. "Fictional Consensus & Female Casualties," in *The Representation of Women in Fiction*, eds. Carolyn G. Heilbrun and Margaret R. Higonnett (Baltimore: Johns Hopkins University Press, 1983).
[3] Publications Quinto Sol, S.A., Berkeley, California, 1971. Citations from this work will be to this edition.
[4] For further details see Iris Blanco's article entitled "Participación de las mujeres en la sociedad pre-hispánica," *Essays on La Mujer*, (Los Angeles: Chicano Studies Center Publications, University of California, 1971), 48-81.
[5] See the account of the Indian wise men's *huehuetlatoles* dedicated to woman in Miguel León Portilla, *La familia nahuatl prehispánica* (Mexico City: Instituto Nacional de Protección a la Infancia, 1967); and by the same author, *Precolombian Literatures of Mexico*, trans. Grace Lobanov and Miguel León Portilla (Norman: University of Oklahoma Press, 1969).
[6] See Carlos Monsiváis, "Sexismo en la literature mexicana," *Imagen de la mujer*, ed. Elena Urrutia (Mexico City: Sep-Setentas, Diana, 1980).
[7] Further investigation that urgently needs to be pursued concerns the women since 1821 who have militated for civil rights of women, the female workers who organized to demand labor rights, and the women in command positions as organizers of armed groups in recent times; see María Antonieta Rascón, "La mujer y la lucha social," *Imagen de la mujer*.
[8] Monsiváis, 106.
[9] (Barcelona: Ediciones Zeus, 1971), vol. 1, chapters 12 to 14.

The Discourse of Silence in the Narrative of Tomás Rivera

Lauro H. Flores

> . . . is productivity to be equated to leadership?
> Tomás Rivera

Brief indeed was the life of Tomás Rivera, the man, the teacher, the university administrator, the friend. Also brief, although this does not diminish its importance, is the literary legacy that Tomás Rivera, the writer, leaves behind.

His book, . . . *y no se lo tragó la tierra*, winner of the first "Premio Quinto Sol" National Chicano Literary Award, in 1970, still stands as the author's major accomplishment.[1] A number of poems, short stories, essays, and some excerpts of his novel, *La casa grande*, complete the list of his literary achievements. And, while his readers may still be hopeful that this second novel will be posthumously released, the fact remains that, in the nearly fifteen years between . . . *y no se lo tragó la tierra* and his untimely demise, Rivera never published another substantial work.

Physical death, therefore, makes silence definitive for a narrator whose critics were beginning to wonder if he would ever publish another novel. But *silence*, as it relates to this negation of production or, more accurately, to the lack of publishing, is not new in the literary milieu. It is certainly not new in the Latin American world, where indigenous literatures, for example, were suffocated and remained ignored for a very long time.

The roots of literary silence vary, however, as also vary the manners in which this silence is expressed. Censorship, for one, has been, and still is, a powerful instrument utilized by the powers-that-be—although with a relative degree of efficacy, it must be admitted—in order to quiet down "subversive" (and at times not-so-subversive) literary voices. The first example that must be cited in this respect is the widely known case of the *Real Cédula del 4 de abril de 1531* which prohibited the passage of novels from Europe into the Americas. This measure obviously left an indelible mark in the history of the development of hemispheric literature by not allowing this genre, the novel, to flourish and fully develop in these lands until almost three centuries later and only in the midst of the War of Independence from Spain.[2]

More recently yet, we witnessed the self-imposed, and fortunately short-lived, narrative silence of the Nobel laureate Gabriel García Márquez as an explicit protest against the fascist regime that overthrew the government of the late President Salvador Allende in 1973 and has ruled over Chile since then.

The examples could continue into a very long list. But, more relevant to this discussion, since Rivera's narrative has often been compared to his, is the "inexplicable silence" that Juan Rulfo, the Mexican master-narrator, had maintained for nearly thirty years. To the undeniable similarity of themes, style and narrative technique existing between these two writers—a similarity that, as Joseph Sommers observed on one occasion[3], one must add their shared negation of writing after producing succinct but extremely important works. As in the case of Rivera's *La casa grande*, Rulfo also had an unfinished novel, *La cordillera*, of which little is known.[4]

Although it evidently bears a substantial amount of importance in Rivera, it is not this "external" silence that this paper wishes to address. Instead, the following pages will focus on the role that silence plays as an organic part of the narrative discourse developed by the author of *. . . y no se lo tragó la tierra*. It is my belief that a close examination of this aspect will illuminate other aspects of the novel, such as the author's manipulation of structure, style, and narrative technique, all of which, in the end, come to postulate a particular vision of the world.

. . . y no se lo tragó la tierra was written in the late 1960's, a time when, in Rivera's own words, "the Chicano Movement was a complete power already."[5] Admittedly, the author's motivation was to save for posterity "the suffering and the strength and the beauty" of the "people who existed in the migrant stream between 1945 and 1955" (161). The novel as a whole, then, is a retrospective view of a time-gone-by, of that decade in his life which the author attempts to congeal. In 1967-68 he says

> I began to see that my role—if I want to call it that—would be to document that period of time, but giving it some kind of spiritual strength of spiritual history. (. . .) Not just this and that happened, but to give a spiritual dimension to the people of that time. I see myself more as a documentor of that period of time when the migrant worker was living without any kind of protection. There was no legal protection and without legal protection there is nothing. I saw a lot of suffering and much isolation of the people. (148-9)

It is clear that Rivera conceived his writing task as an "objective" exercise, attempting to reproduce a reality as he perceived it: "Right away it's a historical documentation that I want to deal with" (148). Such "documentation," however, is filtered by the author through a "spiritual dimension" which emphasizes feelings, the human condition, and finally emerges in the text of *. . . y no se lo tragó la tierra* as a quasi-existentialist vision of the world well within the currents of modern subjective prose (Kafka, Proust, Mansfield, first, and then Camus, Sartre, Rulfo). "Por que nosotros nomás enterrados en la tierra como animales sin ningunas esperanzas de nada?" ("Why should we always be tied to the dirt like animals without any hope of anything?" 68).This anguished question posed by the central character in ". . . y no se lo tragó la tierra," the piece giving its title to the entire novel, "sets the tone of the book," as Ralph Grajeda has observed.[6] More than setting the tone, a function that is really performed by the introductory section, as we shall see later on in this work, it brings it to a climax. The "we" lying in the nucleus of this sentence refers to the main character and his immediate family, his parents and his brothers. Therefore, it is demonstrative of the process taking place in the novel, a motion in which the anguish which predominates in the tone of most of the narrations moves from the individual to the group and back to the individual.

Correspondingly, the discourse articulating Rivera's novel oscillates between two opposing and seemingly contradictory poles. On one hand, it gravitates toward an interiorization of experiences as the only possible recourse that the characters can perceive to be able to order the confusion unfolding around them. In this case, the actions they repeatedly perform throughout the novel are of a passive and silent nature: "to think," "to recall," "to forget," "to see," "to feel," etc. On the other hand, the same discourse moves the characters toward a limited and at times quite feeble attempt to communicate and share their experience—even if this is merely anguish—, and, in such cases, their actions become active: they "talk," "call," "say," and, as it occurs at the end of the novel, they "move." Making a final assessment of the development of the characters, the techniques, points of view, and style utilized by Rivera, a dense subjectivity is what transpires in the novel.

The informed reader will recall that . . . *y no se lo tragó la tierra* is structured into fourteen main sections and thirteen vignettes which precede all but the opening "chapter." The first and the last main pieces ("El año perdido" and "Debajo de la casa"), as critics have proposed before, function respectively as an "introduction" and a "recapitulation" of the themes treated in the twelve basic sections, which correspond to the twelve months of that initially "lost year," and which comprise the main body of the book.[7]

Two features of the novel that reflect well the subjective vision of the author are his treatment of time and silence, two intertwining elements in the book. The importance of these two elements becomes apparent from the very outset of the narration: "Aquel año se le perdió. A veces trataba de recordar y ya para cuando creía que se estaba aclarando todo un poco se le perdían las palabras" (1). With these two opening sentences, the third-person omniscient narrator relates the protagonist's loss of time, memory and words, placing the reader in the midst of a subjective environment highly charged with ambiguity. As the narration advances, the air of ambiguity increases and reaches an oneiric dimension when the boundaries between consciousness and unconsciousness are also erased: "Casi siempre empezaba con un sueño donde despertaba de pronto y luego se daba cuenta de que realmente estaba dormido" (1). And very rapidly the character, who will significantly remain nameless throughout the novel, falls into a type of limbo: "Luego ya no supo si lo que pensaba había pasado o no." Thus, in four sentences Rivera manages not only to erase time and the possibility of verbal communication, but also to cast a doubt on the authenticity of the thinking process itself. Silence, symbolic of the character's alienation, has reached an almost absolute point.

But, as if not enough had been done already to negate all external references, the narrator provides us with a slightly modified version of the extreme situation his character confronts: "Siempre empezaba todo cuando oía que alguien le llamaba por su nombre pero cuando volteaba (. . .) quedaba donde mismo" and, a little later, "hasta se le olvidaba el nombre que le habían llamado." By the end of the second paragraph, then, in addition to time and speech, tne anonymous being has lost his very identity.

As the narrator continues to guide the reader through the apparent chaos, he leads us into the original source of the crisis faced by the character. And, at this point, the intrinsic relationship between time and silence ("year" and "words"), already announced in the first sentences of the chapter, becomes clear. The character, the narrator relates, "Una vez . . . se dio cuenta de que él mismo se había llamado. Y así empezó el año perdido." If we had thought that the character's concern with time, the losing of a year, is what triggers his meditation and later on makes him "lose words," now we know that it is in fact *silence*, the realization that no one other than himself had been calling him, which makes him lose perspective of time and fall into a deep state of alienation.

At the end of the first chapter, out of that false dynamic in which silence and vocalization carry out an apparent tug-of-war, what finally prevails is silence carefully wrapped up by Rivera in the interior of his character. And, considering that the character is present more by the allusions of the omniscient narrator than anything else, Rivera's exacerbated efforts to negate things, making them difuse and blurry to the point of near disappearance, can be fully appreciated. Silence, as it appears in this introductory section, can be subdivided into two different levels: a conscious level ("pensar") and an unconscious realm ("dormir"). Working his way through a series of concentric circles structured in descending order, Rivera first places his character before the vague possibility of verbal communication, then in the conscious level of silence ("Se dio cuenta de que siempre pensaba que pensaba y de allí no podía salir"), and finally sinks him into total unconsciousness ("Luego se ponía a pensar en que nunca pensaba y era cuando se le volvía todo blanco y se quedaba dormido"). Silence becomes absolute.

With the last and deceiving sentence of this first section, "Pero antes de dormirse veía y oía muchas cosas . . ." (which, it must be said, does not modify but only reaffirms the air of passivity and inactivity surrounding the narration, as demonstrated by the verbs included in it: "dormirse," "veía," "oía"), the narrator provides an opening and invites the reader to accompany him on the character's Proustian and voyeuristic journey.

It has been correctly noted by various critics that the ghostly character who loses the year at the beginning of the book is the same one we encounter in "Debajo de la casa" at the conclusion of the novel. Furthermore, critics conjecture that it is indeed this central figure who, in the highly symbolic shape of the child, wanders through the rest of the chapters, sometimes as an actor and other times as a mere observer, thereby providing one of the necessary elements of narrative unity in the book. Pursuing this line of reading, it can be safely assumed that nothing in the novel really occurs. The central character, as a grown-up man, spends a certain amount of time under a house and, there, half-asleep and half-awake, quietly recalls a series of traumatic experiences he has lived or witnessed in the past.

In fact, the only brief interventions on the part of the central character are toward the end of the book when he silently meditates in the dark and wishes he had arms long enough to embrace all the people he has recalled. This desire to see all of those people together, coupled with his declared recuperation of the "lost year," has been generally interpreted as the point in which the character symbolically begins to overcome alienation and to acquire a social consciousness.[8] However, a close reading of the text clearly demonstrates that the character never really rejects solitude and silence—on the contrary, he enjoys them and makes clear his purpose to pursue his search through meditation:

> —Quisiera ver a toda esta gente junta. (. . .) Pero eso apenas en un sueño. Aquí sí se está suave porque puedo pensar en lo que yo quiera. (. . .) Yo creo que es lo que necesitaba más que todo. Necesitaba esconderme para poder comprender muchas cosas. De aquí en adelante todo lo que tengo que hacer es venirme aquí, en lo oscuro, y pensar en ellos. Y tengo tanto en que pensar y me faltan tantos años. Yo creo que hoy quería recordar este año pasado. Y es nomás uno. Tendré que venir aquí para recordar los demás. (168)

This silence is finally broken, quite abruptly and violently, at the very end of the novel: "Volvió a la situación del presente cuando oyó que un niño gritaba y al mismo tiempo sintió un golpe en la pierna" ("His thoughts returned to the present and he heard a child yelling, and at the same time he felt a blow on his leg," 168). Having discovered his presence under the house, a group of noisy children throw rocks at him. The children, their mother, armed with some boards, and a neighbor's dog force him to leave his hiding place: "Tuvo que salir. Todos se sorprendieron que fuera él. Al retirarse de ellos no les dijo nada" ("He had to come out. Everyone was surprised that it was he. He didn't say anything when he walked away from them," 169). Human contact does not make him abandon his comfortable silence. He walks away quietly; he only listens and becomes very happy when he hears the children's mother say she believes he is going mad, that he is losing the years, "Está perdiendo los años." His happiness is due to his sudden realization that he had not lost anything, "no había perdido nada," he had found something, he has been able to discover how to interrelate things, the narrator says. And the novel ends when the anonymous character arrives home, climbs up into a tree and *imagines* that somewhere in the distance, up on top of a palm tree, there is somebody looking at him. He raises his arm and waves it back and forth signaling that he knows that the other one is there.

Very noticeable and highly significant indeed is the fact that the only interaction the character is able to sustain with other human beings is by means of his imagination. His only real contact with concrete people, which takes place despite his resistance, becomes frustrated and, aside from its violent nature, only contributes further to his alienation. Silence, although briefly interrupted, triumphs in the end and thus comes to close the circle of subjectivity that structurally and thematically rules the novel.

Not unexpectedly, silence is also fundamental throughout the pieces composing the main body of the book. Combining and alternating descriptive and dramatic narration, Rivera organizes the stories in the form of "descriptions" by the third-person omniscient narrator, monologues by individual characters, and dialogues sustained by voices that, for the most part, remain anonymous. It is interesting to note, however, that even those selections narrating an external event and strongly based on dialogue ("Los niños no se aguantaron," "La noche que se apagaron las luces"), are continuously permeated by silence. The author skilfully achieves this effect through the utilization of a laconic speech, as illustrated by the following example:

—Dicen que el viejo casi se volvió loco.
—¿Usted cree?
—Sí, ya perdió el rancho. Le entró muy duro a la bebida. Y luego cuando lo juzgaron y que salió libre dicen que se dejó caer de un árbol porque quería matarse.
—Pero no se mató, ¿verdad?
—Pos no.
—Ahí está.
—No crea, compadre, a mí se me hace que sí se volvió loco. Usted lo

ha visto como anda ahora. Parece limosnero.
—Sí, pero es que ya no tiene dinero.
—Pos sí. (7)
(They say that the boss almost went insane.—Do you really think so?—Yes. He's already lost his ranch. And he's started to drink very heavily. After the trial when he was set free he jumped off a tree because he wanted to kill himself.—But he didn't kill himself, right?—Well, no.—There you are.—You wouldn't believe it, compadre, but I really think he went crazy. You've seen the state he's in nowadays. He looks like a beggar.—Sure, but it's only because he doesn't have any money any more.—I guess you're right.)

and also through the reiterated introduction of the vague "dicen" which, given the ambiguity of the information source, casts a doubt on the veracity of the information itself and thus tends to negate it. But the resources Rivera uses to weave elements of silence into his stories are not limited to these two techniques. The richness and diversity of elements that come together in order to form a discourse of silence in his texts becomes evident upon a careful reading of virtually any of the selections in the novel.

In "La noche que se apagaron las luces," for example, we know that Ramón, the central figure in the story, did not talk much, "no hablaba mucho," (106). So, the information regarding the events leading up to Ramón's suicide reaches us through the accounts of a third-person omniscient narrator, the dialogues of various unknown voices and excerpts of retrospective monologues and apparent conversations sustained by Ramón and Juanita.

Curiously, even the unknown voices we hear doubt of the accounts they are referring to: "Dicen que apenas la había vuelto a ver en cuatro meses . . . no se sabe, no se sabe . . ." ("They say that he had hardly seen her for four months . . . no one knows . . . no one knows," 106), replies another voice who intervenes two paragraphs later. But the latter immediately falls back into a position which also leaves a margin for doubt: "A mí me platicaron otra cosa. A mí me dijeron que . . ." ("They told me something else. They told me . . .," 107). To reiterate, the insecure source makes the information questionable and thereby contributes to quiet down, if not to erase, the voices. Similarly, even the third-person narrator leaves his omniscience momentarily aside toward the end of the story in order to contribute in fomenting the doubt: "Dicen que estaba bien achicharrado . . . También los que habían estado cerca de Ramón y Juanita oyeron que le dijo que se iba a matar por ella" ("They say he was burned to a crisp . . . Those who had been near Ramón and Juanita also had heard him say that he was going to kill himself on account of her," 109).

The tragedy of this story has its roots in the rupture of silence. All is well as long as Ramón, away from Juanita, performs a contemplative action: watching her picture "después de cena hasta que oscurece. Y al mediodía durante la hora de la comida también" ("After supper until it gets dark. Also at noon during the lunch hour," 107). Despite the concreteness of the photo, memory begins to fade away: "Pero lo que pasa es que ya no me acuerdo tanto de cómo es de veras" ("The fact is that I can't really remember how she really looks,") says Ramón. And the technique of repeating the same motif, the same words, not only illustrate the pathological obsession of the introvert man but also have the effect of slowing down the narration: "Veo el retrato pero ya no me acuerdo de cómo es aunque vea su retrato" ("I see her picture, but I don't recall her features even though I see her picture"). Ramón finally casts the photo aside and, as we saw in the case of the character in "Debajo de la casa," he also takes refuge within his own imagination: "Me prometió serme fiel. Y sí lo es porque sus ojos y su sonrisa me lo siguen diciendo cuando me la imagino" ("She promised to be faithful. And that's the way it is because I can still see it in her eyes and in her smile every time I think of her").

Ironically, Juanita is not "true" to Ramón because she *talks* to another man whose name, Ramiro, blends with Ramón's. "Pues no es que no quiera a Ramón, pero éste habla muy suave, y es todo, nomás hablo con él" ("It's not that I don't love Ramón, it's just that this other guy is a smooth talker, and that's all there is to it," 108), Juanita confides to an anonymous listener. And Ramiro in turn writes in a letter to Juanita, "ya sé que andas con otro pero me gusta mucho hablar contigo" ("I know that you're going around with somebody else, but I like to talk to you").

Not only is *talking*, the breaching of silence, responsible for triggering the fatal chain of events in the story, it is also talking, in the form of gossip, which carries the incident a little closer to its climax: "Unos amigos de Ramón se lo contaron todo" ("Some of Ramón's friends told him all about it," 107). Finally, talking is the single action which precipitates the debacle in at least two different manners. First, when the couple reunites after four months, despite the gossip, everything seems to be fine as long as Ramón performs a passive action, that of "seeing": "Le dio mucho gusto al verla y se le quitó el coraje que traía. Pero después de hablar con ella un rato le empezó a entrar el coraje de nuevo. Allí mismo y en ese mismo instante perdieron" ("He was overjoyed to see her, and all of his pent up anger disappeared. But after talking with her for a while his anger started building up again. Right then and there they broke up," 108) Later, when they meet again at the dance, "Se dijeron palabras por un rato. Ella le dio una cachetada, él le gritó quién sabe qué y salió casi corriendo del salón" ("They exchanged heated words for a while. She slapped him; he called her heaven knows what, and hurried out of the dance hall," 109). The final outcome, as we know, is tragic.

The extreme situations of silence we find in the novel, however, are best exemplified perhaps by the selections in which Rivera uses the interior monologue as an exacerbated technique to illustrate the alienation of the characters. "Un rezo," for example, as Daniel Testa has put it, "is a prayer spoken by a Chicano mother intimately troubled by a lack of news from her soldier son".[9] Whereas it can be argued that the mother does indeed "speak" the prayer, perhaps in a soft, almost imperceptible voice, insofar as it is a monologue it is part of the discourse of silence in the book. But more significant for the purpose of the present discussion is the fact that *silence*, the lack of news, is what triggers the anguish and the subsequent prayer of the woman: silence engenders silence. Similarly, the anecdote preceding the story also depicts a woman, presumably the same one in "Un rezo," whose concern over her son missing in action leads her to visit a medium, an *espiritista*. Lost words, lost years, lost sons, whether in the war or in an accident: "Lo único que no se quemó fueron los guantes" ("The only thing that didn't burn were the gloves"), we read in "Los quemaditos"; such is the nature of the world we encounter in Rivera.

The thesis elaborated in the previous pages proposes that Rivera's characters, despite sporadic attempts to break silence, move toward an interior time, into an intimate space devoid of noise and words. An argument that might be used to counter this thesis would be that the two central selections in the book, "La noche estaba plateada" and ". . . y no se lo tragó la tierra," are "rebellion" stories in which the central characters break silence. However, a close examination of the texts rapidly reveals that both of these stories not only do not violate the pattern of silence established by Rivera but, on the contrary, fit quite well into it.

For reasons of space and without any claims to exhaustivity, let us look only at one of these selections. "La noche estaba plateada" tells the story of a young man who, moved by his own curiosity, decides to one night summon the devil (we note that the protagonist of ". . . y no se lo tragó la tierra," who might very well be this same character, curses God). Waiting until his whole family is asleep, he slips out of the house "sin que nadie le sintiera ni le viera [. . .] Salió muy despacio sin hacer ruido" (". . . without anyone seeing or hearing him [. . .] He left without making the slightest noise," 54-5), and once he is at a prudent distance from the house he begins to talk to himself very quietly. Struggling between keeping silence and vanquishing his fears, he accidentally utters the name in a loud voice "accidentalmente se le salió el nombre en voz alta." Silence is "broken" but nothing happens: "Todo se veía igual. Todo estaba igual. Todo en paz" ("Everything was the same. Everything was the same. Everything peaceful").

The narrator has played a trick on the reader. The character seems to break silence but his vocalization is empty insofar as it does not reach anybody but himself. "En dos o tres ocasiones sintió que alguien le hablaba pero no quiso voltear, no de miedo sino porque estaba seguro de que no era nadie ni nada" ("Two or three times he sensed someone calling him, but he refused to turn around, not because he was afraid but because he was sure that no one was there"). The story ends, as it opens, when the young man slips back into the house and lies down again "con mucho cuidado, sin hacer ruido" (". . . being very careful not to make a sound"). And, at this point, he realizes the full significance of his actions: " 'No hay diablo, no hay nada.' Lo único que había oído en la mota había sido su propia voz" (" 'There is no devil, there is nothing.' The only thing he had heard in the field had been his own voice.") The reader evidently faces the very interiorization process which appears in the first page of the book; a false vocalization which is directed to nobody.

As a final point it must be noted that the small anecdotes used by the author to introduce the main chapters of the book are all written in italics. Typologically, therefore, they become associated with the interior monologues that abound in the novel and, being told by an anonymous voice, their authenticity becomes diffuse. The anecdote preceding the selection entitled "La noche que se apagaron las luces" for example, describes the conclusion of a wedding and its last sentence says: *"Enfrente de ellos venía un montón de niños corriendo y gritando.—Ahí vienen los novios"* *("In front of them was a group of youngsters running and screaming:— Here come the newlyweds,"* 105). The "yelling" of the children, however, is diluted into the ghostly background provided by the voice which, ironically, is supposed to be "exteriorizing" the event. Furthermore, the outcome of the events depicted in the chapter itself (the breaking up of the couple, Ramón and Juanita, and the subsequent suicide of the jealous boyfriend, as we saw earlier) come to negate the idyllic scene painted in the anecdote.

Silence, in various forms, filters even into the anecdotes with a clear satirical and at times humorous intention. For example, the one which sketches the story of a man sent by one of the local protestant ministers to teach carpentry to the migrant workers: "Traía de ayudante a la esposa del ministro para que le interpretara. Pero nunca les enseñaron nada. Se pasaban todo el día dentro del trailer. A la semana se fueron sin decir una palabra" (65). Or in those vignettes with a moral and didactic air, like the one relating a conversation between an old man and his grandson. The old man asks the young one what his greatest desire in life is. When the boy answers that he wishes the next ten years of his life would go by immediately, the dialogue ends abruptly: "El abuelo le dijo que estaba bien estúpido y ya ni le siguió hablando" ("The grandfather told him that he was very stupid, and he didn't talk to him after that," 81).

Clearly, in trying to recreate and document aesthetically the reality of the migrant farmworkers, as he knew and lived it himself in the 1940's and 1950's, Rivera's sensibility and deep insight into his people's culture compelled him to render a deeply subjective interpretation of that slice of life. More than one critic has attempted to see in . . . *y no se lo tragó la tierra* the social awareness that the 1960's would bring about among farmworkers and other segments of Chicano society as well. However, Rivera's characters, whether we like it or not, predate the Chicano Movement. They inhabit a harsh world in which exploitation and denial are still the fundamental traits of their existence and which leaves them with no other exit but to express their anguish through a discourse of silence.

[1] *. . . y no se lo tragó la tierra* (Berkeley: Quinto Sol Publications, 1971).

[2] I am referring here to Fernández de Lizardi's *El periquillo sarniento*, generally considered as the first novel of the Americas. Some scholars, however, suggest that earlier works like Francisco Bramón's *Los Sirgueros de la Vírgen sin original pecado* (1620) and Joaquin Bolaños' *La portentosa vida de la muerte* are "first samples of the novel in New Spain." Agustín Yañez, in the prologue to his edition of the two works (México: Universitaria, 1943), says that the provisions of the *Cédula* were not respected and that "not only were novels read in these domains, but they were also written, and with profane themes," viii.

[3] Joseph Sommers, "Interpreting Tomás Rivera," in *Modern Chicano Writers*, Joseph Sommers and Tomás Ybarra-Frausto, eds. (Englewood Cliffs: Prentice-Hall, 1979), 95. In a footnote appearing in this page, Sommers mentions Charles Tatum's work "Contemporary Chicano Prose Fiction: Its Ties to Mexican Literature" as an exception.

[4] In recent declarations, Rulfo made clear his intention of not finishing the novel. At the most, he said, he would condense the material into a short story.

[5] Juan Bruce-Novoa. *Chicano Authors: Inquiry by Interview* (Austin: University of Texas, 1980), 148. The quotation of Rivera that I use as an epigraph for this work is also taken from this book, 161.

[6] Ralph F. Grajeda. "Tomás Rivera's Appropriation of the Chicano Past," in *Modern Chicano Writers*.

[7] Herminio Ríos, in his "Introduction" to the first edition of the novel, advanced this notion, x and xv. Others, like Ralph Grajeda, op. cit., elaborate further on this idea.

[8] Juan Rodríguez's "The Problematic in Tomás Rivera," is an exception, in *Revista Chicano-Riqueña*, 6:3 (1967), 42-50.

[9] Daniel P. Testa. "Narrative Technique and Human Experience in Tomás Rivera," in *Modern Chicano Writers*, 89.

Chicano and Hispanic
Literature of the United States

Growing up Chicano:
Tomás Rivera and Sandra Cisneros

Erlinda González-Berry &
Tey Diana Rebolledo

We all grow up and our childhood is part of our history, our cultural baggage, and our definition of self. The recovery of the past through memories of childhood, the coming into knowledge of the person now by examination of the growing up period, and identification of social and cultural forces that shaped and influenced thier lives: these are some of the forces that lie behind the series of "growing up" poems and stories or *bildungsroman* written by Chicano writers.

The adventures of the hero/heroine that shape his/her destiny and bring self-knowledge and self-realization are part of the genre of self development through schooling or other forces of society, the *bildungsroman*, which could also be called *entwicklungsroman* or the novel of development since, as Anais Pratt points out, "they delineate a turning point in the hero's life, that is of both personal, psychological import and social significance."[1]

The growing up stories and poems written by Chicanos are part of a chain of searching for moments of insight into what made the Chicano what she/he is that forms a general theme in Chicano literature. Rolando Hinojosa, writing about Khail City, Tomás Rivera in . . . *y no se lo tragó la tierra*, Rudolfo Anaya in *Bless Me, Ultima*, are tales of young boys growing into manhood or self-knowledge through the acceptance of the symbols, happenings, and circumstances of the past, and the subsequent integration/unification of these as their destiny. For them the coming of age explains and signifies the winning of the kingdom of consciousness, heritage, and self. Characteristics of this male *bildungsroman* may include the following: 1) the hero leaves home or goes to school, 2) undergoes a trial by his peers, 3) is either accepted or learns to deal with his situations, 4) overcomes adversity, 5) in some way is successful at some heroic act, 6) discovers who he is, as a man and as a person in society, and, 7) at the end of the novel has integrated his consciousness, thus achieving self definition and is ready to deal with the world on his own terms.

Traditional growing up stories for females have quite a different scenario and outcome. The female adolescent may or may not go off to school, but in any case, in these stories the young woman also undergoes trials and tribulations which teach her how she must behave in society, what she must learn in order to assume her expected position. In contrast to the young male hero who at the end of the *bildungsroman* comes into a complete sense of integration and freedom, the female adolescent is carefully schooled to function in society, to lose her freedom and her sense of individuality in order to become a loving wife and mother. She thus integrates her destiny with that of a man who will protect her, defend her, and create a life for her. Whereas in their rites-of-passage, adolescent males encounter tests of strength and valour, Pratt points out that younger girls were given "tests in submission" while their older sisters were provided with models of behavior appropriate for success in the marriage market (14). Thus, rather than achieving maturity, young women of the traditional coming-of-age novels are lead down the path to a second infancy. Consequently, the female *bildungsroman* has tended to culminate in images of imprisoned women. When escape is an option, it is most often found through death or insanity. While elements of this fare may have been typical of the writings of early Chicano writers, the contemporary female growing-up story focuses on a more general sense of loss, around the realization that innocence is gone, around awareness of death and mortality, of the inability to retreat back into childhood and, at times, of the necessity to conform to a life not necessarily chosen by them. Many of these stories find the woman in the child and represent the voice of reflection. Seeing their own process of growing older, they monitor woman's going forth into the world. They also chronicle the world in which the adolescent heroine's expectations conflict with the dictates of the surrounding society. As Pratt further points out, "every element of her desired world-freedom to come and go, allegiance to nature, meaningful work, exercise of the intellect and use of her erotic capabilities" clashes with the norms of a strongly family and male oriented society (20). These clashes are chronicled in rebelious thoughts or actions against the church, or in secretative sexual actions in the exploration of body and sexuality. Clearly, in the following two poems by Margarita Cota-Cardenas, the state of freedom, innocence and naturalness is reflected *vis-a-vis* the contained persons the lyric speaker and her sister have become.

"Oohh the Boogyman

in Mesilla   New Mexico
   in the summer
         when I was very young
we would go to play   in the old cemetery
         and I would chat very happily
            with my dead relatives
         and I would dance on top

                              of a big cement
                              tomb
              stepping on dancing, dancing
                  a black painted skull
from delicious fright   my cousins would laugh
                  and my little brother el
Plonquito
                  and my little sister la Billie
and among dust   mesquite dried flowers   and tombs
              they'd be nervously shouting and shouting
              and I'd be dancing and singing
                  singing and dancing
but last night
              when the ghost of that poor soul buried
              in my former platform of cement
              came looking for me
I had to deny myself voice trembling
                  three times
                  ¡No, I am not that daring young girl!
                  ¡No I am not the happy Plonquita!
                  ¡No I am not the same!

          "To a Little Blond Girl of Heber, Califas"

      that little sister of mine
      was pretty, small tender
          but also very brave
          she wore cowboy boots
          a cowboy hat t-shirt and levis
      she was always followed
          by little Wienie dogs
      the Chapo the Chapa and the Chapitos
      once she tried to take a molar from one
      with a large pair of mechanic's pliers
      and during Holy Mass
      when communion was offered
      to be precise
      she said to Father Jean Vincent
      —Cabrón. I am going to tell my papa
      that you didn't want to give me the
      white cookie.
      Now
          well   she's a mother   wife
              and she behaves herself.[2]

This paper will examine two Chicano novels which are part of the *bildungsroman* genre for their similarities to each other as well as their differences and for their relationship to the traditional *bildungsroman*.

Tomás Rivera's *. . . y no se lo tragó la tierra* consists of twelve short narratives preceded by even shorter vignettes, all preceded by a prologue and followed by an epilogue. The twelve episodes represent the twelve months in a year and the symbolic time that passes in this novel/collection of stories. Of the twelve narratives, four are first person narrations (a young boy telling the story). The two middle narratives (the most significant ones in relation to the boy's sense of self *vis-a-vis* society and religion) are narrated by an observant third person—a device for lessening the intensity of the experience and one which strengthens the I/he dichotomy to be discussed later. The remaining narrative voices are various stories from a collective history or memory. What ties the entire narrative structure together, as we discover in the epilogue, is the conscious thought process of a young man who, by the end of the narration, has become a man. The emphasis on the emergence of the adult is clearly illustrated when a child sees someone exit from under the house and cries, "Mami, mami, aquí está un viejo debajo de la casa. Mami, mami, mami, pronto, sal, aquí esta un viejo, aquí está un viejo" ("Mami, mami. There's a man under the house. Mami, mami, come outside quick. There's a man here, there's a man here").[3] This allusion to an old man, when we in fact know it is a boy under the house, imbues this story with ambiguity. However, if we read the story on two levels the ambiguity is resolved. On the one hand, the story is that of a young boy seeking refuge, a place to reflect, remember, and order his life. On the other, this story acts as a metaphor for the process of writing, and the figure of the young protagonist (boy) and the narrator/author (man) merge when the child calls out, "There's a man here."

Why is he under the house? The first chapter consists of a rather ambiguous narration in which we are introduced to a character who seems to be suspended in limbo between reality and fantasy: "Casi siempre empezaba con un sueño donde despertaba de pronto y luego se daba cuenta de que realmente estaba dormido. Luego ya no supo si lo que pensaba había pasado o no" (1). This person hears a mysterious voice call, but each time he turns there is no one there. Finally he realizes that it is his own voice calling to him. Clearly this call beckons to an examination of the subconscious and/or metacultural.

At the beginning of the last story, a third person narrator introduces a young boy hiding under a house. While isolated under this house the boy has been reconstructing the memories of his past year. At this point the change from third person narrator to the boy's interior consciousness is indicated by italics and a graphically indicated box. Having entered the boy's interior world, we discover, via a stream of consciousness technique, a summary of all the stories of the book. In addition to bringing the reader in direct contact with the center of consciousness of the novel, this narration serves as a metaphor for Rivera's vision of the creative act. Inherent in that metaphor is the archetypal labyrinth motif which Rivera claims to be synonymous with the form and structure of literature.

> The labyrinth was and is a man-made structure full of intricate passageways that make it difficult to find the way from the interior to the entrance or from the entrance to the center. In essence, the important element here is that the labyrinth provides a setting for a search . . . Literature represents man's life, it also reflects his inner search and his outward search. It is in a sense an intricate maze to provide either exteriorization or interiorization of the human involvement and evolvement.[4]

In the last story of . . . *y no se lo tragó la tierra*, Rivera's literary theory and his creative work coincide perfectly. By situating the boy under the house, the author alludes to the center of the dark recesses of the labyrinth. The exterior of the labyrinth is suggested by a thin line of light which is visible to the boy, "De donde estaba nada más se veía una línea blanca de luz todo alrededor" (118). If the labyrinth is indeed a structure designed for search, and the light can be interpreted as understanding, then the boy must find his way out of the dark maze to reach the level of the light/knowledge. Now, then, we can return to the first story and understand that the voice is the voice of his *alter ego* calling him to enter the labyrinth in search of his "other." According to Rivera that search should lead to the discovery of the human condition,

> for it is a vicarious notion of humanity, or man, to attempt to search for the other, "alter ego," in order to better comprehend himself. Again the labyrinth represents a structure into which his life can and does fit. In essence, is it not life in search of form—a conquest, a labyrinth in which to reflect his human condition? (1971, 13).

Thus at the end of the story, not only has the nameless hero discovered who he is, but in the face of negative time, "he's losing his mind," he discovers "something" (127). Instead of "losing" himself, he knows that he has found himself and is in touch with that other part of himself, in the true meaning of uncover. This I/he dichotomy, reinforced in the form of the narration, is illustrative of the man-child separation, which through the process of the narration, through the thought process, find each other and are united for always: "Luego cuando llegó a la casa se fue al árbol que estaba en el solar. Se subió. En el horizonte encontró una palma y se imaginó que ahí estaba alguien trepado viéndolo a él. Y hasta levantó el brazo y lo movió para atrás y para adelante para que viera que él sabía que estaba allí."

Rivera's book represents not only the coming of age of the protagonist and the coming to terms with the adult/child part of the narrator, but also the collective narrations of Chicano experiences, and the injustices that accompany them; they deal with the repression that religion brings, racism, suffering, laughing and crying—in sum all that makes up life, and in particular the life of the Chicanos known to the narrator. Whose stories are these? Are they all connected to the narrator? Sometimes it is a child narrator whose present adult consciousness sees through reality as if from behind a double veil, the adult experience with a child's perception of the events.

All the stories in . . . *y no se lo tragó la tierra* are complete in themselves, that is, they stand by themselves; yet they are tied together by the common thread of the child/man narrator, under the house, in the labyrinth of memory collecting, synthesizing, creating.

In *The House on Mango St.* by Sandra Cisneros, the structure of the novel is similar to that of Tomás Rivera. First, the symbol of the house as consciousness, as collective memory, as archetypal labyrinth, as a nourishing structure within which (or in Rivera's case under which) the child comes into a sense of his/her own being is clearly presented in both texts. The outside community is also reflected in both texts. Cisneros' text is limited to Mango Street but, nevertheless, both childhood communities are the nucleus and the microcosm for the larger world.

Like Rivera's text, Cisneros' is a collection of smaller texts which can be read separately but which are related to each other through the narrative speaker as well as by characters who pop in and out of the stories. There are important differences between the two texts, however, just as there are similarities. One of the most important differences is in the narrative voice used by the female protagonist in *The House on Mango St.* While she narrates the lives, struggles and concerns of her immediate family, neighbors and friends on Mango Street, her voice is clearly and consistently that of a child—a child who reports life as it is: full of ambiguities, the possibility of misinterpretation, mysteries, fears and uncertainties. We see the world through this child's eyes and we also see the child as she comes to an understanding of herself, her world, and her culture.

The first vignette begins with a negation of her "house": it is not a real house, it is not a nice house, actually it is a disgrace. All six family members share rooms, there is only one bath, it is in a poor neighborhood. But, more important, the house on Mango Street is not her house. "I knew then I had to have a house. A real house. One I could point to. But this isn't it. The house on Mango Street isn't it. For the time being, mama said. Temporary, said Papa. But I know how those things go."[5]

At the end of the story, however, the narrator comes to understand that despite her need for a space of her own, Mango Street *is* really a part of her—an essential, creative part she will never be able to leave. In this realization, Rivera and Cisneros coincide. While the protagonists of both narratives evolve in their journey or quest, beyond encapsulating cultural mores, both search in (as narrators) and return to (as authors) their neighborhoods for the human and historical materials of which their stories will be made.

A second difference is that in Rivera's text, the narrator is unnamed; perhaps this lack of naming is meant to indicate the universal condition. In Cisneros' text from the beginning the female protagonist knows who she is, and what her name is, Esperanza. Yet, even this name she would like to change.

> In English my name means hope. In Spanish it means too many letters. It means sadness, it means waiting. It is like the number nine. A muddy color . . . It was my great-grandmother's name and now it is mine. She was a horse woman too, born like me in the Chinese year of the horse—which is supposed to be bad luck if you're born female—but I think this is a Chinese lie because the Chinese, like the Mexicans, don't like their women strong . . . At school they say my name funny as if the syllables were made out of tin and hurt the roof of your mouth. But in Spanish my name is made out of a softer something like silver, not quite as thick as sister's name Magdalena which is uglier than mine. Magdalena who at least can come home and become Nenny. But I am always Esperanza.
>
> I would like to baptize myself under a new name, a name more like the real me, the one nobody sees. Esperanza as Lisandra or Maritza or Zeze the X. Yes. Something like Zeze the X will do. (12-13)

Both texts are similar in the coming to terms with sexuality. For both young protagonists, the fear, mystery, and finally, understanding of sexuality—particularly the implications of their own, is important for the full realization of their being. However, the encounter with sexuality is experienced quite differently by each of these protagonists. Rivera's young boy emerges from his first encounter feeling that he has discovered something so marvelous as to compare it to the grace of God. This exposure to sex, in fact, frees him of culturally and religiously induced guilt and serves as a catalyst for further curiosity *vis-a-vis* the larger world: "Tenía ganas de saber más de todo" ("I had a strong desire to learn more about everything," 64). Esperanza's first exposure to sex is an equally positive experience, one that points in the direction of acceptance. The story entitled "Hips" shows Esperanza and her young friends coming to terms with their bodies, as they feel themselves blooming like crocuses in the spring.

> One day you wake up and there they are. Ready and waiting like a new Buick with the keys in the ignition. Ready to take you

where? . . . If you don't get them you may turn into a man. Nenny says this and she believes it. She is this way because of her age. But most important, hips are scientific, I say repeating what Alicia already told me. It's the bones that let you know which skeleton was a man's when it was a man and which a woman's.

They bloom like roses, I continue because it's obvious I'm the only one that can speak with any authority; I have science on my side. The bones just one day open. Just like that. One day you might decide to have kids, and then where are you going to put them? Got to have room. Bones got to give.

But don't have too many or your behind will spread. that's how it is, says Rachel whose mama is as wide as a boat. And we just laugh. (47-8)

Their second exposure, however, functions as a warning of the nefarious implications surrounding female sexuality. Anxious to play grown up, the young girls put on high heeled shoes and parade down Mango Street only to confront male lasciviousness: "Bum man says, Yes, little girl. Your little lemon shoes are so beautiful. But come closer. I can't see very well. Come closer Please" (39). Here we see echoes of "Little Red Riding Hood." However, the experience does function as an explicit warning, "We are tired of being beautiful. Lucy hides the lemon shoes and the red shoes and the shoes that used to be white under a powerful bushel basket on the backporch, until one Tuesday her mother who is very clean throws them away. But no one complains" (40).

That female biological coming-of-age is frequently established by physical violation is suggested in the story "Red Clowns": "Why did you leave me all alone? I waited my whole life. You're a liar. They all lied. All the books and magazines, everything that told it wrong. Only his dirty fingernails against my skin, only his sour smell again . . . He wouldn't let me go. He said I love, I love you Spanish girl" (94). An equally violent vision of sexual abuse of young women is alluded to in the following passage: "Until the way Sally tells it, he just went crazy, he just forgot he was her father between the buckle and the belt. You're not my daughter, you're not my daughter. And then he broke into using his hands" (85-6).

Despite these negative experiences, and the disillusion that accompany them, Esperanza dreams of physical love that is exciting, beautiful and fulfilling: "Everything is holding its breath inside me. Everything is waiting to explode like Christmas. I want to be all new and shiny. I want to sit out bad at night, a boy around my neck and the wind under my skirt" (70).

This passage, however, is not sufficient to allow us to interpret the rites of passage leading to sexual awareness as equal for male and female. Rivera's young protagonist has only to separate sexuality from religion in order to achieve a positive integration of the former into his gradually expanding world view. Young Esperanza, on the other hand, must suffer some very negative experiences, or knowledge of them, which in the end leave her, and the reader, with a very strong impression of female sexual vulnerability.

Of the two authors, Cisneros is more clearly conscious of the act of self exploration through writing in the text itself. Esperanza is explicitly a teller of tales, a budding writer of poems. It is only at the end of Rivera's text that we have a hint of narrative self consciousness. Following the summary of the boy's memories, wandering through the maze of discovery, there is a monologue in which the protagonist/narrator becomes the surrogate voice of the author: "Encontrar y reencontrar y juntar. Relacionar esto con esto, eso con aquello, todo con todo. Eso era. Eso era todo. Y me dio más gusto" (127). Happier than what? The superlative here refers to an earlier discovery: "Quisiera ver a toda esa gente junta. Y si tuviera unos brazos bien grandes los podría abrazar a todos. Quisiera poder platicar con todos otra vez, pero que todos estuvieran juntos. Pero eso apenas en un sueño" (125).

In a dream, or perhaps in the invented world of fiction. By bringing all those people together between the covers of the book, Rivera is in fact able to embrace them all. Thus, writing, for Rivera is an act of love for his people.

> To write is a total experience, like life itself. It is an original experience, like of a complete and splendid act of sexual union, of birth, of death, of the joy one has in loving mankind, because of these feelings involved—compassion and brotherhood. (1971, 19)

Esperanza's act of love for the inhabitants of Mango Street will likewise manifest itself in the stories she will one day write:

> One day I will go away. Friends and neighbors will say, what happened to that Esperanza? What did she do with all those books and paper? Why did she move so far away?They will not know I have gone away to come back. For the ones I left behind. For the ones who cannot get out. (102)

Both Cisneros and Rivera utilize the rich oral tradition of stories told and incorporate it into their narratives; they simply choose different facets of that oral tradition. Rivera uses Catholic belief and mythology as well as folk beliefs, folk tales, tall tales and gossip—all that body of values and societal dictums which the boy must rebel against in order to understand. Cisneros incorporates children's games and rhythms as well as the female-to-female tradition into her narrative. The use of female childhood belief, half-truths, mis-truths, and attempts at self affirmation entice the reader into the hilarious world of childhood. In the section titled "Hips," the girls jump rope while chanting not only the traditional rope verses but inventing new ones which enrich and enliven the narrative and bear witness to their imagination and wit:

> The waitress with the big fat hips
> who pays the rent with taxi tips.
> Nobody in town will kiss her on the lips
> because . . .
> because she looks like Christopher Columbus!
> Yes, no, maybe so. Yes, no, maybe so. (49)

And, finally, both authors use myths to understand their narratives. Rivera's characters search for a lost paradise, just as the hero does, in genuine quest for his mythic self. A universal paradise is denied because of social injustice, racism and economic suffering. Yet the individual is successful in his quest for himself. Cisneros plays upon fairy tales such as Rapunzel, Sleeping Beauty, Little Red Riding Hood, and imprisoned fairy princesses. Thus in her narrative, woman after woman is denied her freedom and her ability to make something of herself by society. Esperanza clearly knows that that is not the destiny she wants for herself. She, like Rivera's protagonist, participates in the mythic search for self, and in so doing, she breaks with the traditional female *bildungsroman* to portray her heroine as a true hero. Much against societal and cultural codes, she refuses to accept gender determined limitations. "I have begun my own quiet war. Simple. I am the one who leaves the table like a man, without putting back the chair or picking up the plates."(82). And she refuses to acknowledge her father's house as her own (and by implication that of the man to whom her father will some day give her), continuing steadfast in her search for her own house—that is in pursuit of the creation of an authentic self.

This consciousness of a "different" destiny is as evident in much of contemporary Chicana writing as it is in that written by Sandra Cisneros. An example would be the following poem by the New Mexican poet, Demetria Martínez titled "Troublemaker (for all who ask what I plan to do with my degree)":

> I want to be
> a mango seed
> that men trip over,
> those innovators!
> cradling print-outs
> for the production
> of pink liquid soap.
>
> Once on a train

I complained to a man:
We should make bread
not pink liquid soap.
He said:
That's not the
American Way.
If we didn't innovate
those Mexicans
would be in worse shape
than what they are today.

I want to be a mango seed
in the street
grow into a tree
towering in the tar
to stop dead all trucks
full of pink
liquid soap.

Mother, father
there's no passing
the cup
I'm going to be a troublemaker
when I grow up.[6]

Thus the work of Tomás Rivera and Sandra Cisneros is reflective of a rich, varied and complex series of texts on growing up by Chicano writers. Both authors use a traditional form to indicate that the Chicano *bildungsroman*, both male and female, has come into its own.

[1]Anais Pratt, *Archetypal Patterns in Woman's Fiction* (Bloomington, In.: Indiana University Press, 1981), 13.

[2]Margarita Cota-Cárdenas, in Tey Diana Rebolledo, "The Bittersweet Nostalgia of Childhood in the Poetry of Margarita Cota-Cárdenas," *Frontiers*, 2:2 (1980), 33-34.

[3]Tomás Rivera, . . . *y no se lo tragó la tierra* (Berkeley: Editorial Justa, 1977), 127.

[4]Tomás Rivera, "Into the Labyrinth: The Chicano in Literature," *New Voices in Literature. The Mexican American* (Edinburgh, TX: Pan American University Press, 1971), 13.

[5]Sandra Cisneros, *The House on Mango St.* (Houston: Arte Público Press, 1983), 9.

[6]Demetria Martínez, unpublished poem.

Fragmentation in the Chicano Novel: Literary Technique and Cultural Identity

John C. Akers

If Tomás Rivera's description of Chicano Literature as "a ritual of immortality" and "a ritual of the living" is to bring meaning to literary criticism, it must be backed by insightful analysis and commentary of texts.[1] What particular demands do works of Chicano fiction present to the reader and the critic? What conclusive observations can be made about these texts? Rivera's "rituals" are there: how can we understand them?

It is significant to learn that in Chicano prose fiction one of the few constants in narrative and structural design has been the frequent use of what is generally referred to as "fragmentation." Rodríguez del Pino, for example, in his study of the novels of five Chicano authors, concludes specifically that:

> La técnica en todas estas obras es fragmentaria y experimental. Para poder abarcar al pueblo en su totalidad y en su diversidad, ha sido necesaria la experimentación y, como requisito, la fragmentación. Esta técnica fragmentaria va desde una sencillez expresiva (Hinojosa) hasta una complejidad comprometedora (Brito) en la que se requiere la inmersión y colaboración del lector. Morales incorpora la teoría literaria objetivista de Robbe-Grillet con elementos cinematográficos, y Méndez convierte un maremagnum de personajes y vidas en un acertado mosaico en el que las historias y sus protagonistas se funden en una gran visión.[2]

Of course, not all of Chicano fiction uses techniques of fragmentation, nor is Chicano literature the sole contemporary advocate of its application. Critics have noted that the Chicano novel has relied on many sources for its inspiration—from the novel of the Mexican Revolution, to the Latin American novel of the "boom," to the anti-novel of the present—and while it is incorrect to state that there is one source that predominates in the development of Chicano prose, it does seem that there is something special in the technique of fragmentation that responds to the needs of the Chicano author to perform the "ritual" that Rivera mentions.

Guillermo Rojas, to cite one author, has looked to the novel of the Mexican Revolution and decided that, based on a comparison of several characteristics of these writings and those of a few examples of Chicano fiction, the latter are a continuation of the former.[3] While indeed structural and technical similarities are found by Rojas, it is evident to most critics that Chicano literature is developing its own creative experiments and that no specific influence alone explains its growth and varied expression.

Fragmentation as a novelistic technique has become a commonly accepted feature of the modern Latin American novel in general. One critic has suggested that fragmentation itself is one of the fundamental structures of present-day Hispanic American narratives;[4] and Fernando Alegría in writing of the Latin American "anti-novel," which I believe would include some works of Chicano fiction, presents a useful observation that serves to explain in general terms the function and effect of fragmentation: there is, he summarizes, "an attempt to disassemble narrative in order to make it fit into the disorder of reality."[5]

The process of fragmentation to be considered in this study will be limited primarily to that affecting narrative development; linguistic or other dimensions of fragmentation that do not directly relate to narrative trends will not be emphasized here (although they too are relevant to a comprehensive appreciation of the phenomenon of Chicano literature).

Besides serving as a focus of analysis of Chicano prose fiction, the study of fragmentation helps to link novels in a way that presents more logic than a chronological or thematic grouping might, simply because it elaborates creative methods of writing—a more meaningful way to approach a body of works of art than through consideration of extraneous features such as date of publication or presence of social commentary. Thus, while the novels to which I will limit my comments fall generally into Charles Tatum's "second group" of Chicano writings—those published approximately in 1971-75—they do so only because they share narrative fragmentation.[6] I shall include another novel that Tatum excludes from his second group: Raymond Barrio's *The Plum Plum Pickers* (1969); and I shall exlude others that Tatum presents: Rudolfo Anaya's *Bless Me, Ultima* (1971)—because this novel does not overtly experiment with narrative fragmentation—and Rolando Hinojosa's *Estampas del Valle* (1973). Of Rolando Hinojosa I will mention only *Generaciones y semblanzas* (1976; originally published as *Klail City y sus alrededores*), not because Hinojosa's other novels are not representative of the processes of fragmentation, but because the fragmentation found in *Generaciones y semblanzas* is perhaps the most fully developed of his novels and encompasses the fragmentation techniques he uses elsewhere. The remaining novels I shall add to my grouping are Miguel Méndez's *Peregrinos de Aztlán* (1971); Tomás Rivera's *. . . y no se lo tragó la tierra* (1971); Alejandro Morales's *Caras viejas y vino nuevo* (1975), and its English translation, which has important structural changes: *Old Faces and New Wine* (1981); and finally, a novel not usually said to be fragmented but that does use an important variant of fragmentation, Ron Arias's *The Road to Tamazunchale* (1975).

I do not intend to analyze each novel's fragmentation in exhaustive detail, although a study of all the dimensions of fragmentation in these works is needed.[7] More of an attempt is made to gain a general understanding of fragmentation in Chicano literature and to suggest that there is critical relevance to its presence in a significant number of Chicano novels: it is a technique tied to a search for cultural identity.

It is important to note that fragmentation as a literary technique both in Chicano and other modern literatures has had its share of negative criticism. The universally acclaimed novel *Pedro Páramo* (1955) by the Mexican author Juan Rulfo is one example of where experimentation with narrative structure through disintegration has drawn reserved praise from respected critics. The comments by the Mexican poet and critic Alí Chumacero are representative of the hesitancy with which some writers regard narrative experimentation. He writes of Pedro Páramo that "the principal flaw of the novel is to be found in the plan utilized to write it . . . Without a nucleus, without a central point around which the action can be integrated, its reading leaves us at the end with a series of scenes put together only by the isolated value of each one."[8]

This same criticism to varying degrees has been leveled against Rivera's . . . *y no se lo tragó la tierra* and Hinojosa's *Estampas del Valle, Generaciones y semblanzas*, and the other works in his Klail City series. Usually the critique of these works has sought to emphasize the independence of the parts of the novel to the detriment of the whole. In an early article by Juan Rodríguez, to cite an example, the critic refers to Rivera's . . . *y no se lo tragó la tierra* as primarily a collection of short stories.[9]

Other theoretical work outside of Chicano literature has attempted to define the transformation of the established novelistic craft as a conscious and threatening movement away from traditional narrative strategies. Noé Jitrik finds, for example, that the narrator is taking a more limited role in the new novel, that the narrator's omniscience is to choose and "convoke real elements to give form to an imaginary world; the narrator, within the story, is the one who unifies elements which would appear in total disorder if they were not placed into contact and relationships and if they were not given a meaning."[10] Significantly, he entitles his article "Destruction and Forms in Fiction."

Even in more general studies of art there has been a concern for fragmentation as a disintegration of form and aesthetic content. The classic study of Erich Kahler, *Disintegration of Form in the Arts* (1968), presents a negative assessment of avant-garde modern art (including literature) in which the continuity of aesthetic creations is seen as being sacrificed to a directed emphasis on the construction and independence of parts. He affirms that the "anarchically multifold artistic endeavors" of his day are manifested in movements that are contributing to what he sees as "an extremely dangerous trend of events."[11] He urges an aggressive assertion of rationality in all art forms, concluding: "As long as we sense in a work that effort, that captive road toward the achievement of a coherence, as long as we can retrace in the work this striving to disclose the innermost structure of phenomenality, or to express an innermost, most delicate psychic experience, we feel assured of its artistic authenticity and can relive a creative process" (Kahler, 95-6).

The ritual of Chicano fiction, in all its vitality and variety, does not forsake Kahler's coherence nor advance Jitrik's "destruction." At its heart is a powerful, singular search, one of meaning and integration where disparate experiences and splintered dreams are reunited in creative experiments. The use of fragmentation does not signal chaos or disintegration in Chicano literature; to the contrary, its development is a reflection of a consciously chosen path to bring readers to a deeper experience of the unique cultural identity of the Chicano.

The Novels

One of the points of departure for this study is to review some of the catchwords that have been applied to the fragmented approaches of the Chicano novels previously listed. These words range from "web," "tapestry," "mosaic," and "collage," to "time and space montage," and a "complex of echoes, reminiscences, cries of pain."[12] They are limited in their critical usefulness because they describe in a general and impressionistic fashion what often is a complex literary phenomenon.

It is Vernon Lattin in his article "Paradise and Plums: Appearance and Reality in Barrio's *The Plum Plum Pickers*" who first elects the word "web" to describe the fragmented presentation in Raymond Barrio's early novel of the migrant farmers' experience.[13] His description, repeated by Charles Tatum in his book-length study of Chicano literature, reads: "The novel is a web of appearances, facades, dreams, hopes, fantasies, and aspirations that are played off against and contrast with the nightmares, disappointments, and death" (Tatum, 109). The problem with this description is the use of the word "web" applied to the structure of the novel. "Web" generally implies both a certain symmetry and a purpose of entrapment, and neither of these concepts fits the narrative pattern of *The Plum Plum Pickers*. The presence of symmetry is not part of Barrio's fragmented structuring of the world of the migrant farmers; perhaps the opposite is true, that Barrio employs a fragmented narrative, replete with multiple points of view, to reconstruct a world where there is no continuity other than that of deception and exploitation. Even the "editorial" structuring of the novel—the division of the work into thirty-four numbered units—has no symmetry; some units are very brief (little more than a paragraph and less than a page), while some are ten or more pages. There is no consistent ordering of long and short fragments. This is in evident contrast, for example, to Rivera's structuring of novelistic form in . . . *y no se lo tragó la tierra* where there is symmetric unity: an introductory framing chapter; twelve internal narrations—each preceded by a reflective vignette—; and a final, conclusive framing chapter that joins the whole. Although Barrio's fragmentation shows no structural consistency, it is used decisively to recreate a sense of the migrant's disillusioning reality. One of his most effective techniques is to splice anecdotes with what can be called "para-literary" material: graffiti, bulletin-board announcements and newsclippings. The effect of such splicings is to put the reader into what seems to be a more direct, immediate contact with real objects and events relevant to the migrant's world. The traditional distances between reader and reality, and narrator and that which is narrated (or author and subject matter) are minimized. Thus, Barrio has introduced another form of fragmentation, narrative splicing, into his original fragmentation—the separation of narrative development into numerous anecdotes presented from multiple points of view—thereby apparently condensing and intensifying his work, and heightening the reader's perception of a Chicano reality.

The novels of Alejandro Morales, specifically his *Caras viejas y vino nuevo* and its edited and revised English translation *Old Faces and New Wine*, contain a complex type of fragmentation akin to that of Barrio in that it incorporates a decisive attempt to approach reality through a manipulation of the novel's form, not just its content.[14] An initial reading of the novels has the reader sensing both chaos and order in Morales' fragmentation, as on one hand the author is determined to break up traditional narrative patterns by 1) obscuring the presence of a consistently discernable narrator; 2) infusing dialogue into narrative or descriptive text; and 3) ignoring the mechanics of structure, such as chapter separations or punctuation; while on the other he is evidently aware of structuring his fragmented discourse with interspersed, key passages of lyrical, emotive and narrative qualities.

One of the issues that continues to complicate an evaluation of Morales' fragmentation is why the translation by Max Martínez with editing and revision by Alurista and José Monleón differs substantially from the Mortiz publication of the original Spanish (1975). One has to question whether Morales acquiesced to the changes in the English version, which will be outlined here; whether or not Morales would agree that the structural changes affect the novel, yielding in fact a significantly different novel; and even whether the Mexican publishing house, Mortiz, requested the modification of Morales' original work. While speculation is all that can be directed to these questions, certain issues are clear: the Alurista and Monleón revision of the novel assumes that the novel lends itself to a structural reshuffling without altering the basic coherence of the entire work. This assumption should be questioned, even if in fact Morales himself allowed the editors of the Englsh version to make the alterations.

The major changes that are found in the revision are the reversal of order of fragments two through thirty-two of the Spanish edition to the

English text, and the breaking of fragment nine into two parts, which gives the English edition a total of thirty-three fragments. There are also two significant printing errors in the English text; on pages 16 and 83 there are repetitions of previous paragraphs, apparently due to printing and proofing oversights and not editorial aims. With a text as complicated as that of Morales, exacting attention to detail in editing is crucial to avoid further reader confusion.

By leaving the positioning of the first and last fragments of the Spanish original the same, Alurista and Monleón appear to be granting particular importance to the placement of their events, indicating their primacy as the first and last constituents of the novel. By then reversing the overall order of the interior fragments (two through thirty-one became thirty-one through two) without varying their relative order, the editors again would seem to be acknowledging some continuum in the relationship of one part to another, although without necessarily relating this relative continuity to the presentation of all the parts together. They also consciously or unconsciously have used the first and last segments to "frame" the interior.

I postulate that the relationship that the editors found in fragments two through thirty-one was one of perceived time. Erlinda González-Berry, in her article "*Caras viejas y vino nuevo*: Journey Through a Disintegrating Barrio," described what she analyzed as a reversed chronological ordering of the narration; she sees Morales' Spanish text proceeding from fragment one backwards in time, somewhat structurally similar to Alejo Carpentier's *Viaje a la semilla* (1971).[15] While the novel does possibly move backwards chronologically between the first fragment and the last, this chronological movement is by no means clearly linear; in fact, there are several sections of the novel that either indicate no definable temporal ordering or else that actually suggest a precedence, chronologically, over subsequent fragments. The editors of the English edition, in a playful sense of editorial responsibility, may have mistakenly reinforced the notion of strict chronological ordering of these fragments.

Regarding the issue of the English version's division of one of the fragments (fragment nine in the Spanish edition) into two fragments, it can be surmised either that the English editors detected a necessary break in the Spanish original or else that they were victims again, as in the case of the repeated paragraphs on pages 18 and 83, of printing and proofing oversights.

The problem raised by the reordering of fragments is of course should the structure of Morales' Spanish edition be tampered with? While Alurista and Monleón may have had the complete support of Morales in their edition, it does seem plausible that their work has been one of creative consequences rather than faithful representation of the Spanish original. A more detailed investigation of the relationship of the fragments of *Caras viejas y vino nuevo* may reveal more startling contradictions in the two versions of the novel. Certainly the placing of what in the Spanish text is the penultimate fragment in the second position in the English translation already changes the tone and momentum of the novel in the early stages of the reading. The Spanish text (fragment two) is lyrical, objective, and powerful in its description of the barrio, which is the backdrop to a young man's (Mateo's) nocturnal sexual fantasy. The second fragment of the English text is less momentous, less relevant to the barrio per se, and ultimately innocuous in its positioning relative to the first fragment, which involves the violent confrontation of father and son. It deflates unnecessarily and illogically the strength of the novel's beginning as it narrates the trials of Julián remembering his conflicts in barrio school-life.

Fragment positioning can be decisive, and playing with the ordering of fragments may have results not intended by a given author. Only in the case of a work like Julio Cortázar's *Rayuela* (1966), where the reader is actually instructed in rereading the novel with a reordering of its pages, can one be assured of following an author's original designs. Fragmentation does not preclude relative relationships of at times apparently discordant parts.

In the case of Rolando Hinojosa's *Generaciones y semblanzas* (Berkeley: Justa Publications, 1977) the result of fragmentation has been what is described as both a montage, a mosaic, and a tapestry. Francisco Lomelí, in commenting upon the structure of *Generaciones y semblanzas* and the earlier *Estampas del Valle*, writes that the novels "have a similar result in that they represent a series of montages; however, the reader must go beyond the fragment and play on words to see the whole as a mosaic of a people consisting of many personalities in their respective milieu."[16] The word "tapestry" was used by Hinojosa himself in an interview by Salvador Rodríguez del Pino (with Luis Leal and Francisco Lomelí).[17] What is relevant in the use of the words "montage," "mosaic," and "tapestry" is that they are all taken from the terminology of the visual arts. "Montage" is commonly used to describe a particular photographic or design outlay; "mosaic" refers to a specific construction technique and effect, again from the visual arts; and the word "tapestry" conjures up images of textile art. Conspicuous by its absence is the term "mural," because this artistic technique more than the three other cited descriptions of fragmentation has cultural roots closest to home for the Chicano author in the works of the Mexican muralists Siqueiros, Orozco, and Rivera; although again "mural" is a term generally assigned to visual phenomena. What is called for in the study of fragmentation in Chicano literature and literature in general is a new set of terms that suit literary strategies rather than visual ones.

A further problem with the visual terminology is that on occasion it does not quite capture the *essence* of the novel, in the sense that a word like "montage" inadvertently places the prominence of fragments, the parts, on an equal plane with the overall effect of the whole, the coherence. A montage is comprised of equally significant or insignificant parts, where the totality of the parts is not necessarily greater in aesthetic impact than the sum of the individual parts. Referring back to Erich Kahler's observation regarding the goal of coherence as the key to the integration of fragmented artistic expressions, it is clear that the Chicano novel does strive for this coherence; and that, yes, the "whole" of works like Hinojosa's is greater than the sum of the parts: he writes novels—links in a five-part series (the Klail City Death Trip Series)—not short stories.

Hinojosa can be seen as an author who concertedly uses fragmentation (whatever its description: montage, mosaic, or tapestry) as an authorial prerogative; that is, he appears to be developing its possibilities all the while he accepts its usage as a basic tenet of his writing. His writing is fragmented in such a way that,of all the Chicano works to be discussed in this study, his is the most flexible in terms of the ordering of the fragments. Again, it is the author himself who has defended this possiblility ("Encuentro"). At the same time he evolves his novelistic art through the use of independent fragments, which are linked at times only via recurring characters, locales, or themes and characterized by changing narrators and perspective, he overtly projects his work as a novel and not a series of unrelated vignettes or short stories. He likes to give the reader indices of sorts, such as those found on pages 10 and 60 of *Generaciones y semblanzas* in which he outlines the coming fragments. He also breaks up these narrative fragments, most of which are titled, with further fragments such as letters (84) and a poem (20) by one of the novel's characters. Another fragmentating device is his intrusion as author (67-8, 99-100) in which, ironically, he writes of his own method in building his novel, relying on humor to defend himself: "These two parts of . . . *Notes from Klail City and its environs* (sic) are included here because they broke out like the measles: first the fever, then the itching followed by the spots, and not because this writer had foreseen that they would fit here. What's more, numbers four, five and six were written first, then number one and now two and three. One never knows how these things come out" (68).

In Hinojosa's recent addition to the Klail City series, *The Valley* (Ypsilanti, Michigan: Bilingual Press, 1983), he continues his experiments with fragmentation by stating in his introduction that this novel is "a re-creation in narrative prose of a portfolio of etchings, engravings, sketches, and silhouettes by various artists in various styles, plus a set of photographs from a family album" (3). It is as if now he has come to take his association of literature and visual arts even more seriously, as he lists several words—portfolio, etchings, engravings, sketches, silhouettes, photographs—that are of obviously visual reference. In fact *The Valley* represents an increasing "visualization" of Hinojosa's fictionalized southwest Texas, "Klail City and its environs," as exemplified concretely by the author's insertion on page four of his novel of a supposed map of the area from where many of his characters come and live out their days.

In attempts to analyze Tomás Rivera's *. . . y no se lo tragó la tierra* (Berkeley: Quinto Sol Publications, 1971) there has been further confusion surrounding its fragmentation, in part due to improper terminology. On one hand, it has been regarded as "difficult to describe structurally" because traditional narrative guideposts (a set narrator, a logical progression or succession of events, a readily identifiable denouément) are apparently absent; and yet, on the other, critics have tried to make its structure overtly simplistic: the twelve fragments of the novel correspond to months of the year and relate the temporal setting of the migrants' farming experiences.[18] The conclusion is that Rivera has aimed for a cyclical format, which in turn evokes the futility of the migrants' existence: a never-ending cycle of back-breaking work, forced exodus, and disillusionment. Rivera has not, however, made his novel that simple for analysis, and it is far more ambiguous—though not structurally "difficult"—than often admitted. As outlined before, his structural fragmentation is strongly patterned, more than that of any other Chicano work to date; it is in the "binding" of the pattern that problems of comprehension arise. As has been explained in other critics' interpretations of the novel (Testa, 86), the last chapter entitled "Debajo de la casa" gives structural cohesion to his work, bringing together the initially discordant fragments of experience of chapters one through twelve (or thirteen, if the introductory "El año perdido" is counted as a chapter). What has grown from the interpretation has been the tendency to delineate more temporal cohesion to the novel than the author may have intended. While the first fragment is called "El año perdido," and there are twelve subsequent chapters, not necessarily is the cyclical nature of the work the correct reading. Temporal sequence between chapters does not exist, as there is little or no indication of time or season in many of the twelve segments. Furthermore, the novel as a whole is misread if the sense of a cycle is perceived to preclude the fact that the boy who is the protagonist has broken out of a cycle: that of accepting passively his role as disadvantaged. I believe Rivera secondarily creates a temporal cycle in his work and that the only primary cycle is that of oppression, which the boy consciously destroys in his coming to grips with his own world.

In discussions of fragmentation in Chicano literature, one rarely mentions the novel by Ron Arias, *The Road to Tamazunchale*, (Reno, Nevada: West Coast Poetry Review, 1975), although perhaps from the reader's viewpoint this is one of the novels that by experience leaves the most distinct impression of fragmented discourse. "With different modes of discourse continually interchanging throughout Fausto's on-again, off-again struggle with death, the consequent disorientation the reader suffers is also a constant throughout the novel."[19] Reader disorientation caused by the novel begins almost from the onset, where in the first episode it is not clear whether reality, fantasy, or a combination of the two will be the projected level of experience from the narrator. (In the initial pages of the text, Fausto is found pulling dead skin off his body: is this happening? Is Fausto really dead? Is this the author's imagination that we as readers are to accept as real?) While episodes, no matter if fantastical or realistic, are linked by key recurring symbols in the text (the flute music of the Incan that symbolizes a call to a remote past; snowfall in Los Angeles that symbolizes the at times incredulous side to reality—because it *has* snowed in Los Angeles—etc.) and do give a sense of some unity to the novel, the actual reading of the novel is quite difficult, as the reader is forced to sift through the author's playful juxtapositioning of apparently real events with others generated by Fausto's imagination.

Many of the episodes of the novel are short, although in the reader's retrospect—because he is left with a vivid image of often fantastic occurrences—they seem longer. There are thirteen chapters in the novel, introductory quotes from a chronical of the New World and a Nahuatl poem, and a postscript in two parts; all of this in approximately ninety-seven pages of text.

While the mixing of dream and reality, or fantasy and realism, is a constant never fully resolved in the novel, reader confusion is compounded because the play of these opposing modes is gradually intensified over the course of the text to the point that in the last narrative sequences, beginning with the "performance" of a play entitled "The Road to Tamazunchale" until the last words of the novel, Fausto appears to have died on two or even three occasions, if he wasn't already dead to start with!

This pattern of confusion in the text begins early in chapter seven, which describes the discovery of a dead *mojado*, David, in the Los Angeles River, and his eventual "stay" (as a guest corpse) with the lonely old maid, Mrs. Rentería. The chapter has realistic elements: the discovery of the body, the disclosure that the individual is an "illegal," the barrio's shared concern over his death and its implications to all of them; and it has decidedly fantastical qualities: was the body really dressed and housed by Mrs. Rentería? With this chapter, Arias sets the stage for his following concentrated experiments with dream-reality disjuncture. Unaware perhaps, he has determined that his novel will be an experience of fragmentation: the fragmentation of reality into dreams and fantasy and back to reality again.

The last novel to consider here is Méndez's *Peregrinos de Aztlán* (Tucson, Arizona: Editorial Peregrinos, 1974). Critical comments about its fragmentation have taken another route than that of the other novels of this study, trying to find the coherence of the novel not in a specific pattern that can be labeled "web" or "tapestry," but rather in the novel's language and reliance on oral tradition. The two studies that predominate in this view are Juan Bruce-Novoa's "Miguel Méndez: Voices of Silence," and Aristeo Brito's "El lenguaje tropológico en *Pergrinos de Aztlán*."[20]

What I would like to suggest, taking as a starting point the emphasis on figurative language and oral tradition in Méndez, is that with *Peregrinos de Aztlán* critical evaluation of fragmentation should look for analogies not in the visual arts but possibly in music, granted of course that a terminology of fragmentation in literature has yet to be established. A case can be made for his having created a carefully *orchestrated* fragmentation, where characters and events enter as solos and choruses: all variations on a theme of suffering and exploitation. While detailing correlation between literature and music is, as criticism, at best a challenging exercise and at worst an exercise in metaphor, at least it does provide an alternative to the association with visual arts and phenomena that has been used with other Chicano novels. It accents Méndez's particular art, allowing its unique qualities independence from others' experiments.

Fragmentation and Cultural Identity

To begin to relate a literary technique, that of fragmentation, to cultural identity it is best to generalize certain experiences of literature, particularly those that deal with the transferral of chaotic reality into harmonious fiction. The idea that the author initiates his work with an underlying chaotic reality at his disposal is reiterated by Juan Bruce-Novoa in his article "The Space of Chicano Literature," in which he begins his discussion of Chicano literary efforts with a summarizing interpretation of man's experience of modern life: "The contingency of discontinuous reality devours man's reflections and images so quickly that his only perception of them is at best partial, fragmentary, resulting in an even more pernicious revelation of his self-image as irrevocably lost and meaningless within that speeding, one way time progression. Man seeks to avail himself of recourse with which to combat the menace of chaotic discontinuity."[21] A literary work then, especially one within Chicano literature where precedents for authentic expression of the Chicano reality have not been as numerous—or at least as readily accessible as those of majority literary currents—has to struggle to respond to this "chaotic discontinuity." This same struggle, of course, is true of the poet, as Juan Bruce-Novoa, in another study, notes when he aptly entitled his analysis of Chicano poetry, "A Response to Chaos."[22] Joseph Sommers would call this response to chaos "a form of cognition," for a literary text "refers to and interprets human experience" (Sommers, 36). The Spanish critic, Andrés Amorós, believes that an author's creation is inevitably a *visión del mundo*, and that an author always possesses a special and personal way of seeing life.[23] Like Sommers, he recognizes the novel in particular as a means of knowing and appreciating reality.

Having accepted these premises of creative literary expression and recognizing the predominance and variety of uses of fragmentation in the six novels touched upon in this study, it can be postulated that this literary technique has in some way facilitated the Chicano novelists' efforts. What are the advantages and suitability of the technique to capture the Chicano *visión del mundo*, and how does this sorting out of chaotic reality become transformed into the expression of a cultural identity?

One of the first effects of fragmentation is that it enables a writer to cover a vast array of experiences in various temporal settings with numerous characters. Most of the novels cited in this study for example present the reader with an almost countless number of episodes of Chicano life. The Chicano author's purpose often seems to be an act of retrieving and appropriating what is rightfully his in his particular understanding of the Chicano identity. Hinojosa's "tapestry," for example, is more an artistic inventory of his past, where some events and people have grown from his own background in Texas and the Midwest, and where others are what would logically, and often with a twist of affectionate humor, fit into the Klail City Chicano microcosm of fiction.

But to assert that fragmentation has only a unidimensional benefit to its application—i.e., to retrieve and appropriate the past—is to lose sight of another result of the technique: to fix images and affirm identities. When Rivera writes his novel in twelve segments that are, at first reading, narratively independent, he allows those segments to be secured on their own grounds. The reader is fully cognizant of the depth of feeling of, in one case, the mother's separation from her son (in the chapter "El rezo"), of the symbolic and real suffering of the migrants in the chapter "Cuando lleguemos," and the deception and cruelty of "La mano en la bolsa" (chapter six). He is left with not one narrative image inspired by Rivera's novel, but rather with several, regardless of Rivera's final tying together of the segments through the revelations of the last chapter.

Ron Arias also has a capacity in fixing images for the reader. His protagonist Fausto, wandering by Elysian Park in Los Angeles and implausibly spotting a herd of alpacas is poignant in that the reader senses the longing of a humble, dying man for respite for the immediacy of his disillusioning environment. Another "herd" of the novel, the undocumented workers that Fausto and his "Sancho," Mario, lead up from the border through San Diego toward Los Angeles, are portrayed as hapless victims in a both comic and tragic march to nowhere.

Fragmentation, while not necessarily to be associatedd with chaos, also serves to parallel and directly imply the chaotic reality of certain exeriences. Hence Morales in his *Caras viejas y vino nuevo* may have intentionally explored the potential of techniques of fragmentation and disintegration to construct the fragmented and disintegrating reality of an East Los Angeles barrio. In early reviews of Morales' work this was the first impression received: the chaos of life was becoming the chaos of literature. One early review finds, contrary to Gonzales-Berry's previously cited article in which more definitive structures are detailed, that general chaos is the salient characteristic of the novel: "[The novel is] structurally organized into brief fragments or episodes in the form of [a] montage with no simple time or space. [The author] utilizes contemporary experimental techniques: a persistent superimposition of events where there is no separation of dialogue from narrative, a free association of ideas, a series of flashbacks, interior monologues and shared narration by first person or omniscient narrators. The general chaos is compounded by the ambiguous use of 'those,' 'here' (sic), [and] unknown 'he's".[24]

Also in Barrio's *The Plum Plum Pickers*, fragmentation may have been the most functional technique to convey the sense of there being not one protagonist in his narrative, but many: the pickers and those controlling their lives. In fact, fragmentation in most works of fiction is a key in widening the scope of the author, permitting him to span a vastness of life that would be more difficult to recreate with more traditional methods of narration. Ironically, breaking a narrative into parts actually allows an author to expand his narrative scope, because the process of breaking often introduces new perspectives, places, people, emotions, and time periods. All of the novels considered in this study can be characterized by their capacity to take in and portray a large segment of the Chicano experience.

Usually this "large segment of the Chicano experience" is presented in the fragmentation of these novels as a progressive detailing of deception through an episodic unfolding of life. Indeed, an individual's life, or that of a group of people, is most authentically communicated when the concrete events (episodic fragments) of that life are presented. Life is not expressed in terms of continuity, but rather in those of conflict with adjustment to new and different challenges. In the case of the Chicano past, where there has been constant struggle with the limiting designs of the dominant Anglo culture, there is an abundance of material for fiction, best related through an episodic discourse that is by nature fragmented.

Finally, together with the attempt to document in fiction the cultural identity of the Chicano through the detailing of Chicano life, fragmentation serves another "pragmatic" purpose: it is a vehicle of recollection and vicarious return. So often the novels of Chicano authors, especially those using fragmentation, can be seen as cultural receptacles of the Chicano past; that is, they are efforts to identify those significant parts that have brought the Chicano to his present experience of life. Readers look to Hinojosa to be re-linked with the "Tex-Mex" reality of the last forty years; Méndez speaks out for the forgotten of the Southwest and the border towns; Barrio and Rivera remind us of the complex world of suffering behind the peaceful facade of migrant pickers' lives; Morales reveals the inherent struggle of the urban ghetto; and finally, Arias depicts the swansong of an aged Chicano dreamer.

¹Tomás Rivera, "Chicano Literature: Fiesta of the Living," *The Identification and Analysis of Chicano Literature* (New York: Bilingual Press, 1982), 19.

²Salvador Rodríguez del Pino, *La novela chicana escrita en español: Cinco autores comprometidos* (Ypsilanti, Michigan: Bilingual Press, 1982), 142.

³Guillermo Rojas, "La prosa chicana: Tres epígonos de la novela mexicana de la revolución," *The Identification and Analysis of Chicano Literature*, 317-28.

⁴Zunilda Gertel, "Tres estructuras fundamentales en la narrativa hispanoamericana actual," *Nueva narrativa hispanoamericana actual*, 5 (1975), 215-27.

⁶Charles Tatum, *Chicano Literature* (Boston: Twayne, 1982), 103.

⁷The Hungarian Hispanist Laszlo Scholz has begun work in this area and recently presented a paper on Rolando Hinojosa's *Klail City y sus alrededores*, entitled "Fragmentarismo en Klail City y sus alrededores," (University of Mainz, Germany, Conference on Chicano literature, July 1984).

⁸Alí Chumacero, "El *Pedro Páramo* de Juan Rulfo," *Recopilación de textos sobre Juan Rulfo* (Habana: Casa de las Américas, 1969), 109.

⁹Juan Rodríguez, "Short Story," *A Decade of Chicano Literature* (Santa Barbara, California: Editorial la Causa, 1982), 42.

¹⁰Noé Jitrik, "Destruction and Forms in Fiction," *Latin America in its Literature*, 167-8.

¹¹Erich Kahler, *The Disintegration of Form in Fiction*, (New York: George Braziller, 1968), 3.

¹²Most of these catchwords have been gathered in Charles Tatum's chapter on the Chicano novel in *Chicano Literature*, 102-37.

¹³Vernon Lattin, "Paradise and Plums: Appearance and Reality in Barrio's *The Plum Plum Pickers*," *Selected Proceedings of the Third Annual Conference in Minority Studies* (La Crosse, Wisconsin: Institute for Minority Studies, 1976), 165. The edition of *The Plum Plum Pickers* referred to here is the first (Sunnyvale, California: Ventura Press, 1969). A recent edition published by the Bilingual Press (Binghamton, New York, 1984) is valuable for its introduction and bibliography related to Barrio.

¹⁴Alejandro Morales, *Caras viejas y vino nuevo* (Mexico: Joaquín Mortiz, 1975); and the revised, translated edition by Max Martínez, José Monleón and Alurista, *Old Faces and New Wine* (San Diego, California: Maize Press, 1981).

¹⁵Erlinda González-Berry, "*Caras viejas y vino nuevo*: Journey through a Disintegrating Barrio," *Latin American Literary Review*, 7:14 (1979), 64.

¹⁶Francisco Lomelí, "Novel," *A Decade of Chicano Literature*, 35.

¹⁷This is from a video-taped interview, "Encuentro #18 (1977), available through the Center for Chicano Studies, Santa Barbara, California.

¹⁸See Ralph Grajeda, "Tomás Rivera's Appropriation of the Chicano Past," *Modern Chicano Writers* (Englewood Cliffs, New Jersey: Prentice-Hall, 1979), 74; Daniel P. Testa, "Narrative Technique and Human Experience in Tomás Rivera," 91; and Joseph Sommers, "Interpreting Tomás Rivera," 99, both in *Modern Chicano Writers*.

¹⁹Mariana Marín, "*The Road to Tamazunchale:* Fantasy or Reality?," *De Colores* 3:4 (1977), 34-8.

²⁰Juan Bruce-Novoa, *Chicano Poetry: A Response to Chaos* (Austin, Texas: University of Texas Press, 1982); and Aristeo Brito, "El lenguaje tropológico en

'Peregrinos de Aztlán,' " in *La Luz* 4:2 (1975), 42-3.

[21] Juan Bruce-Novoa, "The Space of Chicano Literature," in *De Colores* 1:4 (1975), 23.

[22] Bruce-Novoa, *Chicano Poetry: A Reponse to Chaos*.

[23] Andrés Amorós, *Introducción a la literatura* (Madrid: Castalia, 1979), 67-72.

[24] This review is by the editors of Alejandro Morales' *Caras viejas y vino nuevo, De Colores* 3:4 (1977), 80.

This article is the result of research supported in part by the National Endowment for the Humanities.

Bilingual Poetry:
A Chicano Phenomenon

Susan Bassnett

In considering Chicano literature as a whole and Chicano poetry in particular, the single most significant feature that should be borne in mind is the fact that it is an emergent literature, with a relatively short history. Most of what has come to be termed Chicano literature has been produced within the past thirty years, and centres for the study of this literature are only about a decade old. For anyone attempting to analyse this phenomenon, there are immediately apparent advantages and equally obvious disadvantages. On the one hand, the case of a literature that is emerging together with the growth of cultural consciousness makes it possible for certain types of patterning to be observed. So, for example, we have the frequent use of a child or adolescent as narrator in Chicano prose works, as happens so often in Anglo-African literature; we have theatre that combines agit-prop elements with folk dance and music; we have a range of attempts to create an *epic* poem. On the other hand, the problem of determining influential sources is made particularly complex, since the writers of the texts straddle linguistic and cultural boundaries and draw on a range of different, often contrasting traditions.

One such tradition in conflict is the case of the function of poetry outside the intellectual establishment. In the Anglo-Saxon world, the functions of poetry are extremely restricted. Poetry is produced by a minority and read by a minority and that minority tends to be middle class and academic, often ideologically biased towards the right. The challenge to this traditional poetry establishment by the Beat poets, by male and female new wave writers in the United States has remained a minority issue. If the President of the United States were ever to quote poetry, it would be lines from Longfellow or, at best, selected lines from Whitman, well-known texts whose familiarity serves as a comfort and panacea to the general public. The poet who disturbs is marginalized as an undesirable in the American establishment.

In Latin America, the tradition of the poet's function is completely different. We need only think of the number of writers who have acted as ambassadors for Latin American nations, of the huge sales of books of poems, of the way in which the works of some poets achieve massive circulation. When the death of President Allende in Chile in 1973 is recalled, his name is immediately linked with that of Víctor Jara, poet and songwriter executed by fascist troops, and Pablo Neruda, Chile's most famous poet whose death coincided with the loss of his hopes for a free socialist state.

The Chicano poet, then, is heir to two traditions that are not only different but are actually in conflict. On the one hand, there is the US tradition of intellectualised versifying, of poetry being a voice through which a minority speaks to a minority, whilst on the other hand there is the Latin American tradition of the poet who occupies a prominent place in the struggle for freedom and national unity. And to this problem of differing functions can be added the linked problem of oral and written poetic forms. For whilst in the Anglo-Saxon tradition, poetry has come to be predominantly a written genre, in Latin America it still remains an art that crosses boundaries between the spoken or sung, and the written. *El canto* is both poem and song, a form that exists on two levels. For the oral tradition implies a reading experience that is totally other than the experience which happens between reader and printed page; the oral forms involve more people, they are communal in a way that the solitariness of reading the written cannot ever be. So when Ricardo Sánchez entitles his book *Canto y grito mi liberación*, he is immediately involving himself and his readers/listeners in a communal experience, where poetry does not belong to high art, but to daily reality.[7]

It would be far too simplistic to attach value judgements to these different traditions of writing and reading. What matters is that their existence feeds into the complexities of Chicano poetry, adding yet another dimension of intertextuality. The problems become more difficult to resolve if we consider Chicano poetry from the point of view of the receivers, for the first question to pose is simply: who are they? who buys and reads Chicano poetry? the inhabitants of the barrios? the migrant workers? the literate bilinguals in urban areas? the expanding Chicano middle classes? non-Chicano intellectuals? I do not propose to attempt to answer this question, but it should remain as an unresolved enigma behind everything that I may say about Chicano poetry, because it seems to me that it is crucial, just as similar questions can be asked about English and Francophone writing in Africa. What makes the questions so vital is the fact that, without a clear idea of the readership and its criteria, the writer writes in a position of particular difficulty, and I would suggest that the position of the Chicano writer is actually more difficult today, in the mid-Eighties, in spite of the diffusion of Chicano literary studies as an area of academic respectability, than it was in the mid-Sixties for precisely this reason.

Twenty years ago, issues seemed to be more clear-cut, at least on the surface level. Luis Valdez' work, together with the other theatre activist groups that sprang up in the wake of the Teatro Campesino, emerged in a very precise context: the California grape strike and the impulse for exploited Mexican-American agricultural workers to organise in effective trades unions. Later, this issue became linked to the anti-war movement and to the general question of minority rights across the US, but the driving force behind writers in the Sixties can be summarised by the first verse of Rodolfo Gonzales' *I am Joaquin*, his attempt at creating a Chicano epic poem, published in 1967.[2]

> I am Joaquin,
> lost in a world of confusion,
> caught up in the whirl of a gringo society,
> confused by the rules,
> scorned by attitudes,
> suppressed by manipulation,
> and destroyed by modern society.
> My fathers
>   have lost the economic battle
> and won
>   the struggle for cultural survival.

Tracing the history of the Chicano peoples through their Spanish Christian ancestors, Indian ancestors and, in an interesting gesture of solidarity with another racial group, through their Moorish ancestors, Gonzales explores the tragedy of a people who are descended from two groups that fought and killed each other and who have since become the servants of another nation. But throughout the poem he insists on the endurance of the Chicano people, and expresses his belief that at last things have begun to change for the better:

> And in all the fertile farmlands,
>   the barren plains,
>   the mountain villages,
>   smoke-smeared cities,
>   we start to MOVE.

Today, twenty years later, with Ronald Reagan serving a second term in the White House and with massive unemployment in the Chicano community and in the United States as a whole, with the problem of illegal migrant workers still unresolved, the question of Chicano movement forward has to be seen in context. Of course, the establishment has taken some note of the existence of Chicano culture, some money has been put down towards the subsidising of publishing houses, education, and the arts generally, but the amorphous nature of Chicano culture and the lack of organisation around precise issues has combined with the general loss of militancy in the US to create a climate that is far from fulfilling Gonzales' hopes. Ricardo Sánchez' poem "los doldrums" written in 1970 might be equally written today:

>   post election
>   when patronismo retains
>   its choking hold
>   sobre   la humanidad;
>   cannon fodder people
>   work out
>   daily drudgery
>
>   politician megalo-maniacs prepare
>   the artful desecration
>   of all we term humanity
>
>   the day drolls on,
>   blasely walloping us
>   with random buffs and puffs
>
>   the day after
>   elections
>
>   and
>
>   no one
>   gives
>   a damm . . . .[3]

If the picture so far painted is somewhat black, then I must acknowledge this as a deliberate ploy, an attempt to get away from over exaggerated claims for progress and development based on the proliferation of published, printed texts. Apart from the question of the readership, there is also the question that an emergent literature often relies heavily on content orientation at the expense of formal criteria, a criticism that can also be levelled at minority interest literature. So, for example, a poem or novel may depict a social situation that the author perceives as a burning issue that needs to be brought to the attention of the reading public, but that text may be clumsily written and full of cliches. And where there is a problem of finding a tradition out of which to write—indeed, where there are doubts as to whether writing, as opposed to singing, is the best way forward anyway—then the risk of creating well-meant but bad poetry is increased.

Now, truism though it is, poetry is made up of words arranged in a sequence that increases the density of language, the phenomenon described by the Russian Formalists as "making strange," or thickening language. The placing of words in a line, the use of patterns of assonance, alliteration, rhythm, repetition, the structures of syntactical components and lexical items are part of the process of making, or shaping a poem. We have already noted that the Chicano poet has more than one tradition of the poet's social role to contend with; in addition there is the question of the choice of language in which to shape the poem itself, a problem faced by neither the English language poet, nor the poet writing in Spanish. The Chicano poets have at their disposal English and Spanish, and in addition they have a particular form of Spanish that may be said to constitute a separate dialect. And here the question of who reads the poems becomes important again, because obviously some groups of readers are going to have greater or lesser access to one of these language systems. Moreover, although many Chicanos are roughly bilingual, that in itself creates difficulties, since the suppression of Spanish in schools and the general downgrading of Spanish socially in the US has created an inequality between the two languages. Hugo Baetens Beardsmore, in his study of *Bilingualism* (1982), talks about the phenomenon of *vertical* and *horizontal* bilingualism, where in the latter case the two languages have equal status for the speaker, but in the former case the two languages co-exist in a hierarchical relationship with the other.[4]

For many Chicano poets, the question of linguistic parity is of general importance. From a position of vertical bilingualism, they are attempting to move towards the horizontal, and out of this particular struggle has come what I consider to be the most original and most startingly creative texts in Chicano literature: bilingual poetry. In other words, where poets have focused on the task of crafting two linguistic systems into a coherent whole, they have been able to work with form and content, rather than simply concentrating on the overt "message" contained within the text.

There is a whole range of different types of bilingual poetry, and I would like briefly to look at some of these. The first type is the poem printed with a translation on the facing page. A case in point would be *Perros y antiperros* by Sergio Elizondo (1972) which has an English translation facing the Spanish text (although the title of the poem is not translated at all).[5] This kind of solution aims at making the poems available to two separate readerships, the English and the Spanish, and where the translator has had difficulty with dialect terms and left them in the original, this then becomes a kind of local colour that the English language reader has to necessarily overlook. The problem is that in the process of interlingual translation all kinds of changes happen and the bilingual reader actually has a less satisfactory experience in that comparisons are made between the two versions.[6] A case in point would be *Grito*, by Sergio Elizondo.[7]

A second type of bilingual poem is typified by "I am Joaquin," where the author provides two versions and where there is an additional text, a third language, through the use of photographic material. What happens here is that the poem can be read in several languages or across boundaries, and there is a new kind of interlingual process. So, for example, the last verse of the poem offers an illustration of the different dimensions that can be obtained when the same lines are written twice, and in such a way as to use differing patterns in each language:

I am the masses of my people.	Yo soy el bulto de mi gente y
I refuse to be absorbed.	yo renuncio ser absorbido.
I am Joaquin.	Yo soy Joaquín.
The odds are great	Las desigualdades son grandes
but my spirit is strong,	pero mi espíritu es firme,
my faith unbreakable	mi fe impenetrable,
my blood is pure.	mi sangre pura.
I am Aztec prince and Christian Christ	Soy príncipe azteca y Cristo cristiano
I SHALL ENDURE.	YO PERDURARE.
I WILL ENDURE.	YO PERDURARE.

The third type of bilingual poem is perhaps the least typical of a blending of two systems. In this type, the predominant language is English, and the Spanish elements are used for colour, for the creation of a sense of otherness. If the words or phrases used are untranslateable, terms that are specifically Chicano, then I would see the poem as belonging to another category, where the bilingualism is a functional, integral part of the composition and that would be a different case.

It is the fourth type of bilingual poem that is the most innovative and the most interesting, for in these poems the two languages interlock structurally, creating a text that reflects the way in which bilingual Chicano speakers use language in their daily lives. I realise that here I am touching upon another huge area of research, the question of the relative degree of bilingualism in the Chicano communities, given the differing uses made of English and Spanish in society at large. Ulrich Weinreich in *Languages in Contact* (1968) summarises the problems perceptively:

> . . . under a foreign occupation or in migrating to a new country, the adult members of a mother-tongue group may come to use a new language in its dealings with governmental authorities, while the children use it at school; at the same time, the old language may live on in the homes and at informal gatherings of the group. In such a case we might speak of a *partial* rather than a *total* shift. While language shifts among urban communities in America are usually rapid and total, the language shifts among rural immigrant communities are often rather of a partial type for two or three generations, at least.[8]

In the fourth category of structurally integrated English-Spanish poems, various sub-sections can be ascertained. One such sub-section is the poem where the two languages are used to show the gaps between the cultural traditions. An obvious example is Alurista's "address," where English is the language of authority and Spanish is the language of politeness and caring, with the Spanish speaker insisting on the significance not only of his name, but also of his family name.⁹ The harshness of the Anglo categorization system is exemplified through the listing of nouns: "address/occupation/age . . . height/hobbies/i.d. number/rank . . .," a system that reduces human individuality to zero. Faced with this kind of language, the Spanish speaker tries to change the level of communication. Three times he interrupts, politely using "perdone; the first time he gives his Christian name only, the second time he repeats this and adds his surname, and finally he gives details of his family name: "perdone mi padre era / el señor ortega / (a veces don josé)." Unlike the bureaucratic form language, he replies with complete sentences. The Anglo voice ignores him, and continues with the list of nouns, culminating in the symbolically loaded word "race." There is no communication between the speakers of these two languages, separated not because of the distinctions between English and Spanish, but because of the ideology within those two language systems.

In Ernie Padilla's "Ohming Instick,"¹⁰ a similar device is used, only here English is the language used by the teacher who, like Mr. Gradgrind in Dickens' *Hard Times*, is describing a peacock in arid, academic, factual terms, while Spanish is the language used for the child's interior monologue as he dreams about the beauty of birds and recalls his own pet pigeon who flew away. At the end of the poem, which is conceived almost as a scene from a play, the two languages come together in a culture clash, as the child is told off for daydreaming and is unable to speak English:

ALRIGHT.
Are you kids in the corner paying attention?
Armando, what is a peacock? What does homing instinct mean?

A MI ME HABLA?
¡SOY MUY TONTO!

Aohming instick eis . . . eis . . . como Lenchita . . ."
"Armando haven't I told you not to speak Spa . . ."
¡Caramba,
me van a pegar! . . .
"It's bad for you . . . Go see Mr. Mann"
. . . Mañana
sí iré con papá.

Piscaré mucho algodón . . .

The two languages in this type of poem typify two conflicting systems of value. English denotes undesirable qualities, authoritarianism, alienation; whilst Spanish denotes the inner world, the imagination, feeling. The crudity of this contrast is obvious: the reader identifies with the Spanish elements, and has no sympathy for the Anglo values. But in terms of the formal structure of these poems, the dichotomy is not so obvious, for the use of the two language systems implies a knowledge on the reader's part, so that the reader is implicated in the English speaking world by virtue of understanding the language it uses.

José Montoya's poems introduce another type of bilingual poetic technique: the placing side by side in the same text of Spanish and English sentences (or complete verses) with the obvious implication for the reader that they must be able to move freely in and out of both linguistic systems. His poetry requires the reader to be able to handle the two languages with equal control, but also utilises elements from the differing English and Spanish traditions. So, for example, the confession device of the new wave poets combines with the highly coloured abstract imagery of writers like Paz and Neruda, and this in turn is often combined with a discourse that reminds us of Ginsberg. Montoya's poetry blends both languages and styles, resulting in a complex writing that is a long way away from street songs and "popularity."

So in a poem entitled "Lazy Skin,"[11] Montoya glides in and out of both languages:

> Ambiente-
> Transparente como
>
> Una jolla, opaca como
> El carbón, heavy like
> A feather—carga fija
> Del hombre marginal.
> Aflicción arquetípica
>
> Reposando en los armarios

The bilingual reader follows this process with him, shifting linguistic gears through the progress of the poem. The juxtaposing of English and Spanish occurs simultaneously with the juxtaposing of the different traditions. In the passage quoted the I-speaker of confessional poetry coexists with the tradition of powerful symbolic language usage that we find in many Latin American writers. Montoya's poetry is a skillful blend of languages and traditions; it is committed poetry of great intelligence.

Of all the Chicano poets, my personal favourite is Alurista who, it seems to me, has found a genuinely new way of combining English and Spanish into an innovative whole. Alurista's poetry, like that of someone such as Ricardo Sánchez, can be placed in a third sub-category, that of unifying the fragments. What happens in Alurista's writing is that he acknowledges basic features of bilingualism and works from this basis. One of the most obvious features of bilingualism, for example, is the slight degree of incompleteness in the speaker's knowledge of both languages. Whereas a native speaker may be said to have 100 percent control over her/his language, the bilingual may have 99 percent control over two languages. To borrow a term from semiotics, for the bilingual both languages are *troués*—incomplete, not quite whole. The strength of the bilingual comes through access to two cultures, but the weakness comes from the slight degree of insecurity in both. What happens, particularly in a community of people who are all dealing with two languages simultaneously, is that a form of hybrid develops, a kind of third language that amalgamates both systems. The speaker may glide in and out of both quite unconsciously in the same sentence, using instinctively whichever elements come first and most immediately to hand. So, for example, Sánchez' dedication to *Canto y grito mi liberación*:

>This outpouring is dedicated, como toda mi vida
>a Teresa
>   Rik-Ser
>   Libertad Yvonne,
>to the memory of mi jefe, Pedro L. Sánchez,
>   mis carnales Pete y Sefy
>to the love felt from mi madrecita, Lina

I want to take one poem by Alurista, "i can see reality," from *Floricanto en Aztlán*,[12] as an example of the kind of complexity that can be achieved by this unifying of fragments, while at the same time the poem remains absolutely accessible to all readers.

>i can see reality
>without lifting the eyelids of my will
>inerte
>fijo—like my sign
>contemplating
>i can see
>everything's free in amerika
>excepto amerika misma
>constricted by its tripas
>amerika is bound to hide
>organic suicide
>en masa—de gula
>   la nación se consume
>   gnawing away its own life
>the system serves no more
>but it binds freedom
>   en barrios; de polvo y veneno

> i can see reality
> sin levantar los párpados de mi voluntad
> contemplo el suicidio de amerika (y su dieta inhumana)

This poem works on several levels. The i (uncapitalised) sees in his imagination this image of *amerika* (with k) as a gigantesque, fat being eating itself to death. The food terminology—tripas, gula, dieta are Spanish, but the key verbs *gnaw* and *bind* are in English. *Suicide/suicidio* is given in both languages, but the English term *freedom* is contrasted in the very next line by the Spanish *en barrios de polvo y veneno*. Significantly, the first language used is English, but the i speaker shifts into Spanish for the last two lines, repeating the second (English) line of the poem and concluding with the longest line of all that is also an explicit statement about the state of American society.

The statement made by Alurista is polemical, but the polemics are contained within the skilfully constructed structural pattern. What results is a text that is available to both Anglo readers of the left, in sympathy with the Chicano cause, or to Chicano readers accustomed to language shifts, without necessarily switching ideological codes. For in his use of Spanish and English in this poem with the witty ironical quote from *West Side Story*, English is not used in order to be read negatively, but rather to be read together with the Spanish units to create a kind of new, third language. In this respect, the utilisation of different language elements in the same textual composition reflects what is undeniably truly innovative about the Chicano experience: that because language is itself dynamic, it follows that where two language systems are in daily use together, such a dynamic process is accelerated. A good deal has been written on the changes wrought upon English by Spanish in the Southwest and on the West coast, as has happened with the impact of English on the Spanish language, both in terms of lexis and syntax. And as these changes occur in the spoken form, it follows logically that literary forms will begin to emerge. In fourteenth-century England, Chaucer wrote in a mish-mash of southeast Middle English dialect, overlaid with Francophone borrowings and has come to be termed the father of English poetry. Perhaps, as Alurista and his fellow writers begin to blend their diverse linguistic usages together in poetry, we are witnessing the beginning of something more far-reaching than can as yet be imagined.

---

[1] Ricardo Sánchez, *Canto y grito mi liberación* (El Paso: Mictla Publications, 1971).
[2] Rudolfo Gonzales, *Yo soy Joaquín* (Bantam Books, 1972).
[3] Ricardo Sánchez, "los doldrums," *Canto y grito mi liberación*.
[4] Hugo Baetens Beardsmore, *Bilingualism* (Chiveden: Tieto, 1982).
[5] Sergio Elizondo, *Perros y antiperros* (Berkeley: Quinto Sol, 1972).

⁶See Roman Jakobson, "On Linguistic Aspects of Translation," in R.A. Brower, ed. *On Translation* (Cambridge, Mass.: Harvard University Press, 1959), 232-9, and Susan Bassnett-McGuire, *Translation Studies* (London: Methuen, 1980).

⁷Sergio Elizondo, *Perros y Antiperros*.

⁸Uriel Weinreich, *Languages in Contact* (The Hague: Mouton, 1963), 107.

⁹Alurista, "address," in *Floricanto en Aztlán* (Los Angeles: University of California, 1971), 28.

¹⁰Ernie Padilla, "Ohming Instick" *El Espejo*, ed. O. Romano-V. and H. Rios C. (Berkeley: Quinto Sol, 1972), 255-256.

¹¹José Montoya, "Lazy Skin," *El Espejo*, 227-228.

¹²Alurista, "i can see reality," *Floricanto en Aztlán*, 31.

The Presence of Native Americans in Chicano Literature

Heiner Bus

In his *Chicano Manifesto*, one of the most comprehensive texts of the Movement, Armando B. Rendón states: "Not only . . . do the brown men and the red men have common bonds to the land and in blood from ages past, we have the common experience of the white man's deception and brutality whenever land, money, and cultural supremacy are at stake."[1] Rendon's call for a united effort of the two groups is founded on the ideas of the Chicano heritage as "a Spanish-Mexican Indian confluence of civilization" (70). Although this definition has become a commonplace, the profound exploration of the individual components has yet to come: "We have hardly begun to investigate the fathomless inheritance that is ours from our Indian forbears, the Nahuas, the Toltecs, the Aztecs, and the North American Indians" (280). Readers of Chicano literature are familiar with Alurista's *indigenismo*, "drawing from the Mexican indigenous heritage and the actual realities of barrio living in the United States."[2] They are also acquainted with the efforts of critics and anthologists to provide a wider context for Chicano literature.[3] Besides Alurista, the novelist and short story writer Miguel Méndez M. particularly stresses the Indian aspect: "As a characteristic that binds our literature, one could well cite the acknowledgement and full acceptance given in it to the Indian, in the glorification of his past as well as in the pride taken in inheriting his color."[4]

In his prose Méndez is preoccupied with the Indio, the Meso-American roots of his *Peregrinos de Aztlán*. A tendency to concentrate on this segment and to neglect the Native Americans is quite obvious, although lately a shift of emphasis can be noticed. Ricardo Sánchez strongly contradicted Alurista's 'indigenismo' which he called "pollyana indianness," "pyramided jive and distortion" and accused him and others of unrealism: "No, there are no pyramids nor fancy ideas at the Navajo nation, just as our barrios are not beautiful and edifying."[5] This line of argument includes a rather restrictive temporal and regional perspective which Alurista certainly could not accept.

The great variety of the Chicano experience prohibits such a prescriptive view. We have to acknowledge the different degrees of intensity in the exchange between the two groups. And it is legitimate to approach the present with the help of the myth which, at a first glance, appears to blur and romanticize harsh realities. In his introduction to the Alurista interview, Juan Bruce-Novoa discovers a new reconciliation of the past and present, the 'exotic' and the close-at-hand:

> Although in the earliest poems the indigenous presence was mainly Nahuatl-Mayan—a fact decried by his detractors for its supposed irrelevance to Chicano reality—he later evolved toward a Third World emphasis on one hand, and the inclusion of indigenous peoples more geographically related to the U.S. Southwest on the other. (265)

This part of Aztlán contributes to the theme a long, uninterrupted history of co-existence quite different from the barrio situation. Therefore, writers setting their works, for example, in rural New Mexico are much more stimulated to design recent and apparent scenes of interrelationship.

The immediate presence of the Indian urged many writers and political activists to reflect quite extensively upon the common history. In his fight to reclaim the old Spanish-Mexican land grants, Reies López Tijerina affirmed the bonds by separating historical fictions from truth: "We have not robbed the Indian, as some accuse us, nor do we seek harm for the Indian. The Indian is our brother, and that same law of the Indies commands us to live as brothers with the Indians."[6] And in another statement Tijerina described his ties to the land: "The Indian was our mother. The Spaniard was our father, yes, but the Indian was our true mother. Our father, the Spaniard, left us. We decided to stay with our mother, the Indian, here in New Mexico. This was our country. The land was our birthplace. We were a New Breed."[7] Such ideas are supported by Rudolfo A. Anaya who characterized New Mexico as the meeting place of the individual and the communal traditions.[8] This special quality of the place has been equally accepted by the Chicano and the Indian: "In a real sense, the mythologies of the Americas are the only mythologies of all of us, whether we are newly arrived or whether we have been here for centuries. The land and the people force this mythology on us. I gladly accept it; many or most of the American newcomers have resisted it."[9] Their common history, political demands, and the overlap of their systems of values have moved Chicanos and Indians to unified actions on various practical levels, for example, the Poor People's Campaign of 1968, the founding of D-Q University at Sacramento in 1971, or the commemoration of the 1680 Pueblo Revolt documented in Rudolfo A. Anaya and Simon J. Ortiz eds., *A Ceremony of Brotherhood, 1680-1980*.[10]

As we have already noticed, a number of Chicano writers have paid homage to their Native American heritage, still it is not easy to define the visible results of such confessions in their literary products and to relate them to the achievements of recent Native American literature.[11] It is significant that in his *Chicano Writers* Juan Bruce-Novoa asked his partners: "Does Chicano literature share common ground with Black literature? Differences?" but did not inquire about their affinities to Native American literature, although some of the writers laid down their opinions in another context.

Of all authors interviewed Alurista related his poetry most closely to his Indian background:

> Poetry is the traditional means of philosophical, theological, and scientific expression in the Indian world. The Indians wrote in poetry, not because they did not write prose, but simply because they thought that poetry was more realistic, more dialectic, more dynamic . . . in poetry we find reality depicted in its dynamic sense. Everything moves, changes in the world. Everything is experiencing constant transformation. Nothing is static. We are constantly dying and constantly being reborn. This applies to our material world, our psychological world as well as our spiritual world . . . That is the beauty of poetry. The continuum, the process is what is important in poetry. It gives us a glimpse of what reality is all about. Reality in motion. (274-5)

In answering the next question Alurista continued to specify the necessity of re-constructing the Chicano self in his poetry, mainly by revitalizing Indian world views: "We do believe that part of our responsibility, as creators, is to humanize, and this is to live in harmony with all other beings who are our brothers. Human beings are not superior to plants. Human beings are not superior to animals" (278). Thematic choices are involved when Alurista agrees with the Indian concept of "the mythological time-space that unifies the personal and historical time-space" (279). The poet goes beyond perspective, theme and world view by referring to the responsibilities of the creator in and for society. This notion comes very close to the role of the writer in the Indian storytelling tradition. In his article "An Overview of Chicano Letters: From Origins to Resurgence," Francisco Lomelí comments on this common ground: "This style of transmission is particularly appropriate to our Hispanic heritage as well as to our Indian background, both rich sources of oral tradition whose literatures sometimes depended on it almost totally."[12] The critic Vernon E. Lattin confirms this background information in his analysis of novels from both literatures:

> Moreover, in Anaya and Momaday, the novels themselves are also forms of rediscovery, attempts to return to the sacred art of storytelling and myth-making that is part of Indian oral tradition. They are attempts to push the secular mode of modern fiction into the sacred mode, a faith and recognition in the power of the world."[13]

In the following paragraphs I want to discuss five selected Chicano literary texts published between 1976 and 1984 to find out how and in which context Chicanos depict Native Americans. I shall proceed chronologically to avoid general classifications obscuring the individual approach.

Rudolfo Anaya has indeed applied some of the techniques of oral storytelling in his novel *Heart of Aztlan*, for example, the legends and myths he intersperses, the open ends, and the loose episodic structure. The Chicano and Indian qualities of the book are highly visible in the character of Crispín, the old blind seer who plays a crucial role in Clemente's search for identity in an urban environment. He evidently represents the agrarian, land-based component in the hero which has to be strengthened to help him cope with the challenges of the barrio in general and the demands of his social group for leadership in particular. Crispín spiritually connects him with the mythology of the land: "The earth was the new covenant between the people and their gods," and "The mystery of his melody and the magic of his words carried them out of their present time and misery to a time of legends and myths, and in that time he made them encounter the truth of their being."[14] As the Indian and Chicano mythologies are interchangeable, the revitalization of the collective memory of the Chicano with the help of the blind Indian seer can produce the lifting power for the problems dragging down the individual in the modern barrio and factory world.[15]

In his story "The Retribution," Nash Candelaria ironically explains the common New Mexican roots of the two ethnic groups. Through his mode of presentation he also very well illustrates a storytelling technique. The scene is set in 1846: The 'Irishman' Miguel and Tercero of the Rafa clan are sorting out pieces of the family history that they have learned from Grandfather Rafa. When Tercero finds out that Miguel was only informed about the Spanish component of the past, he eagerly fills in the Indian aspect: "So. He did not tell you about his Navajo grandmother. My great-great grandmother. Well, let me tell you, because somehow this is as much the story of the Rio Grande as conquistadors, land grants, and ricos."[16] The Indian connection was established with the acquisition of the Los Rafas land grant by José Antonio I. who had to keep the Navajo warrior Ojo Torcido, Twisted Eye, off his new possessions. Despite its fierceness the fight reveals some surprising facts and attitudes:

> Ojo Torcido could speak Spanish. There were rumors that his mother had been a Spanish settler who had been kidnapped in one of those many raids in which the Navajos captured slaves and wives. Whatever truth to the rumor, Ojo Torcido spared many a life that another might not have. His captives were sheep rather than settlers. His tribe was said to own the largest flocks in New Mexico. Larger by far than the richest Don in the Rio Grande Valley. (181-2)

Both emotionally and materially the Indian is recognized as an equal opponent. Such a remarkable enemy makes it difficult for Don José to achieve retribution. His strategy takes advantage of a custom of the land, the capturing and trading of slaves with its traditional consequences, the mixture of bloodlines.

During the annual fall gathering at Taos, Don José discovers that the Indian chief's daughter is to be sold as a captive. He can purchase her before her father is able to make "his move towards negotation. The general bargaining had not yet begun" (185). The buyer's procedure and motives are described as personal and representative features:

> Don José moved quickly, with the kind of heedlessness that had enabled the Spanish to conquer Mexico and push northward to settle the Southwest. There was still enough vitality in the blood to act out old assertiveness on those rare occasions when one thought of pleasures more immediate than 'mañana' . . . he had no son to carry on the family name . . . It was a curse that he bore in the same way that he suffered sheep stealing by the Navajo chief. Having the daughter of his tormentor as a slave somewhat avenged the loss of sheep, but there was no remedy for his lack of a son. His wife was getting older and tired after bearing nine children of which only the girls survived. (185)

Heedlessness and assertiveness, which the Spanish settlers no longer have to demonstrate in their daily lives, are now employed for the individual macho satisfaction of pleasures, revenge, and the preservation of the male blood line. Two curses are supposed to be lifted; the deadly lust for revenge is combined with a vital desire.

The new household situation is quickly comprehended by Doña María Rafa: "The señora had a grim sense of humor, for she named the slave girl Concepción. Then she watched her like a hawk" (185). The human entanglements are retold in a rather ironic style as the thin crust of civilized manners and moral superstructures are easily broken by self-persuasion. Then the savage human drives are lived out:

> The conception was anything but immaculate. Don José had his way with Concepción as was his pleasure. Partly it was for revenge. There was no question that it was for lust. Perhaps too Don José hoped for that son that he did not have. And, at some level even he did not understand, he might have intuited that any son of his who was a grandson of Ojo Torcido would be a force to be reckoned with. (187)

Don José's behavior and motives indicate that both Spaniard and Indian obey the laws set by the land and its people. The Christian who never tires in pointing out the heathenish nature of the Navajos is reduced to basic emotions and rituals. Tercero, the storyteller, does not condemn Don José; rather, he assumes an ironic point of view by contrasting the spanish reality with its myths. The introduction of Indian blood into his family works miracles as Doña María becomes pregnant to avenge Don José escapade, thus following his pattern of intended punishment and achieved live-giving reality. In this way, she takes the initiative again and actively contributes to the final paradox of the story of retribution.[17] In the end Don José is the proud possessor of two male heirs, one with Irish and the other with Indian blood. But he has lost his wife, his Indian mistress, his favorite horse, his macho stature; later he will even abandon the land grant. The new vitality in his family is gained by the blood mixture and is paid for by his social fall: "Ultimately all things are reconciled in the blood. Since we are all God's children, it is inevitable. Especially here on the Rio Grande (. . .) the family cursed the day he had ever seen Concepción. 'Retribution!' they said. 'We would have been ricos if it had not been for that Indian!'"[18]

The intended revenge tragedy has turned into a tragicomedy. Don José's contacts with the Indians have changed his system of values: preserving life has become more important than securing his material possessions. The spirit of retribution has created a practical model of co-existence of various ethnic backgrounds within one family. The story gains the level of allegory when we think of the Indian, the Spanish and the Anglo elements as constituting the multi-racial character of the Southwest and its long history of retributions.

It is notable that in the end the concept of storytelling is acknowledged as a permanent process of re-interpreting the past, confirming the idea of the Southwest as a multi-cultural region which can only be grasped by interconnecting the past, present and future in the activity of the storyteller. Cultural techniques and the blood guarantee the immediacy of the Indian heritage in this specific environment. This explains why from the beginning Ojo Torcido has been treated as an equal to Don José who initially struggled against this reality of mutual give-and-take.

In his poem "From the North Time, to the South Today,"[19] Sergio Elizondo skillfully incorporates the historical and present day experiences of three ethnic groups in an account of the growth of private values and attitudes. A central event from the Native American past serves as his starting point; the second and third parts link the present situation of the Indians with that of the Blacks and Chicanos through parallel, contradiction, reduction and derivation.

The first line, "Wounded Knee Dakota South," abruptly evokes the place marking and symbolizing the final defeat of the Indians. The inversion "Dakota South" breaks up the familiar syntax and calls back the local dichotomy of the title of the poem, thus combining Wounded Knee with the arguments of the 'we' and 'I' of the conclusion. It is remarkable that in the following lines Elizondo does not directly confront the reader with the massacre but rather depicts a situation of anticipation constituted by two elements, the restlessness of the Indian horses and the feeling of futility among the "old men." Animated nature seems unconcerned with the forebodings of men and animals;[20] it even furnishes a romantic, two-dimensional frame to the scene of coming despair and tragedy:

> White view with dream of
> white birches on the sides
> ahead blue waters which
> come down from wet hills.

The images of serenity and fertility foreshadow the final statement of the poem where liberty and love as healing power for the wounds of the past are symbolized by a "blossom on the tallest rosebush in my garden." On the one hand, the autonomy of nature underlines the grossness of the historic incident; on the other, it vaguely hints at the fundamental creative forces which the unsentimental observer discerns in the reconstruction of a crucial event from the experience of another minority group to establish a sound basis for his argument.

In the second stanza this observer clearly discloses his Chicano identity when he uses the derogatory "Merkins" (Americans)[21] and a typical scene from the collective memory to extend the historical foundation of modern sentiments and strategies of survival. By locating his new facts "100 years later" than Wounded Knee, the poet keeps them pending between the poles of the centennial of Mexican defeat and 1990, thus focusing on the recent past, the present, the near future.

The Indians' desperate resistance against the temptations and confusing classifications of 'first class' culture to preserve their identity by narcoticizing themselves—"Indians in reservations drink red mountain wine to tan the personality which wants to get out of 'second class' culture"—is mirrored in the "Chicanos of East L.A." who "drop pills to change the reality of the Merkin." The poet evaluates the activities and self-appreciation of his own ethnic group by adding "theirs is fine, is OK, they say." Although Chicanos, in contrast to the Indians, have advanced to more active and clever methods of struggle, the ground they stand on is still shaky, largely a matter of pretense as the final modification, "they say," indicates.

The whole second stanza describes and analyzes strategies of defense, both of the minorty and the majority. "Merkins . . . attack" and "take by force" but they also show fear. This instability is well expressed in the lines:

> attack with slave horses
> taken by force from corral
> never on foot,
> fear under Texas

> hats-
> more truth in the eyes
> half out of the sockets.

Their warfare thus reveals itself as yet another strategy of defense.

The complicated structure of the present is characterized by "Images deranged / to confuse- / is defense against dumb ethic." The mutual destruction of prejudice prepares the way for new values as indicated by the concluding "commiseration in action." The truth behind this rather hopeful outlook is a trust in the fact that basic human emotions and cultural background symbolized by the color of the skin are "impossible to change" by "Merkins without class." In this section of the poem once again simple natural agents like the moon and the sun disclose the prevailing values.

The second stanza sees Indians and Chicanos on the same level of emancipation. Only the poet's recognition of mixed emotions in the "Memory of Merkins from afar," that is, in the collective memory of his group, makes available a method of ending the game of hide-and-seek in progress. Elizondo qualifies the superior heritage of "Brother copper tones" as a melting process caused by the moon and the sun which obliges the group to clear the way for new approaches. This duty includes modesty and pride as it deeply respects the state of mind of other minorities and refrains from any act of usurpation. The narrator rejects the role of a spokesman outside his domain, although physical defeat and some remaining energy to fight the total loss of identity unify Indians and Chicanos. This outlook retrospectively confirms the detached perspective of the first lines of the poem where commiseration could not be derived from Indian history.

At the beginning of the last stanza the fundamental differences between minorities and the majority are stated in very general terms:

> Another rhythm,
> outside inside
> colored
> form and time.

Here the poet retreats to the generalities of the beginning of the second stanza. "Impossible to change skin by force." Later this will be specified for "Indians, Blacks and Chicanos" who "Live simple strong sincere, feet on the ground." The three groups also share the characteristics of keeping "eyes closed / the mind closed / so the Merkins' disease / won't enter / heart in bloom." Against the American "dumb ethic" and the "Flames of greed,"[22] the poet establishes a land ethic manifesting itself in contrastive food images like "petals of food for brothers" versus "scorn for fat pigs," and "They parsley garnish" versus "we basic purslane." It is not through the 1962 Black celebrations of revenge that the earth is redeemed "but for our things you know; never mind." In his final command the poet hoists the flag of love represented by a rose as a simple, creative and effective symbol of liberty regained to ask colors, water, air and deer to return to a reformed world.[23]

Although in the third part "Indians, Blacks and Chicanos" are called upon to save their own values, the conclusive gesture remains the individual act of a poet in command with a distinctive Chicano voice celebrating his personal power of transcending his memory of past and present oppressions. Obviously the rose symbol can hardly be applied to an Indian background, although the context of the land ethic would suggest this. The poem builds up a series of nature images—water, trees, moon, sun, petals, air, deer—which culminates in the rose blossom, thus indirectly linking up various collective experiences with the process of the individual growth of knowledge. The recognition of a common bond of basic emotions and the conditioning of man by brutalizing circumstances is necessary to formulate the positive message. And in this ethnic triad the Indian experience plays a crucial role as it demonstrates the imminent threat of drowning in the dominant culture. This situation triggers the spirit of resistance and encourages the retrieval of common values. Wounded Knee gets the poet on the way to identifying with his own past and makes him search for people who have traveled parts of the same road. Wounded Knee is the overwhelming symbol of injustice, of mankind gone astray which provokes the creative effort of moral reform, of a new beginning, in the last stanza. Elizondo's personal statement sets an example for the reconciliation of past and present. In this respect it is a didactic poem teaching commiseration and respect.

Alurista's poem "teach not"[24] argues against the fatal combination of didacticism and exploitation, the main stream culture's lack of respect for the Indian world. He proposes the following list of offenses for "you / who did not listen": "teach not / our words and stain them / . . . / suck not its light / . . . / cut not our bodies / . . . / sell not / the wind of warriors breath / . . . / sing not our songs." The addressee is further identified as someone living in darkness, and characterized, of course, by his historical and present day attitudes towards the Indian. As a member of the mainstream society, he does not possess any authority whatsoever to approach the minority; even an intended benevolent gesture is exploitative and thus not welcome.[25] It is quite logical that this radical advocate of indigenous rights excludes his opponents from sharing in a revolutionary concept of humanity springing from the history of suffering and the liberation of the people through the revitalization of tribal traditions:

> winged our heart does soar
> sin más caras that mummify
> while drummers drum the drum
> and singers sing the song

> a world is overturned
> and new manwoman blossom

The poem celebrates the self-contained world of the Indian which cannot be understood by the outsider who necessarily carries his burden of the sins of the past.

In the immediately succeeding poem "i" (47), Alurista takes up the Indian theme again, this time, as the title indicates, in a more subjective manner. In the very first lines a tone of resignation, of mistrust in the effectiveness of Indian mythology is set: "I am tired of chasing coyote with a prayer stick." This confession is confirmed with the following lines when Coyote's profound connection with the natural and human worlds is challenged. He who stands for energy, perpetual motion, for survival and the full range of human potentials[26] is now reduced to normal human dimensions, to someone who deplores his "knowledge lost." One of the most striking signs for his fall is his failure to cope with the white invaders of Indian reservation land: "he not know the beasts / that trespass paper land." In the middle of the poem the 'I' actually ponders on the idea of killing Coyote: ". . . one could . . . / does in deed ask to / kill? kill? / coyote? wolf?" The solution to this dilemma is not brought about by an activity of the disillusioned 'I' but by the Land itself. Alurista undermines the negative context with positive images like "continent / unbound" and "in deer longing/ ocean sands / to sink its hoofs / gently . . ." From these images the final invocatory scene emerges. The essentials of the animal gesture are transferred to the water as the life-giving substance by the technique of syntactic ambiguity:

> to sink its hoofs
>   gently to bring
> the humbleness of water
>   on, to high mesa corn fields
> far, to the land chanting
>   kachina, kachina!
> let life blossom

The Land which comprises man as one component among many others appeals to its own spirits to secure the survival of its creatures. The Coyote figure proves an ineffectual mediator; it apparently prevented the 'I' from total surrender to the cycles of nature.

Comparing this poem with the first one, we can see that both texts argue against the self's tendency to conquer the earth and the universe, to establish the individual as usurper or even creator in his own right. They plea for a system of values in which the harmony of many components of equal status is the ruling principle.

The same reverence for the land and admiration for those who are used to interpreting and respecting its laws pervades the introductory poem "Bribe" of Pat Mora's *Chants*.[27] It contains an Indian woman's chant, an invocation of the land, of Mother Earth to furnish them with the creative energies needed for rug weaving:

> Guide my hands, Mother,
> to weave singing birds
> flowers rocking in the wind, to trap
> them on my cloth with a web of thin threads.

The bribery is presented as a religious ceremony, "chanting . . . kneeling, digging, burying," an act of gentle persuasion in whose course "turquoise threads" are returned to the original provider of this gift. The rug weaving itself is split up into two phases, the re-creation of the beauties of nature and the eventual imprisonment of birds and flowers which deprives them of their external manifestations of vitality. This means that the artists do not solely imitate but take away the consent of nature gained by the bribe of handing back another part of her.

This typical Indian concept of man's activities offers the Chicana a strategy to achieve her own ends. But unlike the Indian women, she buries her writer's tools, "a ballpoint pen and lined yellowing paper."[28] And she closes with her waiting for the magic to work: "Like the Indians / I ask the Land to smile on me, to croon / softly, to help me catch her music with words."

This borrowed strategy includes a re-interpretation of the function of the artist. By giving away the tools of her trade and reducing herself to the unpretentious and largely passive role of listener and recorder, she places the source of her creativity outside her own person. She comes very close to the idea of oral literature in which the individual artist loses his central importance. The emphasis shifts to a delicate equilibrium between the speaker and the listeners, the particular shape of the message and the whole legacy of the tribe. In contrast to the rug weavers, the poet does not intend to remove parts of nature, she just wants to "catch her music with words," to transpose something from one medium into another. Her sacrifice is as valuable as the Indian women's, for she trades in the 'first class' concept of the poet.

Nonetheless, the tone of the poem, determined after all by the curiosity of the poet and the term bribe with its connotative meanings of trickery and even deceit, hints at the eventual futility of her efforts. Although with the Chicana we observe the same closeness to the Land, her act remains but the imitation of a ritual. Her sacrifice is not totally sustained by the personal experience of man and nature moving in harmonious, complete life cycles. She is not able to support her gesture with a traditional chant.[29] As we learned from Alurista, the barriers between individual cultures cannot or should not be easily surmounted. And finally, the 'first class' poetology has a ring of artificiality[30] in contrast to the naturalness of the scene remembered. So the Chicana cautiously tries a slightly uneven deal.

The poem obviously praises and envies the effectiveness of an Indian ceremony unattainable for the outsider. Nevertheless, we should not forget to note that the Indian ritual is set in the past. It is presented as a memory, part of a forgotten world which should be respected but not usurped beyond the confines of the ethnic group.

In conclusion, we note that the Native American theme is relatively rare in Chicano literature. A young ethnic literature tends to concentrate on its own native and urgent problems. As we have remarked in our introduction, the attachment of the Chicano to the Native American can be seen quite differently, depending on the self-definition of the various Chicano groups. The reservedness of the writers can also be explained by the deep respect they hold for the vital goods of another ethnic minority. The long tradition of the distortion of the image of the Indian and the Chicano in American mainstream literature seems to serve as a warning.

But whenever Chicano writers contribute to this subject, their engagement is quite intensive and manifold. Their treatment is related to the individual choice of subject and their point of view. Nash Candelaria dealt with the common roots of the Chicanos and the Native Americans dating back to the period of Spanish colonization. Their contacts eventually resulted in a mutual enrichment securing the continuity of life and the leveling of seemingly irreconcilable differences. As Rudolfo A. Anaya shared this concept of common origins, the old Indian myths were transferable into the modern Chicano world of his novel *Heart of Aztlan*. They were essential for the individual's search for identity. Only his firm embodiment in the history of the group enabled him to participate in a useful social role. Alurista was not so much interested in the social function of the individual but rather in the values of the Native Americans which he wanted to have protected against the oppressor's subtle methods of a new colonialism. In his confessional poem 'i' he insisted on man's submission to the laws of the Land, an attitude which made all human constructs obsolete. The preservation of native wisdom guaranteed the rebirth of mankind.

Pat Mora and Sergio Elizondo looked at the Native American heritage from a more detached and 'less historical' perspective. Pat Mora expressed her admiration for those who had understood and humbly accepted the teachings of Mother Earth. She eagerly longed for identification with the Indian ritual and even sacrificed her own concept of creativity. Elizondo did not make any attempts at identification but used the Native American experience as a means to find new values to build a new world liberated from the oppressions of the past. The poet acknowledged the correspondences between the groups but respected each property as singular and basically non transferable. From his survey of history and the command to bring love into this destructive world, Elizondo derives conclusions and formulates them in a public message through a poetic medium. In this respect, Elizondo's poem was much more inclusive than, for example, Alurista's.

Elizondo's attitude avoided the pitfalls of romanticizing the Native Americans. It clearly drew a realistic line between the two groups. In her sociological study *The Spanish-Americans of New Mexico*, Nancie L. González conceded: "Even though the two groups borrowed freely from each other's cultural inventory in the early days of Spanish conquest and, therefore, share a number of culture traits and complexes today, the differences are considerable."[31] And later she says: "there appears to be little love lost between them."[32] In his interview in *Chicano Authors*, José Montoya already pointed at misunderstandings:

> In my poetry I didn't reject the union with the Native American, I just felt that it wouldn't happen, that the two worlds were very separate. In the last few years I've come to realize that two things are necessary, and they're beginning to happen: one, we as Chicanos must assume the responsibility of our Indianness; two, the Indian must accept our Mexicanness and what it means. That's the next, most important phenomenon in the Movement. New Mexico has had the answer for a long time—communal existence adopted long ago; Indios and Mexicanos joining forces to kick ass; *compadrazco* between the two. It's the next major crisis in our development.[33]

Judging from the analysed texts, one of the most positive results of this mutual awareness and recognition will be a re-interpretation of man in nature and of the rank of the individual in the group. This will also concern the writer himself whose status has to distinguish itself from that in mainstream literature. To this process the rich Hispanic and Indian heritage of oral literature will contribute considerably. This may also undermine the traditional dichotomy between form and content. The treatment of the Native Americans in Chicano literature promises that it will not repeat some of the mistakes of much of American mainstream literature. The deep respect for Native American culture as part of the common history or as a remarkable independent achievement should prevent Chicano writers from usurpation and romanticism.

---

[1]Armando B. Rendón, *Chicano Manifesto* (New York: Macmillan, 1971), 80.
[2]Juan Bruce-Novoa, *Chicano Authors. Inquiry by Interview* (Austin: University of Texas Press, 1980), 265.
[3]Cf. e.g., Antonio Castañeda Shular, Tomás Ybarra-Frausto, Joseph Sommers, eds., *Literatura Chicana. Texto y Contexto* (Englewood Cliffs, N.J.: Prentice-Hall, 1972) which includes texts by "lo mexicano," "lo puertorriqueño," and "lo hispanoamericano."
[4]In Bruce-Novoa, 90.

⁵Ibid., 233.
⁶"From Prison: Reies López Tijerina," in Ed Ludwig and James Santibáñez, eds. *The Chicanos. Mexican American Voices* (Baltimore: Penguin Books, 1971), 215-222.
⁷Stan Steiner. *La Raza. The Mexican Americans* (New York: Harper, 1970), 86.
⁸Cf. David Johnson and David Apodaca, "Myth and the Writer: A Conversation with Rudolfo Anaya," *New America*, 3:3 (1979), 76-85.
⁹In Bruce-Novoa, 195.
¹⁰(Albuquerque: Academia, 1980).
¹¹Lven a publication largely from the outsider's perspective like Dieter Herms and Hartmut Lutz, eds. *Native Americans. Chicanos und Indianer in der USA* (Berlin, 1985), fails to establish a firm link between the cultural products of the two ethnic groups.
¹²In Eugene E. García, Francisco A. Lomelí, Isidro D. Ortiz, eds. *Chicano Studies. A Multidisciplinary Approach* (New York, 1984), 108.
¹³Vernon E. Lattin, "The Quest for Mythic Vision in Contemporary Native American and Chicano Fiction," *American Literature*, 50 (1978), 625-640.
¹⁴Heart of Aztlan (Berkeley: Quinto Sol, 1976), 7, 83.
¹⁵*Heart of Aztlan* serves as a starting point of my investigation. I am fully aware of the fact that the Indian theme in Anaya's works deserves a more detailed study.
¹⁶In *A Decade of Hispanic Literature. An Anniversary Anthology* (Houston: Arte Público Press, 1982), 180.
¹⁷Although, following the tradition that a woman who claims the same liberties as the male has to be seriously punished, she will die giving birth.
¹⁸Candelaria, 188. It would be interesting to interpret this episode as an inverted Pocahontas legend.
¹⁹Sergio Elizondo, *Libro para batos y chavalas chicanas* (Berkeley: Editorial Justa, 1977), 6-9.
²⁰"Waters of the river that undulates, pines that watch from afar."
²¹"Gabachos" in the Spanish version.
²²This feature is again contrasted with the more positive notion of the Americans being thirsty.
²³"Years ago / there were also / colors / but the / water / and the air / fragile they fled—/ frightened deer"
²⁴Alurista, *Spik in Glyph?* (Houston: Arte Público Press, 1981), 46.
²⁵Cf. Geary Hobson, "The Rise of the White Shaman as a New Version of Cultural Imperialism," in G. Hobson, ed., *The Remembered Earth, An Anthology of Contemporary Native American Literature* (Albuquerque: Red Earth Press, 1979), 100-108.
²⁶Cf. Gary Snyder, "The Incredible Survival of Coyote," *Western American Literature*, 9 (1975), 255-272; also Paul Radin, *The Trickster, A Study in American Indian Mythology* (New York: Greenwood Press, 1975, 2nd ed., 1956), and Barre Toelken, "The 'Pretty Languages' of Yellowman: Genre, Mode, and Texture in Navajo Coyote Narratives," *Genre*, 2 (1969), 211-235; reprt. in Dan Ben-Amos, ed. *Folklore Genres* (Austin: University of Texas Press, 1976), 145-170.
²⁷Pat Mora, *Chants* (Houston: Arte Público Press, 1984), 7.
²⁸There is an error in this line; it should read "a ballpoint pen and lined yellow paper;" editor's note.
²⁹Although Pat Mora gave her book the title *Chants*, therefore she unpretentiously

suggests that her prayer of the first poem was well received, that the succeeding poems constitute the music of the land caught in words.

[30]The paper she is digging in is already yellowing. This fact hints at the sterility of her craft. (See editor's note 28.)

[31]*The Spanish-Americans of New Mexico, A Heritage of Pride* (Albuquerque: University of New Mexico Press, 1969), 27.

[32]Ibid., 28, see also Clyde Kluckhohn and Dorothea Leighton, *The Navaho* (Cambridge, Mass.: Harvard University Press, 1946).

[33]In Bruce-Novoa, 130-131.

Chicano Literature:
A European Perspective

Dieter Herms

Surely today, one would not exactly group V.I. Lenin among the towering figures of literary criticism and cultural theory. Yet it was he who said in his *Critical Observations on the National Question* in 1913, that

— in *each* national culture (which meant at the time: culture under a bourgeois-capitalist leadership) there are *elements* (if undeveloped) of a democratic and socialist(ic) culture; for, thus he went on:

— there is in *each* nation, a mass of working and exploited people whose conditions of life, by necessity, create a democratic and socialist ideology. Likewise, he went on to say:

— there is, in each nation, a bourgeois, and in most cases over and above, a reactionary and clerical culture, materializing

— not in the form of elements, but as *the ruling* culture. Therefore the "national culture" is that of the propertied classes: the landowners, the clergy, and bourgeoisie.[1]

Thus far Lenin on the cultural process in classic capitalist European societies at the beginning of our century! Given those particular historical conditions, we have at the same time to realize that the fundamental structure of the capitalist system has not changed all that much. Thus, the assumption seems legitimate, that certain segments of the two cultures thesis may be carried into the present, obviously with modifications and additions taking note of the changed circumstances of what remains basically the same fundamental economic and social condition.

What Lenin was addressing himself to in pre-socialist Russia was principally a multi-national conglomerate of people. From that realization, the two cultures theory carries added importance as applying to a national culture in resistance, a cultural national liberation movement against colonialism and neocolonialism.

The recent ethnicity debate has correctly stated the encounter or the collision of *two cultures*, namely in the U.S.: Black, Native American, Chicano, Puerto Rican, etc. cultures versus North American White Anglo culture, the subordinate versus the dominant, minority versus mainstream. Observations of this kind add up to a descriptive empirical notion of culture which attempts to grasp historical specifics of the ways of life of an ethnic group or a social class and their struggles, in a *horizontal* fashion.

The theory of the two cultures based on Lenin, on the other hand, emphasizes specific ideological qualities *within* a way of life. By first looking for ideological *content*, it adds to a *horizontal* dimension of the descriptive and empirical notion of culture a *vertical* perspective. If *first* culture, in this respect, is a reflection for instance of "rugged individualism," commodity production, a laissez-faire market, rule of the few over the many, privileged ownership (to mention only a few characteristics), *second* culture, then, reflects collectivism, production for use, a market of exchange, democratic community, communal ownership. Second culture, thus, is not synonymous with *any* form of "sub-culture" or "counter-culture".

The specific history of Chicanos shows a continuous struggle of an indio-mestizo native population against the colonial oppression and exploitation of a European "master" race. Barrera and others have pointed out the various phases of this process of colonial subjugation: the dispossession from the land, establishment of the colonial labor system, dual wage system, occupational stratification, creation of a reserve labor force.[2] This process led to a loss of influence over the political process, the loss of communal land, grazing grounds and salt mines. It finally led to poverty, unemployment, starvation, and racism.

Whereas the imperial thrust of the conquering powers was accompanied by a *continuity* of cultural images, the cultural images accompanying protest, resistance, and rebellion are continuously endangered to become lost and buried. This is what was meant by Lenin when he observed that the democratic and socialist culture under capitalism is realized only in "elements," in fragments. This is why an important objective of Chicano literature has been to regain and reappropriate its specific historical/cultural past as a means of finding its identity. The redeeming of Joaquín Murietta as a hero of anti-imperialist rebellion in Corky Gonzales' famous movement poem[3] thus accounts for a specific "second culture" quality within this influential piece of literature.

Literature, by definition, represents a segment of superstructural ideological production, reflecting or anticipating social reality. It thereby represents a significant *sector* or ideological expression *within* the whole way of life of an ethnic or social group. Anthropologists may look at the whole way of life of a people in a direct way. Literary critics can only look at it as it is represented, condensed, reflected, and aestheticized in a literary text. The bulk of literary texts, however, should be viewed within a social context of the circumstances of production, distribution, and reception. Chicano literature since the early 60's has been closely affiliated with, indeed embedded into, the political movement and the social struggle of *chicanismo*. In its larger portion it may be identified as part of culture's contribution to the movement and the struggle, as political culture contributing to the struggle and the movement toward national liberation.

Looked at in terms of the ongoing debate of Chicano literary theory and critical method, the Lenin-based approach of the two cultures fits in between Joseph Sommers[4] and Juan Bruce-Novoa.[5] It may be even suitable to bridge the seeming antagonism of these two positions. The two cultures approach shares with Sommer's historical-dialectical approach the view of the history of the Southwest as a process of economic and social oppression, into which Chicano literary expression is bound up. Moreover, it serves as a method to separate out of a folk tradition those elements, which involve a democratic anti-imperialist dynamic. Thirdly, it opens up—with Sommers—a comparative perspective in that, within the multinationality of the U.S. experience, it helps to define similar patterns of oppression and resistance with regard to Black, Native American and Puerto Rican social history and literature.

The two cultures theory also helps to concretize the rather abstract and open dynamics of the *space* of Chicano literature as perceived by Bruce-Novoa. If Chicanos are continually expanding a space between Mexico and the U.S., claiming from both sides a larger area for their own reality, if this is intercultural and interlingual space dynamically flowing into literature as a progression from chaotic discontinuity, via image retrieval, into a new continuous symbiosis, then the two cultures approach serves to identify that ideology and imagery as democratic and potentially socialist. Furthermore, it serves to define the *rascuachi*[6] perspective from below as the pervasive ordering spirit versus concretizing the "chaotic other" as the U.S. aggressor, not just the gringo as the Anglo master, but his imperialist possessiveness and his capitalist greed. Bruce-Novoa does this himself in his excellent analysis of Alurista's imagery: Fat Mr. Jones getting fatter on the sweat and blood of the Chicanos' labor.[7] The regaining of the past in order to find a human future, a crucial concept in Chicano literature, is also at the core of the two cultures notion. Humanistic (the more modern interpretation of the Lenin formula of democratic and socialistic), it adds to the *ideological* content of literature the *positive emotional*. Humanism (not in the sometimes anti-human sense of classic European bourgeois thinking nor in the almost always anti-human sense of classic European bourgeois doing), but in a sense preserving in itself the historical awareness and the experience of the barbarism which capitalist imperialism has led to: slavery, genocide, fascism.

The two cultures approach is obviously interested in the ideological stance of an author. But as a method applied to literature, it is interested in the ideological quality of a text which, as a cultural document, may be quite separate from its creator and come out with a message objectively different from its author's intention. And since ideological content does not materialize by itself, the approach is also interested in the aesthetic quality of a text, more accurately: the textual dialectic of form and content.

Consequently the *close reading* of a text is a basic first step. It is followed by a discussion and classification of its social and aesthetic determinants or constituents and their interrelations. This all then ideally flows into the *social reconstruction* of the text discussing it against its historical backdrop, and placing its production circumstances into a context of its distribution and reception.

The two cultures approach is therefore interested in the Pocho-Chicano self-reference problem,[8] as it is in the straight and rough stereotype characterizations of the Teatro's early actos.[9] It is interested in their more complex linkage of the farmworker imagery with that of Aztec and Mayan philosphy and mythology, as it is in the "Third World" prison metaphor of Salinas[10] or the tortuga cast representing the alienation and separation of characters in Anaya's third novel.[11] It is interested in Acosta's identity quest satire[12] as it is in Estela Portillo's fine integration of the quest motif with the apocalyptic vision of capitalist pollutionist industry drowning in the flood of scorpions.[13] It is interested in feminist images of La Chicana. It is interested in Elizondo's anti-imperialist images,[14] in M. Méndez' peregrination[15], in Perez' and Delgado's grim pictures of America.[16]

In Hinojosa's *estampas* we discover a minuteness of fictional literary space in his "Yoknapatopha" county: Belken and Klail City, related to the big migratory route of Chicanos. We register the subtle benevolent humor and ridicule with which Anglo characters are presented, but also the stupidity of La Raza who trust Anglos merely because they speak Spanish. We are impressed by a narrative technique which freely associates past and present within a time-span ranging from the Mexican Revolution to the early 70's, a network within which the *generaciones* are pieced together like a tapestry from differing, shifting points-of-view. Chicanos emerge as stoics, like Faulkner's blacks: they endure.[17]

I am impressed by Angela de Hoyos' poetry combining a fine protest quality with nourishment on a wide range of imagery resources: nature, love, death, but also modern world economics and religion:

> Thus a bitterness in your life:
> Wherever you turn for solace
> there is an embargo . . .
> Arise Chicano!—that divine spark within you
> surely says—Wash your wounds
> and swathe your agonies.
> There is no one to succor you
> You must be your own messiah.[18]

There are several works which come out with a clear proletarian class position. The early actos are among them. The form of the exchange-of-role comedy in *The Two Faces* clearly points to the class antagonism in life, work, and ownership conditions between *campesino* and *patrón*. The image is internationalized when, in *Vietnam Campesino*, the two peasant nations emerge as victims of one and the same—here internal, there external—U.S. imperialism. The image is nationalized when, in *Los Vendidos*, the four types (Farmworker, Pachuco, Mexican film cliché type, and the assimilated Mexican American) satirically emerge as the victims of the Yankee political and economic system.[19]

Legitimately, Barrio's *Plum Plum Pickers* has been called the Chicano *Grapes of Wrath*. Impressively, the class antagonism of migrant worker and agribusiness is manifested in the detail of structure, imagery, symbolism and style. The interchange of the sun and dawn chapters, Lupe's care for her avocado tree, Manuelito's beautiful Indian body and other elements of an incipiently intact Chicano life quality contrasts with the interlocking of a psychic and social condition in the form of the internal monologue and the animal metaphor denoting the slave-work of oppression. The campesino has even lost his working capacity as the only exchange value and commodity that he himself governs:

> The competition was not between pickers and growers. It was between pickers . . . Between the poor and the hungry, the desperate and the hunted, the slave and the slave, slob against slob, the depraved and himself. You were your own terrible boss. That was the cleverest part of the thing. The picker his own bone-picker, his own willing built-in slave driver . . .[20]

Eugene Nelson's *Bracero*, although *literatura chicanesca*, may be rightfully termed the Chicanos' *The Jungle*. A documentary reportage narrative strategy reminiscent of Sinclair, unfolds the unspeakable monopoly capitalism disposing over a reserve army of work. The central theme of hunger and starvation is captured in a series of images and situations.

> Nacho felt the hot liquid pass down through his parched throat and then disappear into some mysterious void that registered no sensation other than a continual hollow ache, as if there were a heavy metal tank pressing down upon his bowels instead of organs of human tissue . . .[21]

But it is not to the works with an overtly proletarian quality that the two cultures approach principally applies. We do not need this approach to classify a work such as *Two Ranges* by Medina[22] as assimilationist, reactionary and first culture, and badly written besides. No, our approach addresses itself to complexity of form capturing the complex reality of our time, of Chicanos in this multinational imperialist USA; and there, from a two cultures perspective, three works emerge as almost classic modern Chicano masterpieces: . . . *y no se lo tragó la tierra, Floricanto en Aztlán*, and *La Carpa de los Rascuachis*. This seems to be the view of many Chicano writers and critics. Even if *The Road to Tamazunchale* frequently ranks highest in terms of aesthetic achievement, Rivera does frequently come out first, when you talk of the integration of form and social content. Alurista seems undisputed as the leading lyric poet. There may be some doubt about *La Carpa* as the best drama, which has never been published; one has only watched the Teatro's magnificent production of it but never seen it as a written final document.

All the three works share a basic cyclical attitude, the cycle of time, the cycle of nature, the cycle of literary structure. They are all based on the campesino experience as harsh social reality which they integrate with the finding, the rediscovery, the reassessment of certain elements of a Chicano cultural tradition. Something lost is regained from the past to interpret the present and to envisage a future. Images and people add up to a collective voice reflecting the community idea rather than individual destinies. This is represented convincingly by aesthetically exploring the possibilities of the three genres: prose, poetry and drama.

Rivera's chapters and preceding anecdotes have, most of them, distinctly structural and thematic orientation towards a particular single incident or disastrous event: a sickness, a burning, a death. In that respect they are self-enclosed short stories, but as cumulative evidence they also add up to a unifying experience. They fuse into a novel in that they are woven together by both a single narrative perspective and a collective chorus of the people. Within the experience of a colonized people, certain uninterchangeable archetypal figures are being regained. Despite the tragedies, they infuse an element of hope and optimistic future into the narrative point-of-view:

> Se fue sonriente por la calle llena de pozos que conducía a su casa. Se sintió contento de pronto porque al pensar sobre lo que había dicho la señora se dio cuenta de que en realidad no había perdido nada. Había encontrado. Encontrar y reencontrar y juntar. Relacionar esto con esto, eso con aquello, todo con todo. Eso era. Eso era todo.[26]

This act of relating is then achieved by Alurista in a full scope. Ybarra-Frausto's subtitle, "The Oral, The Bilingual, The Pre-Columbian,"[27] signals quite precisely how this achievement is approached in terms of language experimentation and drawing from the wealth of Nahuatl and Mayan philosophy and mythology. Linguistically, Alurista integrates Anglo English, Black English, Mexican Spanish, Chicano Spanish, Nahuatl and Maya into a unified rhythm of a new creativity unparalleled in U.S. literature. In terms of imagery, symbolism, and metaphor, he infuses surface phenomena of the campesinos' current experience with the richness of Nahuatl life and poetics. If in Rivera's vision the sun was predominantly the source of sweat, toil, blood and death, in Alurista's it is gradually replaced by the positive image of Nahuatl solar centrism. Thus, the red fruit becomes *tenoch*, the *tuna*; the shoes of the company store turn into the wandering nation, but the *cucaracha* gets wings and flies toward freedom. Perfume, at first superfluous capitalist luxury commodity, is changing into the aromatic scent of the goddess and linking with the flower and the song of the "fiesta of the living."

Whereas Rivera rescues from the immediate past a *gachupín* priest, a kind Cuquita, a campesino father, a revolutionary grandfather, Alurista redeems from a pre-Columbian tradition Quetzalcoatl, the god of light and knowledge; Ometeotl, the principle of self-recreation; Tlaloc, the god of rain and vegetation, and Tonantzín, the mother earth principle. The regeneration of Chicanos, the hope principle, is thus given more clarity as is, indeed, the basic anti-capitalist, anti-imperialist stance, at the same time. More clarity in the struggle through more complexity of the literary achievement. And its authenticity is heightened through the author's active involvement in the Chicanismo struggle at the same time when the imagery was being developed.

A historical record of activity, as everyone knows, was also Valdez' and the Teatro's empirical base of merging into *La Carpa*, first of all the *acto* of campesino Jesús Rascuachi, the cycle of his life from immigration to death. Merging it with the *mito* of Tonantzín and Quetzalcoatl, the *corrido* tradition of song and dance, into a complex *historia* of Chicano past, present and future. As Alurista's overall intention is highly didactic, the Teatro introduces into *La Carpa* a scene of Brechtian dimension. In his first life Jesús Rascuachi makes a wrong decision, for the grower, against the union, drawn into it by the evil forces of capital and the state, represented by *calaveras* and *diablos*. So there is a resurrection scene, from which the action is run backwards, as if the play were a movie. Then, with the divine inspiration of Quetzalcoatl, the former decision is corrected in favor of the union. Thus Jesús is able to free himself from the rope which had tied him up with the bosses, and to take an active part in the life and the struggle of his people. Quetzalcoatl is not a *deus ex machina* who makes the decision for him, but he imbues him with the spiritual powers to take his destiny in his own hands, to become the subject of his own history.

The reader may have gathered by now that the two cultures approach does not arrive at results drastically different from hitherto Chicano literary criticism. If it did that, it would be sectarian and politically dogmatic, would alienate itself from the main currents of Chicano thought. What it can do is that it can focus a little more sharply on the anti-imperialist, democratic, socialist, humanist, protest and subversive trends of Chicano literature. It *could* also address itself more to the problems of distribution and reception of literature. It might really become an asset in such cases where the antagonism of the two cultures cuts through the middle of an author's personality or work, or where the contradiction is between creative intention and distribution or reception. Rudolfo Anaya might be such a case.

Armando Gutiérrez, in discussing *Heart of Aztlan*, criticizes the author,—after showing the Clemente family's dispossession from the land—for not presenting any viable solution to the many social problems in the barrios of Albuquerque. The people's bond to the earth is represented as spiritual and mystical. The radical militant Lalo is portrayed as irresponsible, hateful and egocentric. Clemente's leadership to burn away oppression and injustice is built on the fire of love. Gutierrez is a social scientist, not a literary critic. To him literature serves as a political document or as an instrument of immediate social change. As such, he has misunderstood literature in its role; for literature is predominantly an independent productive dynamic force in the complexity of ideological superstructures, namely reflecting a set of images and a symbolic process whose transference into social reality does not happen by direct application. True, there are valuable forms of literature that participate in current issues of the social struggle. But to demand this of all literature would be drastically limiting its creative potential.

Anaya captures, on the other hand, in the cycle of all three novels, of which *Heart of Aztlan* is an integrative part, the epiphany of landscape as a kind of objective literary correlative of the dispossession from the land, a kind of symbolic reappropriation. Through Antonio's narration he redeems *la curandera*, the good principle Ultima stands for. In his edition of the fine volume *Ceremony of Brotherhood*,[29] he displays a sound historical foundation of the rebellion of both Native American Indian and Chicano traditions against the European invaders. On the other hand, however, the epiphany sometimes tends to degenerate into a blood-and-soil mysticism which borders on an ideology that becomes official first culture policy in the darkest phase of my own country's recent history. There might also be a problem with the reading of *Bless Me, Ultima*, in Anglo college classrooms, where it seems to be sometimes perceived as an example of harmless, escapist, exotic, folkloristic Mexican culture, adding to the stereotypes rather than correcting them. There remains, however, a strong element of humanism in Anaya's prose; why this should *not* be built on love as one of the emotional cornerstones, I cannot perceive.

It is a phenomenon of the cultural production system under capitalism that second culture products get channeled through a first culture distribution apparatus. Sometimes this is necessary in order to reach a sizable portion of the audience the product is made for, through TV or the radio. For example, Luis Valdez wanted to reach Hispanics in the East by staging *Zoot Suit* on Broadway.[30] In marketing it, a somewhat cynical incident occurred, a trifling incident really, but indicative of what can happen, once you give yourself over to this process. As *The New York Times* (February 4, 1979) reported, 50,000 Coca Cola bottles were sold in NYC supermarkets which offered "a night on the town;" in exchange for six bottle caps you would receive a free *Zoot Suit* ticket plus a free dinner in a restaurant chain.

Members of the Teatro dismissed this as a publicity gimmick. Its lack of taste becomes apparent when you realize that Coca Cola owns significant chunks of those agribusiness conglomerates which are responsible for the exploitation of campesinos and for mass unemployment in California.

It seems advisable that Chicano culture should control its own distributional infrastructure: small publishing houses, the journals, the TENAZ and *Flor y Canto* festivals, community theater, media. Thus it has control over its own rituals, there is a community bond between the production, the distribution and the reception of its creativity. This will not reach a mass audience as yet, but educating the masses under capitalism is a long and painful process, anyway.

Let me conclude by saying that Chicano literature in its major portion, for me, is a literature of peace. It warms the heart to read Chicano authors' names under "Poets for Peace" appeals. Although Chicano literature is not thematically dealing with chemical warfare, nuclear missiles and the ultimate atomic holocaust, it offers in its intimate space of an alternative living and culture a vision of a world without imperialist wars. Its rituals feeding on a rich cultural tradition are, then, also rituals for survival. For it is not socialism that is on the pragmatic agenda right now for those who struggle in the imperialist western world, but survival, and then decent, dignified living conditions in a functioning democracy. Chicano literature, explicitly or implicitly, is part of that struggle for these goals.

---

[1] See V.I. Lenin, German Edition, *Werke* vol. 20, 8 ff. A more extensive discussion of the connection between the theory and historiography of the two cultures and the production of literature is given in Bremer Forschungsprojekt: "Zur Geschichtsschreibung zweiter Kultur. Konturen einer theoriebildung," *Gulliver* 9 (1981), 9-40. My article was first presented as a paper at the Conference of the National Association of Chicano Studies, Austin, 1984.

[2] Mario Barrera, *Race and Class in the Southwest* (Notre Dame: University of Notre Dame, 1979), especially 7-57.

[3] Rodolfo Gonzales, *I am Joaquin/Yo soy Joaquín* (New York: Bantam Books, 2nd ed., 1972).

[4] Joseph Sommers, "Critical Approaches to Chicano Literature," *De Colores* 3:4 (1977), 15-21; repeatedly reprinted and enlarged.

[5] Juan Bruce-Novoa, "The Space of Chicano Literature," *The Chicano Literary World* (1974), 22-51; also in *De Colores* 1:4 (1975), 22-42.

[6] I am taking the liberty here to broaden the term of El Teatro's *La Carpa de los Rascuachis* into a general perspective.

[7] J. Bruce-Novoa, *Chicano Poetry. A Response to Chaos* (Austin: University of Texas, 1982); especially chapter 4, "The Teachings of Alurista," 69 ff.

[8] I here refer to the novels *Pocho* by Antonio Villareal (1959) and *Chicano* by Richard Vásquez (1970).

[9] Luis Valdez and El Teatro Campesino, *Actos* (Fresno: Cucaracha Publications, 1971).

[10] Raúl Salinas, *Un Trip Through the Mind Jail y otras Excursiones* (San Francisco: Editorial Pocho-Che, 1980).

[11] Rudolfo Anaya, *Tortuga* (Berkeley: Editorial Justa, 1979).

[12] Oscar Zeta Acosta, *The Autobiography of a Brown Buffalo* (San Francisco: Straight Arrow Books, 1972).

[13] See the title story of her collection *Rain of Scorpions and Other Writings* (Berkeley: Tonatiuh International, 1975).

[14] Sergio Elizondo, *Perros y antiperros, una épica chicana* (Berkeley: Quinto Sol, 1975).

[15] Miguel Méndez, *Peregrinos de Aztlán* (Tucson: Editorial Peregrinos, 1974).

[16] Raymund Pérez "Tigre," *Phases* (1971) and *The Secret Meaning of Death*; Abelardo Delgado, *25 Pieces of a Chicano Mind* (Denver: Barrio Publications, 1969).

[17] Rolando Hinojosa, *Estampas del valle y otras obras* (Berkeley: Quinto Sol, 1973), recently revised and translated by himself as *The Valley* (Ypsilanti: Bilingual Press, 1983).

[18] Angela de Hoyos, "Arise Chicano," in *Arise Chicano and Other Poems* (San Antonio: M & A Editions, 1976), 12.

[19] All titles mentioned in *Actos*.

[20] Raymond Barrio, *The Plum Plum Pickers* (Sunnyvale, CA: Ventura Press, 1969), 58.

[21] Eugene Nelson, *Bracero* (Berkeley: Thorp Springs Press, 1972), 207.

[22] Robert C. Medina, *Two Ranges. A Chicano Novel* (Las Cruces: Bilingual Publications, 1974).

[23] Tomás Rivera, . . . *y no se lo tragó la tierra / And the Earth Did not Part* (Berkeley: Quinto Sol, 1971).

[24] Alurista, *Floricanto en Aztlán* (Los Angeles: UCLA Chicano Studies, 1971).

[25] Unpublished. The play evolved through different versions, 1972-78. I am referring to the maturest version which toured Europe in 1978. The basis of the reference is a video recording.

[26] Op. cit., 128.

[27] Tomás Ybarra-Frausto, "Alurista's Poetics—The Oral, the Bilingual, the Precolumbian," in Joseph Sommers and Tomás Ybarra-Frausto, eds, *Modern Chicano Writers* (Englewood Cliffs: Prentice-Hall, 1979), 117 ff.

[28] Rudolfo Anaya, *Heart of Aztlán* (Berkeley: Tonatiuh International, 1976); Armando Gutiérrez, "Politics in the Chicano Novel. A Critique," in Nicolás Kanellos, ed., *Understanding the Chicano Experience Through Literature* (Houston: University of Houston Mexican American Studies Monograph Series No. 3, 1981), 7 ff.

[29] Rudolfo Anaya and Simón Ortiz, eds. *A Ceremony of Brotherhood, 1680-1980*, (Albuquerque: Academia, 1981).

[30] The drama *Zoot Suit* is as such unpublished. It is, however, made immortal through Luis Valdez's own movie of it.

Hispanic Literature in the United States: Self-Image and Conflict

Eliana S. Rivero

The last twenty years have seen an increase in the development and examination of sociological phenomena related to ethnic groups in the United States. Literary and artistic expressions have paralleled, in some instances reflecting and at other times inspiring, a new awareness of ethnicity as it pertains to Blacks, Hispanics, Native Americans, Asian Americans, and other minorities in this country. Among Hispanics, as among other groups, artistic manifestations have been multifold, and as varied as the invididual artist. Yet certain common expressions arise within the different Hispanic nationalities we find in our society.

What are these different groups? Who are the writers among them? How do their works reflect their life experiences as members of a minority group and their consciousness of belonging to a subculture? These and other questions come to mind. In the course of this article an attempt will be made at answering them, as well as to address several other pertinent issues that must be dealt with when thinking about Hispanics in the United States, about their place in society, their life expectations, their self-image, their idiosyncrasy, and the relationships between diverse subgroups of the broad category of "Hispanics."

Since 1848, when the states of Arizona, California, Nevada, Utah, New Mexico, Texas, and half of Colorado passed from Mexican sovereignty to United States ownership, a Spanish journalistic tradition survived in the now Mexican American communities. Some strictly literary pieces appeared from time to time; however, official literary history has until now ignored this activity.[1] In other Hispanic territories now belonging to the United States, such as Puerto Rico, literature has mostly continued within the artistic traditions of other Latin American countries in the Caribbean, namely Cuba and the Dominican Republic. The United States presence has affected Puerto Rican literary expression in the island, but, as it will be shown later, the literature that is culturally comparable to Mexican-American or Chicano literature is that written by Puerto Ricans on the mainland, known as either Nuyoricans, *boricuas*, or Neoricans.[2] Wherever Hispanic immigrants have settled for any length of time, there usually has appeared some form of journalistic writing first, and literature has then been created. In quite a few of these cases, the writing has emerged as a vehicle for demands for social justice: such is the parallel illustration of Chicano texts appearing in Colorado in the 1960's—Rodolfo "Corky" Gonzales, *I am Joaquín*—and Puerto Rican working class chronicles of life in New York—the *Memorias* by Bernardo Vega.[3]

In addition, there is a centuries-old tradition of Hispanic writing done in and about the United States by Latin Americans residing in this country. Their works were mostly for readers in their home countries and written from the perspective of temporary sojourners in American society: José Martí, writing from New York, is a good example. The literature which concerns us here, however, is written by permanent residents of this mainland, insiders who are nevertheless an ethnic and linguistic minority often excluded from the mainstream; and their literary works are, for the most part, directed at, and read by, other permanent residents of the United States.[4]

Racial and ethnic awareness surged to prominence during the 1950's and 1960's, with the rise of the Black civil rights movement. Following closely behind, and greatly influenced by the Black example, came the efforts by Hispanics, Native Americans, and Asian Americans to win the same civil rights. The decade of the sixties shattered the idea of national cultural homogeneity that some had believed realized during World WarII. The U.S. society is still, in fact, mostly a conglomerate of many national groups that migrated to this country in the last hundred and fifty years. Only Indians of North or MesoAmerican origin, and later Spaniards, can claim residence prior to the landing of the Mayflower. Within a setting of unrest, division and social struggle, then, there arose the most recent literary activity of Hispanic groups living in the United States, predominantly Chicanos and Neorriqueños.[5]

In discussing the subject of Hispanics in the United States, the distinction is made here between two categories: the "native Hispanic" and the "migrated Hispanic." The first is a very general way of referring to individuals who have been born inside the U.S. borders; but one must also include in this group those persons who, while having been born in Mexico or on the island of Puerto Rico, have migrated very young, attended school (at least partly) on the mainland, and speak English as natives. Among the writers, they include figures like Alurista and Angela de Hoyos, both Mexican-born, and Pedro Pietri, island-born. This first category comprises the Mexican-American or Chicano population, which lives mostly in the four southwestern states of Texas, New Mexico, Arizona, and Colorado, and the western state of California. The term "native Hispanics" also refers, ironically, to Puerto Ricans. Ironically, because all of them are born with U.S. citizenship in what is geographically a territory far away from the mainland borders, and which constitutes one of the last colonies in this continent. The island of Puerto Rico, a Spanish possession until 1898, was ceded to the United States by Spain after the Spanish American War. Although Puerto Rico is technically given the status of "Commonwealth" (Estado Libre Asociado), its political identity is North American, while its cultural origins, its heritage, and its essence are Spanish American, Hispanic. It must be said that many Puerto

Ricans who reside in the continental United States also consider themselves as immigrants, or even "exiles," for they experience the same sense of uprooting and separation felt by other Latin Americans upon leaving their birthplace and they experience alienation when living in a predominantly Anglo society. Ironically, again, they "arrive" in a country whose citizenship they carry, but whose language they do not speak as natives, and whose dominant culture, ideology, and colonial policies are contrary to their aspirations. Many Puerto Ricans who live now in the continental U.S. have migrated from the island, although a significant portion of their population has been born here.

If, according to the underestimated figures offered by the 1980 census, the Mexican-American population was counted at around nine million, Puerto Ricans living on the mainland number around two million. They reside mostly in the northeastern states of New York, New Jersey, Massachusetts, and Connecticut. The same metropolitan areas of the Northeast contain the most heterogeneous concentration of Hispanics by country of origin; that is, Cubans, Central and South Americans, and Spaniards, in decreasing order of their numbers. Most persons in these last three subgroups are called here "migrated Hispanics," meaning that most of them still belong to the immigrant generation that has been born (and often raised) outside the borders of the United States. But some among their groups, especially the younger individuals, are in the midst of making the transition from emigré, exile, and refugee categories (that is, economic or political immigrants) to that of ethnic minority members. This transition, reflected no doubt in the art forms they produce, entails the development of a sense of "belonging" in a society other than the native, a degree of functionality in the system, a sense of being a cultural hybrid or a bicultural individual, and, to some extent, a feeling of somehow "being able to make it," if not fully within the mainstream, at least on the outskirts of the adoptive society.

The characteristics sketched above, present to some extent in both the immigrant and full-fledged minority groups, are evidenced in the cultural self-perceptions that give a distinctive configuration to their art and their literature. Our intent in these pages is to show how, in the case of Chicanos and Nuyoricans, their cultural identity (and the conflicts it breeds) reflects varying degrees of this transitional stage. In such a spectrum, the Chicano is the full-fledged minority group, without the option of returning to a mother country of origin; the realization of "no return" underlies the poetic creation of Aztlán, mythical land of birth for the Chicano Indian ancestors, but a very real historical territory inhabited later by the Indo-Hispanic forebears of present day Mexican-Americans.

Puerto Ricans, although a supposedly true American minority by the "legality" of their colonial status, still possess the alternative of going back to the insular society. Nevertheless, for some Boricua immigrants or for many mainland-born, returning to Puerto Rico can signify a rejection by islanders, who perceive them as Americanized, "deculturated," bastardized children who are really Spanglish hybrids. This experience is similarly shared by many Chicanos who visit Mexico and are considered alien "pochos," "del otro lado." Such feelings are very adequately expressed in two texts by the Chicana Lorna Dee Cervantes, and the Nuyorican Miguel Algarín, who both use a bilingual medium—or interlingual text, characterized by code switching—to convey their sense of rootlessness, and their sensation of having been robbed of their mother heritage.

Oaxaca, 1974

México I look for you all day in the streets of Oaxaca
The children run to me, laughing,
spinning me blind and silly.
They call to me in words of another language.
My brown body searches the streets
for the dye that will color my thoughts.

But Mexico gags
¡Esputa!
on this bland pocha seed.

I didn't ask to be brought up tonta!
My name hangs about me like a loose tooth.
Old women know my secret,
"Es la culpa de los antepasados."
Blame it on the old ones.
They give me a name
that fights me.[6]

The whole text is based on an ironical premise: false correspondence between the personal poetic subject and her real name—Cervantes (as if an individual for whom English is a foreign tongue were called Shakespeare!). Her color is brown, but her thoughts are couched in a "white language." Heritage escapes the poet; she is a living contradiction of all that her name means for Hispanic culture, and her origins disown her. Miguel Algarín, in New York, will speak the same feelings of non-entity because of linguistic alienation from the mother tongue. Brown has no language of its own; he speaks in the white man's words and feels the need to cleanse himself after the speech act. Language is culture, language is politics; and Nuyoricans speak the words of the colonial conqueror, negating their heritage, betraying their need to be recognized as an independent people.[7]

Inside Control: My Tongue   if a man owns the world

> oh white power hidden
> behind every word i speak
> if the man takes me into his
> caverns of meanings in sound
> if all my talk is borrowed
> from his tongue then i want
> hot boiling water to wash
> out my mouth i want lye
> to soothe my soiled lips
> for the english that i
> speak betrays my need to be
> a self made power[8]

Attention should be called to "mouth" imagery in both poems: Mexico gags on "pochos" and spits them out, inappropriate names are "loose teeth," pieces of language are produced in caverns of sound and generate similarly cavernous meanings—all these are metonymic representations of the tongue as language, principal instrument and symbol of culture.

The idea of not finding a home in the ancestral land, of seeing the original territory occupied by invaders, is also a common thread that runs through both Chicano and Nuyorican literature. Cervantes looks for her heritage in Oaxaca only to find another language. José Antonio Burciaga, in a poem entitled "To Mexico with Love," reminds the mother country of her orphaned, two-tongued children who are like sons and daughters abandoned to their own devices:

> hijos pochos
> hijos huachos
> hijos con el Spanish mochos
> hijos desamparados[9]

And Miguel Algarín, in "A Mongo Affair," does not recognize his native island "filled with Burger Kings," and declares himself homeless, a wanderer:

> I belong to a tribe of nomads
> who roam the world without
> a place that is ALL MINE
> there is no place that I can
> call mi casa[10]

For other Hispanic Americans, the immigrants' return to the homeland is almost always possible, whether for a short visit or a permanent stay (except, of course, when facing violent political persecution). Such is the case of Argentine, Uruguayan, and Chilean writers who have gone back to their countries in recent times. In the case of the Cuban emigrés, and even after return visits to the mother country materialized after 1978, the feeling of belonging to a different world, of being an individual in transition who has ties to two separate realities, prevails. This is a theme pervading some works by the poet, short story writer and essayist Lourdes Casal, who died in 1981 after a prolonged illness. After approximately twenty years in the United States, she returned to Cuba for a visit but remained there after being hospitalized. Her poem "Para Anna Yeltford" portrays the dichotomy experienced by the Hispanic outside her primary cultural milieu; she functions in two different environments, but fits completely in neither. The text, full of recollections and remembrances, tells about her sense of double identity:

Nueva York es mi casa.
Soy ferozmente leal a esta adquirida patria chica.
Por Nueva York soy extranjera ya en cualquier otra parte.
Pero Nueva York no fue la ciudad de mi infancia,
no fue aquí que adquirí las primeras certidumbres,
no está aquí el rincón de mi primera caída
ni el silbido lacerante que marcaba las noches.
Por eso siempre permaneceré al margen,
una extraña entre estas piedras,
aun bajo el sol amable de este día de verano,
como ya para siempre permaneceré extranjera,
aun cuando regrese a la ciudad de mi infancia.
Cargo esta marginalidad inmune a todos los retornos,
demasiado habanera para ser neoyorkina,
demasiado neoyorkina para ser,
—aun volver a ser—
cualquier otra cosa.[11]

For the purposes of this discussion, then, Hispanic literature in the United States is mainly the production of Chicanos, of Puerto Ricans who are permanent residents of the Eastern megalopolis extending between New Jersey, Pennsylvania, and New York (with a few exceptions located in the Chicago area), and of a few Cuban immigrants who arrived in the United States shortly after 1959, while still in their teens or early twenties. These are the most numerous Hispanic subgroups and they represent those variants of the Hispanic culture which have contributed most to an awareness of the presence and significance of the Hispanic heritage within the border of the continental United States.

The majority of Hispanics in the United States today are by far of Mexican origin (sixty percent), and they refer to themselves as either "Mexican American" or "Chicano," depending on a series of factors that relate to tradition, socioeconomic class and political consciousness. Chicano literature, as presented here, is by essence and definition a literature of self-search and a literature of social protest. Chicanos see themselves as searching for their authentic past, their roots in Indian and Spanish-Mexican culture, and they resent and resist cultural domination by what they perceive as the Anglo intruder in their ancestral homelands. Chicano literature, as Black and Nuyorican literature, if taken in the context of American ethnic literatures, represents cultural resistance, or rejection of domination by the predominant white Anglo culture. This resistance also entails, naturally, a refusal to assimilate standard forms of speech, and in the particular case of Chicano and Nuyorican literary works, either the insistence on a bilingual or "interlingual" text that reflects the hybrid, bicultural nature of their world view or the outright use of Spanish.

The process of self-search, of self-building an identity, takes at times the route of preserving tradition by exalting the mythology of Meso-American or Caribbean Indian cultures, or Afro-Spanish syncretism. It dwells on the pre-Hispanic past, reveling in the mythical concept of "earthly paradise" or the fatherland of pristine origins—hence Aztlán, the southwestern lands from which ancient Aztecs migrated back to Anáhuac in central Mexico; hence Borinquen, a beautiful Eden-like island inhabited first by Taínos and then by a mestizo population of Indian, Spanish, and Black African descent. In a sense, this preservation of tradition is indeed a synthesis of both tradition and creation. The political status that both Chicanos and Puerto Ricans perceive as their lot—being a colonized people—makes the writers intensify their search for roots, their affirmation of existence as a cultural entity. It has been said that political crisis intensifies cultural expression as a result of tightened group cohesion and sharper group values,[12] political dissent and cultural resistance reinforce each other. In the "native Hispanic" context, cultural manifestations such as the plastic arts (barrio murals in Los Angeles, Chicago, and New York) and "public" literature (Chicano poetry festivals, like *Flor y canto* are most often linked to a critical consciousness and to a politics of liberation. For the last twenty years or so, the literary production of Mexican Americans and mainland Puerto Ricans exemplify that consciousness and that struggle.[13]

To cite two pioneer texts from both literatures which appeared in 1967, reference can be made to *I Am Joaquín*,[14] by Rodolfo "Corky" Gonzales, and to the Nuyorican work *Down These Mean Streets*,[15] by Piri Thomas. *I Am Joaquín* is a first-person narrated epic poem that attempts to create an historical and mythic overview of a Chicano nation; it literally screams an affirmation of being—"Yo Soy Joaquín!"—which is connected to the Indo-Hispanic past and to the oppressed working class, mostly composed of migrant farm workers and the urban poor. *Down These Mean Streets* is a tale of Puerto Rican life in the Harlem ghetto, offered on the basis of autobiographical testimony given by a young Nuyorican who is also Black. It depicts the underworld of drug addiction, crime, prostitution and prison. Both texts are considered classics of Hispanic expression in the United States, in their diverse variants of linguistic achievement (English and *Spanglish*, or "pocho" interlingual), and in their recreation of life environments that, albeit extreme, portray the possible destiny of underprivileged Hispanic youth in this affluent society. Analysis of these works, and others which followed in their footsteps through the decade of the sixties and early seventies, have led critics to generalized conclusions about Chicano and Nuyorican literatures:

> in general terms, the Puerto Ricans are urban oriented, while Chicanos tend to retain a rural quality. Chicano literature is full of campesinos and migrant workers; one of the prime proponent/protagonists of the literature, the Teatro Campesino of Luis Valdez, began as the propaganda arm of the United Farm Workers. Puerto Rican literature is more concerned with the urban ghetto and the New York style of life. Moreover, western United States traditionally has signified the dream of land acquisition; while the Eastern cities have come to represent the renter's ghetto. Add to this the ideology propagated by much Chicano literature that the Southwest belongs to the Chicanos because it was taken from Mexico through an illegal invasion, and one can understand how Chicano literature would contain a proprietary vein absent in Puerto Rican writing (Bruce-Novoa, "Hispanic Literature").

It is true, nevertheless, that the rich and varied artistic texts produced by both Chicano and Nuyorican authors within the confines of mainland USA cannot all be easily categorized using the parameters pointed out before. In the case of Chicano literature, some very distinguished authors write in standard literary Spanish, with a language that is delicate and colorful in its metaphorical use, even though it seeks to portray the stark reality of undocumented "mojados" and life in the border town. Such is the case of Miguel Méndez, best known for his novel *Peregrinos de Aztlán*,[16] but also the magic weaver of children's tales. From his 1979 collection *Cuentos para niños traviesos/Stories for mischievous children*[17], a reader can glean the sense of poetic enchantment so successfully developed by Méndez as a writer. In the short story entitled "Moro," a child grieves for his horse Moro, who is weak and old, and is dying after many years of hard labor. In the mind of Pablito, the boy, Moro is a metaphor for his father, whose life has also been spent in toiling; both have tilled the soil on behalf of ruthless owners.

Other Chicano authors write almost entirely in English, and create a mythical world in the open countryside, full of the traditions of the Mexican campesinos. Such is the case of Rudolfo Anaya's famous novel, *Bless Me, Ultima*[18], where the author sees the separation of a Chicano community, away from the Anglo world, almost as an idyllic state. Here the reader finds another child narrator, living his life among the migrant workers:

> We always enjoyed our stay at El Puerto. It was a world where people were happy, working, helping each other. The ripeness of the harvest piled around the mud houses and lent life and color to the song of women (. . .) At night we sat around the fireplace and ate baked apples with sugar and cinnamon and listened to the cuentos, the old stories of the people.

But not all Chicano themes are rural. One of the most popular thematic lines for California and Midwest authors is the depiction of life in the urban barrios, where all kinds of street types are found, and where sometimes a hopeless existence gives in to the effects of alcohol and despair, perhaps loneliness. A classic text of Chicano poetry, Jose Montoya's "El Louie,"[19] draws the picture—actually an obituary—of a cool dude from the barrio, el Louie Rodríguez, who spent most of his life in west Fresno, except for a stint in the Army during the Korean War. He was perhaps what has been almost taken to the point of caricature in *Zoot Suit*: the Pachuco, cruising in his 1948 Plymouth, a ladies' man, good dancer, a graduate from barber school, somewhat rebellious and often ready to fight, always looking for a good time. When the poem opens, Louie has just been buried. He has died alone, in a rented room, probably—most likely—in an alcoholic stupor; the speaker in the text reminisces about Louie's life and times as he leaves this world forever. "El Louie" epitomizes the bilingual phenomenon of code switching, where English and Spanish and *caló* are intermingled in the same sentence structure. All interjections typical of the Pachucos' language (*órale, trucha, ése*) are used in this context as a way of actualizing gang fights at a dance club, but even neighborhood rivalries give in to the presence of a common enemy: *la chota*, the police. Dialogues are heavy with argot, while narrative segments in the poem tend to be more an interlingual mixture of standard languages. The repeated refrain, "Hoy enterraron al Louie" serves to convey a sensation of finality to a wasted, if enjoyable, life.

> Hoy enterraron al Louie.
> His death was an insult
> porque no murió en acción—
> no lo mataron los vatos
> ni los gooks en Korea.
> He died alone in a rented
> room—perhaps like in a
> Bogart movie.
> The end was a cruel hoax.
> but his life had been
> remarkable!

Vato de atolle, el Louie Rodríguez!

Among Puerto Ricans in the Northeast, there are those who write totally in English, without the usual barrio or ghetto themes, and without overtly emphasizing the alienating problems of immigration; such is the case of Julio Marzán, who writes poetry that can sometimes be considered "mainstream" if read out of the context of his total production. There are also Puerto Rican authors who write in standard Spanish prose and verse, like Carmen Valle and Pedro Juan Soto. The latter is a unique case, for he returned to Puerto Rico after many years of living in the mainland, but the reality portrayed in his best known collection of short stories, *Spiks* (1957), closely depicts the Puerto Rican migration experience and life in the New York or Northeastern ghettos. Conversely, his novel *Ardiente suelo, fría estación* (1962) describes the arrival of a Nuyorican in the island. In a short poem by Carmen Valle, "Desde mi ventana en el extranjero,"[20] the feeling of nostalgia for the tropics clashes with the naked, cold reality of life in a crowded inner city neighborhood. On a Sunday the poetic speaker looks at the rain coming down softly on trees that are beginning to sprout new growth. The green color of new leaves, and the raindrops falling from time to time evoke another unmentioned environment where it is always green and lush, usually rainy—a tropical island in the Caribbean. Everything is suggested in soft tones, not said explicitly; daydreams to be broken by the concrete sight of steam coming out of the building across the alley—the heating system ever present in a Northern climate.

> Hoy llueve a ratos.
> Los árboles verde tierno
> casi brillan.
> domingo
> y lluvioso es
> conjunción de placer
> con miradas largas.
> Se piensa trópico
> y los ojos chocan
> con el humo
> de la calefacción
> del edificio enfrente.

The view on life is very different, however, from the perspective of a working class Nuyorican barrio woman, who is also proud of her heritage and defends her culturally defined femaleness in front of the society which treats her as a second class citizen on account of her ethnic origin. The poem "My name is Maria Christina,"[21] by Sandra María Esteves, is on its way to becoming a classic for its fusion of the two visions, urban poor Nuyorican and female:

> My name is Maria Christina
> I speak two languages broken into each other
> but my heart speaks the language of people
> born in oppression

But life in the ghetto is always hard. In spite of the women fighting for their children's future, with calm and positive resolution, there is always the desperation of violence. For some, becoming an outlaw is the way out. The anger of young men, jobless and with only the bleakest of hopes ahead, is revealed in the poem "Kill, kill, kill" by Miguel Piñero.[22] After years on the welfare rolls, aggressiveness suddenly replaces resignation, and the desire and/or realization of a violent act constitutes the final reaction to feelings of powerlessness:

> Fired last week man I was mad.
> I don't mean angry or pissed off I
> was mad I wanted to grab the boss
> and the foreman by their
> red necks and kill, kill, kill.

The literature of the "migrant Hispanics," as we call that group of Spanish American, mostly Cuban, writers residing in the United States since the early sixties, presents a different picture. Even so, a few themes and feelings can be found in that literature which parallel those ever present in Chicano and Neorican poetry: namely, the problem of cultural identity. On the whole, however, the reality of the majority of Cuban writers in the United States is another one. First of all, they have migrated mostly because of political reasons, since the way of life they were accustomed to suddenly came to an end. Most of these writers oppose the socialist revolutionary process taking place in their homeland, and they do not identify with the working class, as does the majority of Chicano and mainland Puerto Rican authors. Some of the former are represented by Enrique Labrador Ruiz and Lorenzo García Vega, who belonged to the literary generations of the 1930's and the 1950's, respectively. Another group, who migrated in the decade of the 1960's and the 1970's (for example, Heberto Padilla), or even opted for exile as recently as 1980 (the Mariel generation, including Reinaldo Arenas and Antonio Benítez Rojo), clearly rejects the Third World stance of many Chicano and Nuyorican writers, identifies with the establishment, and does not feel part of an underprivileged ethnic minority. Even some of the younger ones in their midst, who migrated in their teens, embrace middle class values and ignore their subordination to a dominant Anglo culture. This latter group comprises poets such as Octavio Armand and José Kozer, and the prose writer and poet Mireya Robles. Most of the authors cultivate a sophisticated style which has been labeled by Juan Bruce-Novoa as "strictly Latin American." According to the same critic, their literature "neither treats nor engages the U.S. Experience" ("Hispanic Literature in the United States"). Such an observation does not necessarily apply to all of the writers in the above described groups, neither to some of their works; but in many instances they resort to a *nouveau* form which has more in common with avant garde tendencies in Latin American and European literary scenarios. The most recently arrived Cuban writers—Arenas and Padilla, among others—fully belong within a literature of exile and political protest, and are totally alienated from the reality of Hispanic ethnic minorities in the U.S. society.

Nevertheless, as it was mentioned before, thematic similarities can be noticed between some Cuban authors in this country and the other two main Hispanic groups. Mainly, such similarities can be traced to the cultivation of the "lost paradise" motif; much in the same manner that a *xicanindio* present looks back longingly at the *aztlanense* past (a territory that was pillaged, a fatherland that was desecrated), a mainland Puerto Rican dreams of the Indian island of Borinquen—both are left behind in time and space. For some Cuban writers, the island that can be reached only in their dreams becomes a poetic motif (as in the verses of Ana Rosa Núñez and her memories of *palmas*; the same occurs for the Nuyorican Jesús "Papoleto" Menéndez and his "long and slender swaying palm trees"). For the Cubans, nostalgia is a whole modality of poetic creation, either because the paradisiacal lifestyle they knew before the Revolution is no more and distance for the homeland is legitimately linked to feelings of lost roots. Distant childhood experiences, family members left behind, a missing geographical and spiritual landscape that cannot give writers the cultural and emotional sustenance they need; these are some of the images appearing in the work of quite a few Cuban authors who reside in the United States. Thematically, they make up a sizable portion of poetic subject matter even for younger writers, who started publishing mostly in connection to their intellectual activities in North American academic circles, and who, after twenty six years and in spite of the hyphenated name that labels them, Cuban-Americans, cannot feel integrated in U.S. society at large. Some of these writers do not share with their parents' generation an ideological rejection of Third World views; they have become politicized during their confrontation with injustices in the American system, mostly during their college years in the middle and late sixties (the civil rights movement, the Viet Nam antiwar movement). Many of them have come to accept the historical existence of the Cuban Revolution as an irrevocable fact, and although they affiliate with various positions of the political spectrum, most feel identified with the social struggles of minority groups in the United States, and with those of other Latin American peoples.

These younger writers are, by and large, poets; although they also cultivate the essay and short story forms. A prominent figure in this group is the aforementioned Lourdes Casal; other names to be mentioned include Achy Obejas, Emilio Bejel, Enrique Sacerio Garí, Rafael Catalá, Dolores Prida, Ricardo Cobián, Eliana Rivero, E. José Parreño. The last one, who has lived in New York and Puerto Rico, talks about "racimos de plátanos cubiertos de nieve" (Are*íto*, 1977), as a metaphor for the transplated islanders who, after more than two decades, still feel as part of an exotic flora of misfits. Sacerio Garí has a poem entitled "al borde de las Antillas no. 9"[23] which illustrates the described empathy felt toward the poor, the suffering, the victimized:

>Somos uno
>con el mar
>(pégate al agua)
>que no cambia de color
>por las fronteras nacionales (. . .)
>Somos uno
>de polo a polo
>con las potencias de paz
>morimos sin cesar
>de crisis inmemorable
>por zanjar el combate
>tan funesto para todos.
>Pegarse a la lágrima
>de Harlem y Mayaimi
>de Kabul, San Salvador y Varsovia
>a las santas ciudades
>de América
>Santiago, San Francisco, San Cristóbal
>sin aflojar la mano franca
>pegarse a la sangre encendida
>terrorizada
>en las entrañas
>de Barbados
>a la humanidad martirizada
>por el loco viento de los odios

Even for the Cuban American writers who are not politicized in the sense discussed above, a feeling of alienation is resolved in social criticism when confronted with the world of consumerism, material achievements, and rarified pleasures, such as eating dinner while watching the horrors of war on the evening news. The end result is a citizen who will be mesmerized into ignorance and turned into "a braying ass":

> One must have a sense of humor, my friend
> don't take things so seriously,
> rest, enjoy life, enjoy,
> leave for tomorrow everything that is not essential,
> take a vacation, relax,
> if you have to watch the news at dinner time
> pretend that the bombs you hear
> and the artillery detonations
> are the gay sounds of the carnival in Rio[24]

Most works by Cuban American authors are originally written in Spanish; some, like the one cited above, are published in bilingual editions. Other literary texts by writers of this generation, such as the play *Beautiful Señoritas* by Dolores Prida, are not only written in English, but also combine an understanding of the Hispanic minority experience with a feminist overview of women's life in American society. This vision coincides with the one presented in Nuyorican literature by Sandra María Esteves, and in Chicano literature by Sandra Cisneros, *The House on Mango Street*.[25]

Nevertheless, the best known members of the older immigrant generation of Cuban authors, who have chosen narrative prose as their primary artistic medium, do not fall within the parameters of this discussion. Their work does not belong in a review of ethnic minority group writing; some of them have elected to be known as "dissident intellectuals." They belong to the Latin American tradition of "sojourner writers," who perceive themselves citizens of the world although they often resort to themes related to their native countries. Having migrated in their forties and fifties, their worldviews and literary production were shaped and developed under very different circumstances than those discussed here for Chicanos and Nuyoricans, even though their life in Cuba during the decade of the sixties added a new thematic dimension to their work (a good example of this is Antonio Benítez Rojo). Moreover, their social class affiliations and/or status bring a perspective to their work that is quite dissimilar from the world vision found in the literary production of *native* Hispanics. Bruce-Novoa has said that these Cuban writers in the United States, "who consider themselves exiles more than permanent residents, cannot properly be included in *any consideration of Hispanic writings* in the U.S." (op. cit., emphasis ours). We hasten to add: not alongside Chicanos or mainland Puerto Ricans. But some titles would bear mentioning, insofar as they deal with immigrant life—albeit from a political refugee or exile viewpoint; these are the novel *Desterrados al fuego*, by Matías Montes Huidobro, and the journalistic vignettes of Cuban life in the Miami ghetto, *Estampas*, by Eladio Secades.

On the other hand, Cuban *American* writers—those who are already making the transition from emigres to minority group members, and do not consider themselves "exiles"—find themselves at an important point: they are searching for an identity of their own. The conflict they live implies being a minority within a minority, a small group within a subgroup, and this is a heavy burden. Other Hispanics, among them Chicanos and Boricuas, do not feel sympathy for the presumably deferential treatment that Anglos accord Cubans. This is a widely disseminated *social* misappreciation, but it contains a kernel of truth when one considers political perceptions shaped by foreign policy guidelines. As it is commonly known, citizens who migrate from countries ruled by socialist or communist regimes (and writers among them) are seen as readily embracing the "American way of life," and thus their artistic works are not supposed to be antiestablishment. If we define ethnic minority art and literature in the United States as a form of cultural resistance and/or protest, then the works by Cuban immigrants can never be considered. The novels, poems and short stories written by Cubans are indeed seen by many in the Chicano and Neorican communities as reactionary, carriers of a certain ideology which is perceived to be imbued with selfish, materialistic middle class values and easily confused with "the Anglo ways." In reality, quite a few Cuban Americans cannot be subsumed in this category, and their writings are beginning to be recognized as a valid part of the growing literary experience of Hispanics in the United States. It must be admitted, though, that Cuban American writers who do not conform to the dominant ideology prevalent in their national subgroup are placed in the position of having to create their own literature of resistance. In a sense, they must disassociate themselves from the label "Cuban literature in exile" so that they can forge their own intellectual and artistic identity. In this context, the closer they get to an appreciation of minority life in American society, and the more they empathize with Chicanos and Neoricans, the more alienated they become with respect to their original "exile culture." A good illustration of this point is Emilio Bejel, whose texts sometimes reflect a dichotomy of feeling; he is torn between the possibility of a full life in another country outside the native one, and the reality of it being a mere evasionist hope—such were the dreams offered to the sailors in ancient epics, which ended as dashed fantasies in a shipwreck:

> Emigrante
> que vives entre sal y mar
> tocando con los dedos
> los aros de las horas
> el canto de las sirenas te atrae
> con sus números imaginarios[26]

In a very real sense, then, Chicano literature is the only Hispanic literature that "belongs" in American society, by reason of its birthright and by its centuries-old claim of territorial and cultural permanence. The phenomenon of "return migration" by Puerto Ricans, their travel back and forth to the island and its influence on the cultural profile of Neorican art and literature is still being studied. Chicanos are also the only writers who can already claim a degree of recognition by the system: novelists like Rudolfo Anaya and poets like Gary Soto—just to mention two who write in English—are now widely read and published, their works analyzed and studied in university courses around the country. Doctoral disseratations are being approved by faculty committees that, a few years ago, did not deem Chicano literature a worthy area of research. While political trends in the U.S. go exactly the opposite way they went in the 1960's, and even the 1970's, their cultural reaffirmation persists. Conflict arises with the realization of not being fully Mexican, or even fully Hispanic, and at the same time being viewed through the prism of ethnic differentiation by a "white" society which in itself contains large unmelted portions of the fabled pot of nationalities.

Self-concept is an important component of the psychic makeup of Hispanic minorities, and it manifests itself mostly through identity definitions, ambiguity, reaffirmation and even a sense of rage combined with pride, especially among the young: to wit, "La Raza," "carnalismo," "lo hispano," "lo puertorriqueño," Aztlán identification in the West and Southwest; Borinquen, Cuba and *quisqueya* (Dominican Republic) cultural organizations on the Eastern seaboard. In literature, it also takes the form of an affirmation of being different. Not considered white, although sometimes light-skinned and blonde; not fully Indian, or indeed "native American;" not really "Spanish" or even Mexican, and often rejected by those cultural groups as "hybrid," not really Black and all that the term implies, in the case of Puerto Ricans of African descent; not really "Latinos" in the opinion of Latin Americans from outside the United States; and very definitely not "real Americans," according to the majority definition shaped in racist overtones, if one judges the "typical" American to be either Caucasian or Mediterranean European. *What are we as Hispanics?* Answers to this question constitute the lifeblood of many artistic forms created by Chicanos and mainland Puerto Ricans. For the latter, the problem looms even larger on the political horizon: what will happen if the island gains its independence from the United States? Will the Nuyorican alienation then become even more similar to that of the Chicano? What will happen to Puerto Rican writers on the island if Puerto Rico is claimed as the fifty-first state of the Union?

The most poignant form of identity conflict, as we have seen, is related to expressiveness and communication; that is, it relates to language, the essential tool of the writer. Both Chicanos and Nuyoricans feel deprived, robbed of their heritage, and ironically these feelings have to be contained in the language they learned in school, the language that permits them to function in Anglo society, the language that supplanted their mother tongue. Many writers who use English (or an interlingual mixture whose primary code is English) could be named in this context: among the Nuyoricans, Pedro Pietri, Sandra María Esteves, Miguel Algarín. Among the Chicanos, Lorna Dee Cervantes, Alberto Ríos, Pat Mora. At this point, it can be said that Nuyoricans share with Chicanos what has been called their "unifying paradigm": faced with what they perceive as a threat to their culture's very existence, the literary work itself responds, becoming a proof of survival. In this sense, both main groups of Hispanic artists exhibit a linkage with the so-called "exile literature": in the face of negation of their existence, confronted by invisibility and non-entity, writing is an act of self-salvation, words and language become the writer's only true territory. As Lorna Dee Cervantes reflects, in a text with an extremely long title, "Poem for the Young White Man Who Asked Me How I, An Intelligent, Well-Read Person Could Believe in The War Between Races" (Emplumada):

> ... I go to my land, my tower of words and
> bolt the door, but the typewriter doesn't fade out
> the sound of blasting and muffled outrage.
> My own days bring me slaps on the face.
> Every day I am deluged with reminders
> that this is
> not my land.

While mainland Puerto Rican literature still tries to preserve links with the island, and advocates the creation of a new cultural synthesis (la puertorriqueñidad) with a center in the homeland, in the hopes of a future when Puerto Rico will not be a colony of the United States, Chicanos in literature choose to be other than U.S. American or Mexican. In the act of defining themselves, they have configured a non-Mexican national identity. Their literature is the production of what could be called a "border state of mind," a space of intercultural synthesis.[27] To choose one over the other—Mexican over American nationality, Spanish over Indian ethnicity, or viceversa—is to cease being what they are. Therefore, their literature proposes an alternative, an "interior homeland," or a space for a new identity to exist. Compared to this context, Nuyorican literature has a different profile and a different future. It is a literature of transition, created by individuals that conceive their work as coming from a profound sense of national cultural identification with a "true" Puerto Rico; not the colony island of today, but a free and independent society.

It is significant to point out that their literature brings forth in the Chicanos a sense of *chicanismo*: an ethnic, political and cultural identity forged in the sixties and early seventies. For the Puerto Rican, the search for *lo puertorriqueño* goes on: an identity that should encompass both the island's genuine national values as well as the immigration experience. Compared to these phenomena, the most recent "migrant Hispanic" writing, as exemplified by the Cuban Americans, is too new a happening for that literature to be firmly delineated and solidified within a cultural space of its own. This will necessitate some years, and the completion of a transitional process: becoming a full-fledged ethnic minority within the borders of the United States. At that point, Cuban American literature will indeed constitute an expression of cultural survival.

For Cuban Americans, then, the process has just begun. For Chicanos, and for Nuyoricans in varying degrees, the development of their literature is in full bloom. Perhaps it will be the lot of future generations of Hispanics to witness the granting of an important *American* literary award to one of their authors, such as the Pulitzer Prize given to Alice Walker—the Afro-American female writer—for her magnificent novel *The Color Purple*. Whether this can be possible, given our linguistic and cultural idiosincrasies, only time and history will tell.

---

[1] Pioneering efforts in this task of rescuing Hispanic journalistic writings for the early history of Chicano letters can be attributed to Luis Leal and Juan Rodríguez; see their respective "Cuatro siglos de prosa aztlanense," and "Jorge Ulica y Carlos de Medina: escritores de la bahía de San Francisco," in *La Palabra*, 2:1 (Primavera, 1980), 2-15, 25-46.

[2] For an informative and lucid discussion of this ethnic identity situation, see the "Introduction" by Efraín Barradas to *Herejes y mitificadores: muestra de poesía puertorriqueña en los Estados Unidos*, eds. Efraín Barradas and Rafael Rodríguez (San Juan: Ediciones Huracán, 1980), 11-30. I express my gratitude to Efraín Barradas for his assistance in the preparation of this article.

[3] These memoirs, although published posthumously and very late, in 1977, were written in the 1940's; *Memoirs of Bernardo Vega*, César Andres Iglesias, ed. (New York: Monthly Review Press, 1984).

[4] Much of this discussion, with comparable accounting of historical facts, and centered around the origins and development of Hispanic literature in the U.S., can be found in the article by Juan Bruce-Novoa, "Hispanic Literature in the United States," *Media and the Humanities* (Proceedings of the Hispanic Southwest Regional Conference on Media and the Humanities, sponsored by the National Endowment for the Humanities Media Program), José Luis Ruiz, ed. and compiler (San Diego, 1980), n.p. Although I do not necessarily agree with some of the statements Bruce-Novoa makes about non-Chicano writers in the United States, the piece is a reliable source of information and one of the very few in the critical literature that deals with most Hispanic groups. See also Efraín Barradas on "Los chicanos y nosotros," in his review of Tino Villanueva, *Chicanos, Antología histórica y literaria* in *Areíto*, 9:34 (1983), 43-45.

[5] According to historical-literary research popularized in the last few years, the true origins of Chicano literature ("literatura aztlanense") can be traced back to the early days of Spanish settlements in the Southwest, and hence the first

literary works share a common origin with *crónicas* and epic accounts of the discovery and colonization of New World territories. Luis Leal says "Entre las relaciones aztlanenses, la primera y más famosa es la de Alvar Núñez Cabeza de Vaca, titulada *Narración de los naufragios* y publicada en Zamora, España, en 1542," op. cit. See also Bruce-Novoa, op. cit.

[6] *Emplumada*, (Pittsburg: University of Pittsburg Press, 1980).

[7] "Nuyorican [language] is uniquely suited to express the rawness, beauty, and passion of the Puerto Ricans, yet it is not only a new language but also a people and their experience," Joseph Papp, director of the New York Shakespeare Festival, on the backcover of *Nuyorican Poetry: An Anthology of Puerto Rican Words and Feelings* (New York: Wm. Morrow, 1975).

[8] *Nuyorican Poetry: An Anthology of Puerto Rican Words and Feelings*.

[9] *Drink Cultura Refrescante* (Menlo Park: Mango Publications, 1979).

[10] *Mongo Affair* (New York: Nuyorican Press, 1978).

[11] *Palabras juntan revolución* (La Habana: Casa de las Américas, 1981).

[12] See Juan Gómez-Quiñones, "Toward a Concept of Culture," *Revista Chicano-Riqueña*, 5:2 (Spring 1977), 29-47.

[13] But both the Chicano Renaissance and the emergence of Nuyorican literature in the late sixties are preceded by works that literally "blaze the trail." The book *A Puerto Rican in New York and Other Sketches* (1961) by Jesús Colón, constitutes a worthy antecedent of Nuyorican literary writings appearing after 1967. Interestingly enough, it contains the testimony of Puerto Rican migrant life in the New York ghettos of the 1950's and parallels the descriptions present in René Marqués' *La Carreta*, Bernardo Vega's *Memorias*, and Pedro Juan Soto's *Spiks*, all written in the late 1940's and early 1950's. A similar precedent of testimonial and journalistic writings had been established among communities of Mexican immigrants during the *porfiriato* and after the Revolution; this has been partially documented, in anthological form, by Armando Miguélez and Oscar Somoza in *El Gallo Ilustrado*, under the title "Narraciones de la Revolución Mexicana en la prensa chicana" (April 14, 1983). What distinguishes Jesús Colón's "sketches" among all other works, whether by mainland Puerto Ricans or Mexican Americans, is that they were written in English, and so they anticipated the New York-based Puerto Rican literature of the following decades. For a detailed explanation of this connection, see Juan Flores' introduction to Colón's book, in the 1982 edition by International Publishers.

[14] (New York: Bantam Books, 2nd. ed., 1972).

[15] (New York: Signet Books, 1968).

[16] (Tucson: Editorial Peregrinos, 1974).

[17] (Berkeley: Editorial Justa, 1979).

[18] (Berkeley: Tonatiuh International, 1972).

[19] In Luis Valdez & Stan Steiner, *Aztlan: An Anthology of Mexican American Literature* (New York: Random House, 1972).

[20] *Un poco de lo dicho* (Río Piedras: Ediciones Ceiba, 1979).

[21] In Barradas, *Herejes y mitificadores*.

[22] *La Bodega Sold Dreams* (Houston: Arte Público Press, 1980).

[23] *Poemas interreales* (1981).

[24] Luis González-Cruz, *Tirando al blanco/Shooting Gallery* (Miami: Ediciones Universal, 1975).

[25](Houston: Arte Público Press, 1984)

[26]*Huellas/Footprints* (College Park, Md.: Ediciones Hispamérica, 1982).

[27]The significance of the border as "spiritual space," as a state of mind, and as "literary space" has been pointed out by Sergio Elizondo ("Chicano Literature: Spiritual and Physical Homelands," paper presented at the Modern Languages Association 1980 annual meeting, Houston, Texas), and by Armando Miguélez ("La frontera como espacio literario," *Plural*, 4/83).

A Closing Note

On April 6 and 7, 1972, Dr. Luis Dávila of the Indiana University, Bloomington, executed what may have been the first symposium on Chicano Literature. Its significant title was "Chicano Literature and Tomás Rivera: A Symposium." In many ways it augured the development of Chicano literature within the academic setting for the next ten years. The acceptance of Chicano literature as a legitimate area of study, the founding of *Revista Chicano-Riqueña* and, most of all, Tomás Rivera's concerted and tireless leadership in creating the concept and practice of Chicano literature, Chicano literary criticism and Chicano publishing. What was unforeseen, however, was Tomás' death a little more than a decade later. And little did I know then that my symposium paper, "Language and Dialog in Tomás Rivera's . . . *y no se lo tragó la tierra*," written even before I had completed my Ph.D., would eventually be published as part of a posthumous eulogy to the great writer and humanitarian.

Tomás Rivera was one of the founding Contributing Editors of *Revista Chicano-Riqueña* in 1972 and a steady supporter and contributor to our literary magazine until his death. This double issue of *Revista* in his honor marks the last time our magazine will bear this title. *Revista Chicano-Riqueña* ends and begins its run with Tomás Rivera in prominence, the first issue having carried poems and a short story by Tomás. Henceforth, *Revista* shall be known as *The Americas Review* in our desire to expand our focus and create broader audiences, without abandoning our strength and roots, much as Tomás did himself and would have desired for us. *The Americas Review* shall remain in the vanguard of Chicano and U.S. Hispanic literature, but, through volumes like *International Studies in Honor of Tomás Rivera*, shall retain and recall what has been and is the best of us.

Nicolás Kanellos
Publisher

THE UNIVERSITY OF TEXAS AT SAN ANTONIO
4242 PIEDRAS DRIVE EAST, SUITE 250 · SAN ANTONIO, TEXAS 78228

OFFICE OF THE DEAN
COLLEGE OF MULTIDISCIPLINARY STUDIES

Estimado Nicolás,

¡Felicitaciones! El primer número de Revista Chicano-Riqueña está a todo dar. Como dice la raza, "se aventaron." Ojalá y siga el éxito.

Creo que comprendes lo satisfecho que se sienten y me da orgullo en y con ustedes.

¡Felicitaciones! ¡Bien hecho!

Tu amigo,

Tomás Rivera

April 5, 1984

Estimado Rolando,

Recibí tu carta del 27 del pasado. De pronto me pone en contacto con much de lo que aprecio tanto y que a veces olvido por días - cosas del trabajo - tu sabes como es la chinga - the rows get longer, the sun gets hotter, the thistle hurts a little bit more, pero como dices tu Rolando, "It isn't paradise, but it is home" en otras palabras, los chingazos engríen Hay que seguir...no choice. Que más hay que trabajar y de vez en cuando darle gas a la imaginación. Mind you, I am not complaining, but it does seem that the more you work, the more you have to work, and the more things change, the more they remain the same (I guess they remain the same because people work at it,...can you imagine what would happen if they didn't?).

I'm going to try to get to Americo's Party, but it really looks doubtful. I look forward to receiving the invitation.

I note you re-read the essay on the midwest. I really enjoyed writing that piece. El norte was a refuge for many of us physically and symbolically, etc.

I was really sorry I could't make it to the UT permian Basin. Too many conflicts.

Heard that NACS was good and bad. Some people were enthusiastic because the Chicanas blasted them, and others didn't like it. Cansancio, me dicen.

I have received the Texas Humanist. I think it's one of the best issues. During last year's editors meeting, I made sure that one of the future issues would cover the border as a total thematic intent. Marisse McDermott came through. I must write her and tell her.

Well Concha, Javier, Ileana, Irasema and I are finally going to Europe together. We really are looking forward to a great summer. We'll leave for London on June 23rd and return to Los Angeles just in time for the Olympics. We plan to visit London, Amsterdam, Paris and Madrid. Next year we'll take in Germany, Italy and Greece. Times-Mirror Company is sponsoring 357 art and cultural activities from all over the world so Concha and I are going to be tied-up with several events in Los Angeles. So, it's a busy summer, but it's a good start for the next academic year.

By the way, I was invited by Doug Moore, President, University of Redlands, to be a speaker at one of his "President's Round Table Dinners" - (students, faculty, regents, - tu sabes quality stuff - four a year) and he specifically asked me to do a speech on Chicano Poetry. I knew what he wanted, ever sine he heard me read "Old Friends" at a "Lion's Dinner" some 3 years ago, he had wanted to hear it again. So I did my thing and finished with "Old Friends." It's a great poem Roland. I love reading it. I read Chicano Poetry - the best pieces - for 2 hours - y dejé lo mejor para lo último. He was in high heaven, so was everyone else. Le dí la copia que traía de "Old Friends." Cuando tengas tiempo mándale una copia dedicada, se que lo apreciaría mucho.

Bueno - hasta aquí - abrazos a tu familia.

Recibe, como siempre, mis más finos recuerdos.

Tomás

Contributors

James H. Abbott, a David Ross Boyd Professor, was director of Tomás Rivera's dissertation on León Felipe. His "Tomás Rivera—1935-1984—So Proud of You Forever" was published in *Sooner Magazine*. His critical studies of Azorín, Benavente, Julián Marías, Ignacio Aldecoa, Moratín and Antonio Machado have appeared in prominent journals and books published by Espasa-Calpe.

John C. Akers is an Assistant Professor at Saint Mary's College, Notre Dame. He has published articles on the Spanish Novel of the nineteenth century and has participated in an NEH Summer Seminar with Luis Leal at the University of California, Santa Barbara. He received a Lilly Endowment Grant for curriculum development in Chicano Literature and Film.

Susan E. Bassnett is the Senior Lecturer in Comparative Literature at the University of Warwick and Chairwoman of the Graduate School. She is the author of several articles and books in the fields of theatre studies, poetry, translation studies and Women's Studies.

Heiner Bus teaches at the University of Mainz, Germany. He has published books on Saul Bellow and Washington Irving, and numerous articles on Jewish-American, Black and Chicano literatures, on Canadian drama, and on the influence of American English on German.

Lauro Flores teaches Chicano and Spanish American literature at the University of Washington, where he is the Director of the Center for Chicano Studies and Editor of *Metamorfosis*. He is currently a Visiting Scholar at the University of California, San Diego, and holds a Ford Foundation/National Research Council Postdoctoral Fellowship for Minorities.

Patricia de la Fuente holds a Ph.D. in Comparative Literature from the University of Texas, Austin. She is an Associate Professor of English and Mexican American Literature at Pan American University and Editor of the Pan American University Press. Her publications on Chicano authors and other topics have appeared in numerous journals, including *Revista Chicano-Riqueña*.

Erlinda González-Berry is an Associate Professor of Spanish and Chicano Literature at the University of New Mexico, where she also directs the Spanish for Bilinguals Program. She has published numerous articles on Chicano fiction and has recently completed a novel called *El tren de la ausencia*.

Dieter Herms is Professor of American Studies at the University of Bremen. He is Editor of *Upton Sinclair in German* and of *Gulliver, German-English Yearbook*, and author of several books and articles on Chicano politics and literature, the social novel and modern political theatre.

Rolando Hinojosa-Smith is the Ellen Clayton Garwood Professor at the University of Texas-Austin's Department of English. His latest works, *Dear Rafe* and *Partners in Crime* were published by Arte Público Press, which also published *The Rolando Hinojosa Reader*, edited by José D. Saldívar. "Tomás Rivera: Remembrances of an Educator and Poet" is reprinted with the permission of the *Texas Humanist*.

Nicolás Kanellos, Professor of Spanish at the University of Houston, is founder and publisher of *Revista Chicano-Riqueña* and Arte Público Press. His latest publications include *Hispanic Theatre in the United States* and his discovery of and introduction to the first Chicano novel, *Las aventuras de don Chipote o Cuando los pericos mamen*, by Daniel Venegas (SEP and Cefnomex, 1984).

Luis Leal, Professor Emeritus, University of Illinois, is now Visiting Professor in the Department of Chicano Studies, University of California, Santa Barbara, and also Interim Associate Director of the Center for Chicano Studies. He is the author of the recently published book, *Aztlán y México, Perfiles literarios e históricos*.

Sylvia S. Lizárraga received her Ph.D. from the University of California, San Diego, with emphasis on Chicano and Latin American literature. She has published critical articles and short stories in Chicano and Mexican feminist journals, and is presently an Assistant Professor in the Chicano Studies Program of the University of California, Berkeley.

Eliud Martínez, a native Texan, is Associate Professor of Comparative Literature, Chicano Studies and Latin American Studies at the University of California, Riverside. He is the author of *The Art of Mariano Azuela*, and is an artist and art historian.

Julián Olivares, from San Antonio, is Co-Editor of *Revista Chicano-Riqueña* and Associate Editor of Arte Público Press. He has published articles on Chicano and Spanish Golden Age literature, and is the author of *The Love Poetry of Francisco de Quevedo: An Aesthetic and Existential Study* (Cambridge). He presently holds a Ford Foundation/National Research Council Senior Postdoctoral Fellowship for Minorities and is a Visiting Scholar at The University of Texas, Austin.

Américo Paredes, distinguished folklorist and author of *With His Pistol in His Hand: A Border Ballad and its Hero*, is Professor Emeritus of Anthropology and English at the University of Texas, Austin.

Tey Diana Rebolledo is an Associate Professor of Spanish and Director of the Women Studies Program at the University of New Mexico. She has written many articles on Chicana poetry and on Latin American women writers. Currently she is working on a critical anthology of Chicana writers with Eliana S. Rivero, University of Arizona. The project is sponsored by a grant from the National Endowment for the Humanities.

Eliana S. Rivero, born in Cuba, is Professor of Spanish at the University of Arizona. She has published widely on Spanish American literature, and since 1977 has been researching the literature of Hispanics in the U.S.

Evangelina Vigil-Piñón, from San Antonio, is a Chicana poet and author of *Nade y Nade, Thirty an' Seen a Lot*, and Editor of *Woman of Her Word, Hispanic Women Write*.